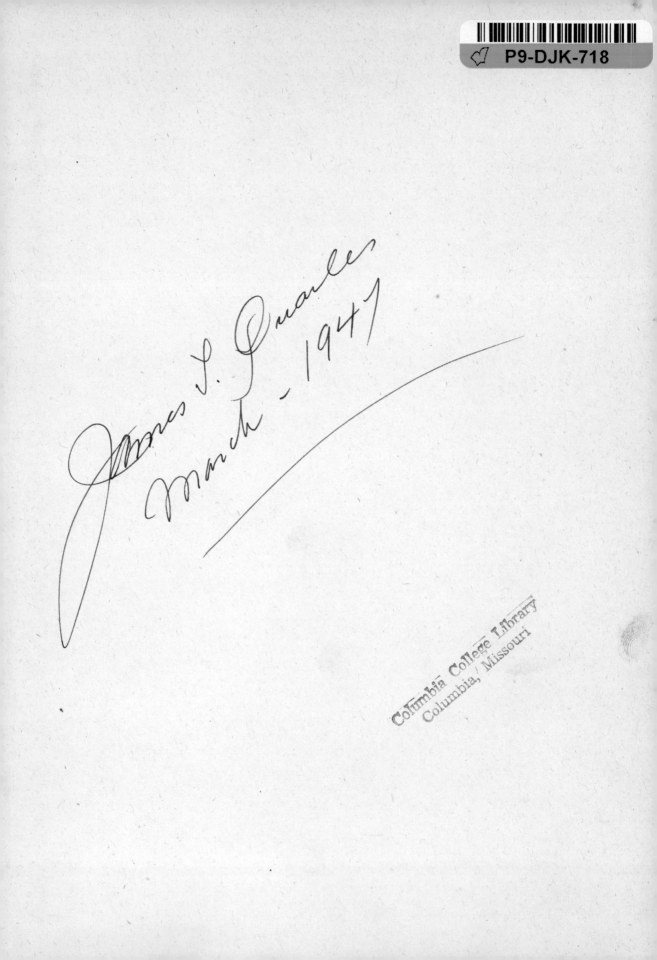

EASTMAN SCHOOL OF MUSIC SERIES

THE CONTRAPUNTAL HARMONIC TECHNIQUE

of the 18th century

By

ALLEN IRVINE McHOSE

1947

F. S. CROFTS & COMPANY

NEW YORK

To
My Father and Mother

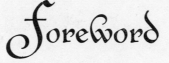

Foreword

The Contrapuntal Harmonic Technique of the 18th Century, by Allen Irvine McHose, in my opinion, marks a new and important development in the teaching of harmonic and contrapuntal techniques. It is the result of many years of teaching in The Eastman School of Music of the University of Rochester, of indefatigable experimentation, and of arduous research. This text has been subjected to the most practical of tests, extended use in the classroom over a period of years, and has proven the effectiveness and validity of the pedagogic principles which it sets forth.

The book is in no sense radical, since it is based upon the harmonic and contrapuntal material of the first half of the 18th century. It is unique, however, both in its completeness and in its detail. The technique of the period is analyzed not as a theory based upon a theory, but through the study of the music itself. Since that music is not solely harmonic nor contrapuntal, the study effectively synthesizes the two correlated techniques and shows one to be an integral part of the other.

The constant emphasis on the study of style reflects the author's firm belief that a technique can be studied only in terms of the style of the period under discussion — that what is "wrong" for one period may be "right" for another. This belief is one which all careful students of music must share, but which in the teaching of so-called "harmony" has been honored more frequently in the breach than in the observance. That the author should choose the style of Bach as a basis for this study seems entirely logical since the music of this master better than any other exemplifies the most perfect synthesis of harmonic and linear writing.

A third characteristic of the text is its insistence that, since music is an art of sound which must be aurally perceived, the analysis of the music must be coordinated with the development of an aural technique. The keyboard and dictation manual which accompanies the text is effectively correlated to develop such a technique.

The carefully organized, progressive presentation of the material is a masterpiece of sound and effective pedagogy. It reflects the fact that Dr. McHose is himself an enthusiastic teacher whose greatest joy is in seeing that his students learn and understand the material which is presented to them. His new book will, I am sure, be greeted with enthusiasm both by the hundreds of teachers of theory who have had the opportunity of studying with him and with the much greater number whom his pedagogic talent has directly or indirectly influenced.

January, 1947

Howard Hanson

Preface

THIS text is based upon the contrapuntal harmonic style of composition in the 18th century, with special emphasis placed upon the music of Johann Sebastian Bach. During this period, the technical elements of the 17th century were evaluated and combined into a type of composition based on the principle of chord progression. This principle of chord progression established the concept of the key center. Without a thorough knowledge of the music of the first half of the 18th century, the development of the art beginning with the Mannheim group and extending through the late 19th century cannot be logically organized in a student's mind.

The approach in the study of the material presented in this text involves emphasis upon the style of the music. This establishes a norm from which comparative studies with other periods may be readily achieved. Having as a basis a thorough knowledge of one technique of composition, one can accurately determine the outstanding characteristics of another style. The author has found that the approach through style leads to greater classroom interest in theory; the teacher and the students are constantly discussing other techniques of composition, which broadens the horizon for the student. Another important feature of the style-approach is that it makes simpler the problem of correcting student errors; questions of this type can always be referred to the practices of the composers of the period being studied.

The salient points to bear in mind when using this text are:

1. The historical approach through examples and discussion of each important element of the 18th century style.
2. The frequency usage of material as it contributes to the establishment of the style.
3. The classification of root movement as it controls the style of two, three, and four-voice composition.

The text is divided into three parts. Part 1 presents the analysis and practice in the use of the material. Part 2 deals with the harmonization of a melody. The author has deliberately kept this presentation as a separate study believing that analysis and practice in partwriting are a necessary prerequisite. Part 3 is a study of the contrapuntal harmonic style of the period.

The following plan shows how the various chapters in the three parts may be used.*

	PART 1	PART 2	PART 3
First Quarter			
	Chapters 1 through 7		
Triads			
	Chapters 8 and 9	Chapter 27	
Non-Harmonic	Chapters 10, 11, 12,	Chapter 28	
Tones	13, and 14		
	At conclusion of 14	Chapter 29	Chapter 33
Second Quarter			
Seventh	Chapters 15, 16, 17,		Chapter 34
Chords	18, 19, and 20	Chapter 30	Chapter 35
			Chapter 36
			Chapter 37
Third Quarter			
Altered	Chapters 21, 22, 23,		Chapter 38
Chords	and 24	Chapter 31	Chapter 39
Fourth Quarter			
Modulation	Chapters 25 and 26	Chapter 32	Chapter 40
			Chapter 41

In using this text, one of the following collections of Bach chorale harmonizations should be available to each student: *Chorale Collection*, Elvera Wonderlich, F. S. Crofts & Company, New York; or *371 Harmonized Chorales and 69 Chorale Melodies with Figured Bass*, Bach-Riemenschneider, G. Schirmer, New York.

A keyboard and dictation manual for use with *The Contrapuntal Harmonic Technique of the 18th Century* is published separately. Instructions for correlating keyboard and dictation practice with this text will be found in it.

The author wishes to acknowledge his appreciation to Dr. Howard Hanson, whose devotion to the art of music and whose interest in education made available all the research facilities of the Eastman School of Music; to Ruth Northup Tibbs, Wayne Barlow, Burrill Phillips, Gustave Soderlund, Elvera Wonderlich, and Donald White for their aid and constructive criticism in the preparation of this text; to the staff of the Sibley Library of the Eastman School of Music; to Wayne Dunlap and Poland Miller, whose dissertations aided the writing of Chapter 12 and Chapter 25; to the students whose contrapuntal exercises are quoted in Chapter 38; and to Paul J. Weaver, Professor of Music at Cornell University, for his counsel in the preparation of the text and his painstaking editing of the complete manuscript.

ALLEN I. McHose

Rochester, New York

* The plan is for a school year divided into four quarters. If, however, this book is to be used over a period of a year and a half, Part 1, Chapters 1 through 9 and Part 2, Chapters 27 and 28 may be begun during the second half of the freshman year. The author suggests that the second year begin with a review of the work covered in the first year.

Contents

xi

CONTENTS

CONTENTS

Introduction

As a prerequisite to use of this manual and its accompanying keyboard and dictation manual, knowledge and training in the following subjects are necessary:

Intervals
Major, minor, diminished, and augmented triads
Major and minor keys
Major and minor scales (all forms)
Keyboard harmony
    To be able to play type triads, scales, and simple cadences (authentic and plagal)
Sightsinging and melodic dictation
    Melodies in major and minor keys containing modulations to the closely related keys and possibly also foreign modulations
Harmonic dictation
    Recognition of at least I, IV, II, and V in major and minor keys.

THE TONAL CONCEPT OF 18TH CENTURY TECHNIQUE

Analysis of the music of the 18th century reveals that its most elementary sonority is a tone cluster. The smallest cluster contains three tones. A melody or two-voice composition will constantly imply two tones or one tone respectively to complete the cluster. A three-tone cluster is called a *triad* and its three tones are spaced a third apart. The tone upon which the triad is constructed is called the *root* or *fundamental*. The names of the remaining tones in order are the third and fifth.

Ex. 1.

The manner in which one analyzes aurally the triad is not to hear a triad as a pile of thirds erected on some root but rather to break it up into intervals related to the root. For example, a major triad contains two important basic intervals both

1

of which are derived from its root, namely the major third (root and third) and the perfect fifth (root and fifth).

Ex. 2.

There are four types of triads. Each one is named according to the intervallic relation of the root to the third and of the root to the fifth.

A major triad is composed of a major third and perfect fifth.

Ex. 3.

A minor triad is composed of a minor third and perfect fifth.

Ex. 4.

A diminished triad is composed of a minor third and diminished fifth.

Ex. 5.

An augmented triad is composed of a major third and augmented fifth.

Ex. 6.

A triad built on any note is identified by the name of that note. For example, the a-major triad identifies a as the root, c-sharp as the third, and e as the fifth. The c-augmented triad identifies c as the root, e as the third, and g-sharp as the fifth.

Composers do not limit the lowest note of a triad structure to the root; the triad appears with the third and occasionally the fifth as its lowest note.

Ex. 7 AND 8.

This practice of scrambling the notes of a triad does not in any way affect the identity of the triad. The chord at 1 is called the *b-major triad*. The chord at 2 is called the *a-minor triad*. The practice of arranging the three notes of a triad in such a way as to have either the root, third, or fifth as the lowest note is called the *theory of inversion*. This theory was established by Jean Philippe Rameau during the 18th century. The student will find that this theory of inversion is the foundation approach to understanding the structure of music during the 18th and 19th centuries.

It was Rameau's belief that major and minor keys were established by chord progression. His approach to proving this theory was through the theory of inversion. His method of attacking the problem confined itself to analysis of the music being composed by his contemporaries. His first step was to write, on a third staff placed below each line of the score, the root of every chord. The following Bach chorale illustrates Rameau's method of procedure:

Ex. 9. Was Gott tut, das ist wohlgetan

The succession of roots written on the accompanying staff below each line of a composition is called the *fundamental bass* by Rameau. The next step in Rameau's analysis is to study the distance between each two bass notes in order as the composition progresses. Considering the interval of a fourth as the inversion of the fifth, the intervals appear in the fundamental bass of the preceding example in the following frequency:

PRIME	FIFTH APART	SECOND APART	THIRD APART
6	26	2	4

That is, there were six repetitions of the same chord, twenty-six progressions with the roots of the chords a fifth apart, two progressions with the roots of the chords a second apart, and four progressions with the roots of the chords a third apart. This table, however, does not give the true facts of the theory of fundamental bass, and further analysis is necessary.

The following chorale is found in C. Heinrich Graun's *Passion:*

Ex. 10.   Der Tod Jesus (No. 11)

Fundamental Bass

PRIME	FIFTH APART	SECOND APART	THIRD APART
4	19	10	6

Comparing this table with the first table of frequencies, we see that there are a few more chord progressions with their roots a second apart and a third apart. If we continue this analysis of Bach, Graun, Handel, and other contemporaries, the following deductions can be established concerning root movement:

PRIME	FIFTH APART	SECOND APART	THIRD APART
16%	52%	21%	11%

Rameau believed that the theory of major and minor keys could be established based on the fact that chord progressions containing their roots a fifth apart are in the majority. He indicates that the major key is established by arranging three major triads so that their roots are a fifth apart.

E G♯ B

A C♯E   B D♯F♯

According to his explanation the e-major triad becomes the chord of rest. The remaining triads are active and must eventually progress to the chord of rest. The rest chord is the tonic. The chord a fifth above the root of the tonic is the dominant, and the chord a fifth below the root of the tonic is the subdominant. In like manner he created his minor key by arranging three minor triads having their respective roots a fifth apart.

f#a c#
b d f# c#e g#

The following Bach example illustrates a phrase of a chorale using the tonic, dominant, and subdominant triads:

Ex. 11.   Lobt Gott, ihr Christen, allzugleich

The error that Rameau and many theorists following him made was to become involved in mathematical and acoustical explanations to prove this theory of the key center. Furthermore, harmonic movement in relation to rhythm has been for the most part neglected.* What should have been done was to continue the analysis of the music.

Since this text confines itself at first to study of Bach's style of composition, and since his chorale harmonizations possess in condensed form his entire harmonic equipment, the continuation of the study of fundamental bass as it clarifies harmonic movement has been through an analysis of many of Bach's chorales, with the following results:

ROOT MOVEMENT TO THE TONIC

1) The tonic chords were located.
2) The interval relation of the root of the preceding chord to the root of the tonic was tabulated.
3) The following was the result of the study:**

---

* This is discussed in Part II, Chapter 27, page 309.

** Only the most frequent roots which precede the tonic are listed. The other roots which appear before the tonic are taken up later in this introduction.

Ex. 12.

ROOT MOVEMENT	DESCRIPTION	FREQUENCY
1 Tonic 1 Tonic	Down a perfect fifth	most frequent
2 Tonic 2 Tonic	Up a minor second	less frequent

At 1, the root movement is dominant to tonic. At 2, the root movement is leading tone to tonic.

Chords built on either the dominant or leading tone progress normally to the tonic, and are called chords of the *first classification.*

The following example illustrates chords of the first classification progressing normally to the tonic:

Ex. 13. Das neugeborne Kindelein   *J. Sebastian Bach (1685–1750)*

The tonic triad may progress to any chord in its key.

ROOT MOVEMENT TO THE FIRST CLASSIFICATION

1) The dominant and leading tone chords were located.
2) The interval relation of the root of the preceding chord to either the dominant or leading tone was tabulated.
3) The following was the result of the study:

Ex. 14.

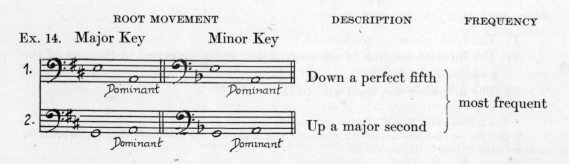

ROOT MOVEMENT		DESCRIPTION	FREQUENCY
Major Key	Minor Key		
1. Dominant Dominant		Down a perfect fifth	most frequent
2. Dominant Dominant		Up a major second	

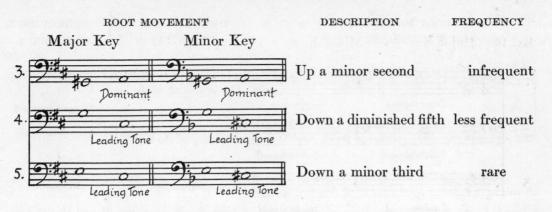

ROOT MOVEMENT		DESCRIPTION	FREQUENCY
Major Key	Minor Key		

3. Up a minor second — infrequent

4. Down a diminished fifth — less frequent

5. Down a minor third — rare

At 1, the root movement is supertonic to dominant.
At 5, the root movement is supertonic to leading tone.
At 2, the root movement is subdominant to dominant.
At 4, the root movement is subdominant to leading tone.
At 3, the root movement is raised-subdominant * to dominant.

Chords which have their roots on the subdominant or supertonic progress normally to chords of the first classification, and are called chords of the *second classification*

The following example illustrates chords of the second classification progressing normally to chords of the first classification:

Ex. 15.   O Welt, sieh hier dein Leben   *J. Sebastian Bach*

Fundamental Bass

Classification:	Tonic	2nd Cl.	1st Cl.	Tonic	2nd Cl.	1st Cl.	Tonic
Root :		Subdominant	Leading Tone	Tonic	Supertonic	Dominant	Tonic

ROOT MOVEMENT TO THE SECOND CLASSIFICATION

1) The supertonic and subdominant chords were located.
2) The interval relation of the root of the preceding chord to either the supertonic or subdominant was tabulated.
3) The following was the result of the study:

* The raised-subdominant is an altered tone. See Part I, Chapter 22.

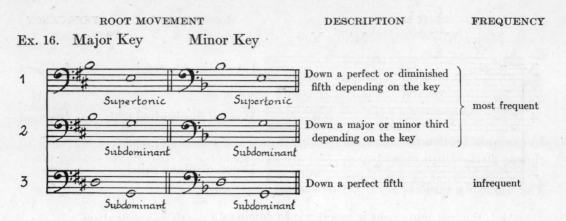

ROOT MOVEMENT		DESCRIPTION	FREQUENCY
Ex. 16. Major Key	Minor Key		

At 1, the root movement is submediant to supertonic.

At 2, the root movement is submediant to subdominant.

At 3, the root movement is tonic to subdominant. In this case the tonic chord must be a dissonance; in the Bach technique it is a seventh chord.

Chords which have their roots on the submediant, and dissonant chords which have their roots on the tonic, progress normally to chords of the second classification, and are called chords of the *third classification.*

The following example illustrates a chord of the third classification progressing normally to the chord of the second classification:

Ex. 17.   Der Tag, der ist so freudenreich   *J. Sebastian Bach*

ROOT MOVEMENT TO THE THIRD CLASSIFICATION

1) The submediant and discords of the tonic were located.

2) The interval relation of the root of the preceding chord to either the submediant or tonic (root of a discord) was tabulated.

3) The following was the result of the study:

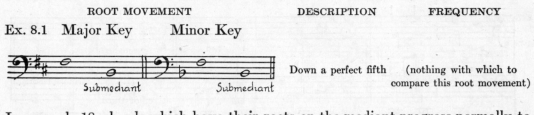

ROOT MOVEMENT		DESCRIPTION	FREQUENCY
Ex. 8.1 Major Key	Minor Key		

Down a perfect fifth (nothing with which to compare this root movement)

In example 18, chords which have their roots on the mediant progress normally to chords of the third classification and are called chords of the *fourth classification.*

The following table illustrates the normal progression:

Fourth Classification
Mediant — III

Third Classification
Tonic — I (a dissonance or altered)
Submediant — VI

Second Classification
Subdominant — IV
Supertonic — II

First Classification
Leading tone — VII
Dominant — V

Key Center
Tonic — I

The Roman numeral to the right of each functional name is used in analysis; it is a symbol to represent the function of the chord. Theoretically, the fourth classification should be followed by the third classification, and so on until the tonic center is reached. The fourth classification is the most remote from the tonic.

Classification of root movement plays an important role in harmonic dictation. It is of extreme importance in the process of chord selection in harmonization of a melody, in improvisation at the keyboard, and in harmonic contrapuntal composition.

The manner in which composers use the tonic harmony is of utmost importance. The fact that the tonic chord is preceded by chords of the first classification has been established. The tonic chord has two other important uses, as follows:

1) The tonic chord may progress to any chord in its key.
2) The tonic chord may be used between two chords which form a normal progression without disturbing their classification.

In the following examples the chorale phrases open with the tonic chord and progress to chords which have their roots in different classifications:

Ex. 19.

In the following example the tonic triad appears between the third classification and the second classification, and between the second classification and the first classification:

Ex. 20. Was Gott tut, das ist wohlgetan　　*J. Sebastian Bach*

Ex. 21. Was mein Gott will, das g'scheh' allzeit　　*J. Sebastian Bach*

At 1, the IV progresses to I, which in turn progresses to V. The I in no way disturbs the normal feeling that the IV actually progresses to the V.

At 2, the VI actually progresses to IV, and the I in no way disturbs the normal progression of the third classification chord. The same is true in connection with IV at 3, which actually progresses to V.

In their music the composers of the 18th century use the normal progression about seventy-six percent of the time. The remaining twenty-four percent of root movement is used as a contrast to the normal progression. The methods used are repetition, elision, and retrogression.

Next in frequency to the normal progression is chord repetition. The functions which are repeated most often are first, tonic; second, dominant; third, subdominant; and fourth, supertonic. The remaining functions are rarely repeated. The following example illustrates repetition:

Ex. 22. Liebster Jesu, wir sind hier

J. Sebastian Bach

If a chord of the third classification progresses to a chord of the first classification, the progression is called an *elision*. The common elisions are as follows:

mediant to subdominant
submediant to dominant
subdominant to tonic

The following examples illustrate elision:

Ex. 23. Wer Gott vertraut,
hat wohl gebaut   Ex. 24. Als der gütige Gott   *J. Sebastian Bach*

At 1 and 2, the VI progresses to V, eliding the second classification chord **II** or **IV**.

Thus far the roots of the chords which were not tonic have progressed in one direction: a chord of the fourth classification progressed normally to a chord of the third classification, and so on; and in the elision the progression has always been toward the tonic center. Occasionally, however, composers interrupt this type of movement by progressing to a more remote classification; for example, a first classification dominant chord may progress to a second classification supertonic. This movement away from the tonic is called *retrogression*. The common retrogressions are as follows:

> submediant to mediant
> dominant to supertonic
> dominant to subdominant

The less common retrogressions are as follows:

> dominant to mediant
> subdominant to submediant
> supertonic to submediant

The following examples illustrate retrogression:

Ex. 25.   Du Friedensfürst, Herr Jesu Christ   *J. Sebastian Bach*

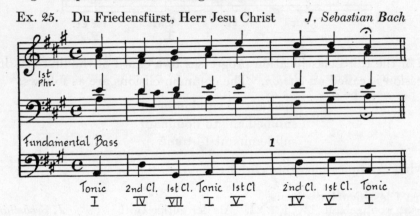

Ex. 26.   Wach' auf, mein Herz   *J. Sebastian Bach*

At 1, a retrogression V to IV occurs, but the movement immediately swings back to a normal progression IV to V.

At 2, a retrogression VI to III occurs, but the movement immediately swings back in the elision III to IV which in turn progresses normally to V.

The retrogression is a forceful harmonic root movement, and two retrogressions are rarely found in succession. Elision and retrogression are much less frequent than repetition and normal progression.

DIATONIC CHORDS IN MAJOR AND MINOR

The key center is determined through classification of root movement. Whether a major or a minor key is identified depends solely on the type of chord used on the roots in the different classifications. Rameau creates his major key center by building major triads on the tonic, subdominant, and dominant roots. The seven tones of the major scale are found in this arrangement.

F A C
Bb D F   C E G

F G A Bb C D E F

It is also important to observe that classification of root movement will fix the tones of the scale. An analysis of music in the key of f-major will reveal that seven different tones may be used as the roots of chords.

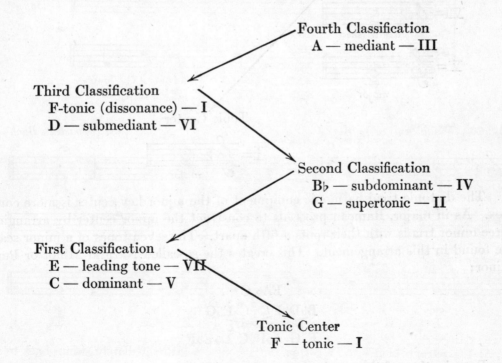

Fourth Classification
A — mediant — III

Third Classification
F-tonic (dissonance) — I
D — submediant — VI

Second Classification
Bb — subdominant — IV
G — supertonic — II

First Classification
E — leading tone — VII
C — dominant — V

Tonic Center
F — tonic — I

Chords found in the scale derived from the three major triads with their roots a fifth apart are called *diatonic chords*.

The basic diatonic triad harmonic equipment used in a major key is as follows:

DIATONIC TRIADS — F-MAJOR

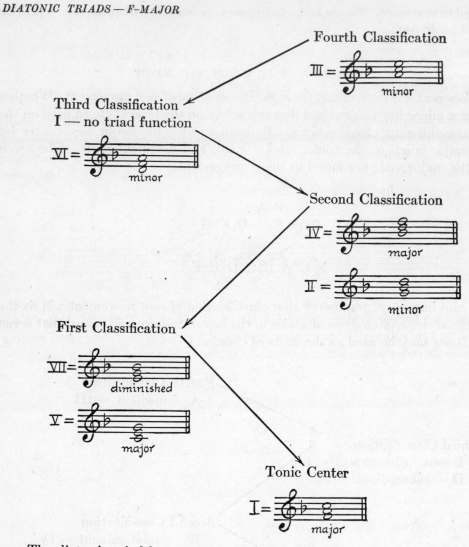

The diatonic triad harmonic equipment of the minor key center is more complex. As in major, Rameau proceeds to construct the minor center by arranging three minor triads with their roots a fifth apart. The seven tones of a minor scale are found in this arrangement. This creates the so-called Natural Minor or Pure Minor:

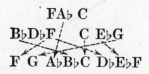

Examination of the music, however, reveals that a major triad is more frequent than a minor triad on the dominant. Likewise, a major triad occasionally appears on the subdominant. These two other arrangements of triads create the Harmonic and the Melodic Minors:

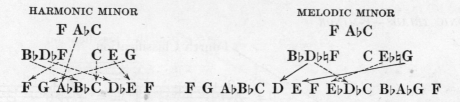

HARMONIC MINOR

MELODIC MINOR

F A♭C

F A♭C

B♭D♭F   C E G

B♭D♭♮F   C E♭♮G

F G A♭B♭C D♭E F   F G A♭B♭C D E F E♭D♭C B♭A♭G F

As in major a diatonic chord in minor will be a chord which has its spelling controlled by any one of the three forms of the minor scale.

Bach uses all forms of minor in his composition. He frequently uses a major tonic triad as the last chord of a composition which is in a minor key. The tones of Bach's minor key may be listed as follows:

Ex. 27.

Scale Tone 1   2   3   ♯3   4   5   6   ♯6   7   ♯7   8

Considering the natural minor as the basis of the minor key center, there are two mediants, two submediants, sub-tonic (whole step below the tonic) and leading tone. The scale steps which differ from the natural minor are defined as follows:

$$♯3 \quad \text{raised-three}$$

$$♯6 \quad \text{raised-six}$$

$$♯7 \quad \text{raised-seven}$$

A ♯ is used to indicate raising a scale step.

The minor key center uses in its diatonic system ten tones.

The diatonic triad harmonic equipment used in a minor key is as follows:

DIATONIC TRIADS — F-MINOR

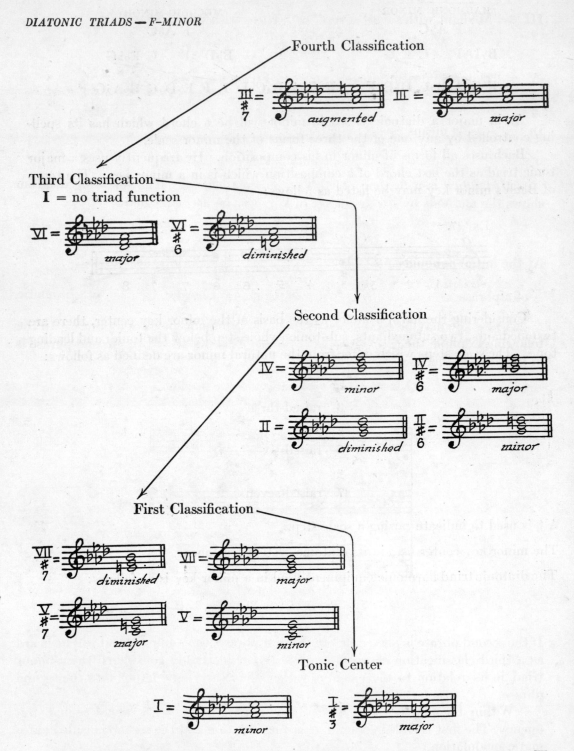

The triads to the left under each classification are the most frequent. The triad symbol with the raised-tone is named as follows:

III = "Mediant with raised-seven" or "Three with raised-seven"
#
7

V = "Dominant with raised-seven" or "Five with raised-seven"
#
7

In this sense ♯ means raised scale tone.

MODULATION

Modulation is a method of effecting change of key.   The following diagram shows the methods by which change of key may be accomplished:

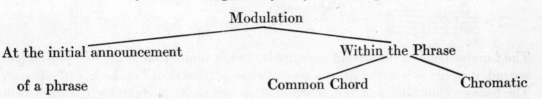

Modulation

At the initial announcement   Within the Phrase

    of a phrase   Common Chord   Chromatic

A new key may be established at the initial announcement of a phrase.   In the following example the first phrase is in the key of a-minor and the second phrase is in the key of c-major:

Ex. 28.   Ach wie nichtig, ach wie flüchtig
J. Sebastian Bach

If the second phrase is played before the first phrase, the a-minor triad will be heard as a third classification chord in c-major.   Bach certainly considered the a-minor triad in its relation to the c-center, rather than carrying a-minor into the second phrase.

Within the phrase two types of modulation occur with about equal frequency. The first is called common chord modulation and the second is called chromatic modulation.

The following example illustrates common chord modulation:

Ex. 29. Gott lebet noch

J. Sebastian Bach

The f-major triad in the second measure is, first, a tonic triad in the key of f-major; second, it progresses normally as a second classification chord in the key of c-major. The f-major chord belongs to both keys. *Common chord* modulation occurs within a phrase when the function of the first key can be supplanted by a function in the new key on a chord common to both keys.

The following example illustrates chromatic modulation:

Ex. 30.   Das neugeborne Kindelein

J. Sebastian Bach

At 1, the f-major triad progresses to the d-major triad. This progression is called chromatic since the f in the f-major triad becomes f♯ in the d-major triad. The phrase begins in b-flat major and the chords progress normally to the first classification chord. At this point the chromatic chord progression introduces the d-major triad. This chord is not found in b-flat major. However the d-major triad is a first classification chord in g-minor.

When a new key is introduced by chromatic chord progression, the procedure is called *chromatic modulation*. If the second chord of the chromatic chord progression does not belong to the first key, it is analyzed as a function in the new key.

If the tonic of the new key is found as a diatonic triad in the original key, the modulation is said to be to a closely related key. If the tonic of the new key is not a diatonic triad of the original key, the modulation is said to be to a foreign key.

In Part I the analysis of examples and the exercises will employ modulation. The analysis of each exercise will give the student practice and experience in analyzing modulations.

VOICE RANGE

Bach's chorale harmonizations have four voices. The ranges and names of the voices are as follows:

Ex. 31.

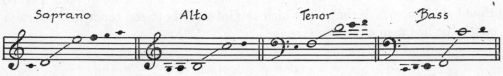

The whole notes and the range between represent the highest frequency. The dark notes on either side of the whole notes vary in size. The largest is more frequent than the smallest.

DOUBLING

In the chorales the triads which appear most often in root position are major and minor. Diminished and augmented triads in root position are extremely rare. Since a triad is composed of three tones, one of the tones must be doubled. A frequency study of Bach's doubling, in major and minor triads which are in root position, is as follows:

MAJOR TRIAD				MINOR TRIAD			
Root	Third	Fifth	Exc.*	Root	Third	Fifth	Exc.*
88%	8%	3%	1%	84%	13%	2%	1%

The above study reveals that there is very little difference in Bach's method of doubling. When major or minor triads are in root position, the root is the best tone to double, the third next, and the fifth last. The first six chapters will stress the doubling of the root and third of a triad.

OPEN AND CLOSE STRUCTURE

The spacing of the tones which make up the triad is of real importance. In the following examples notice the freedom given the bass in its interval relationship to the tenor, alto, and soprano.

* Exceptional triad structures were as follows: Three roots and a third; two roots and two thirds.

Ex. 32.

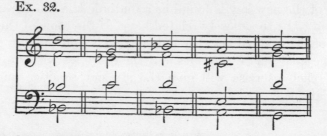

Although Bach usually keeps his bass within an octave below the tenor, he sometimes has the bass exceed an octave to an octave and a fifth below the tenor. This freedom is not permitted between the upper voices. He rarely has an interval greater than an octave between any of the adjacent upper voices.

An examination of his spacing the soprano, alto, and tenor reveals two conventional structures. A chord in which the interval between tenor and soprano is an octave or less is in *close structure*.

Ex. 33.

CLOSE STRUCTURE

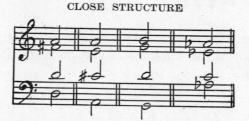

A chord in which the interval between the tenor and soprano is greater than an octave is in *open structure*.

Ex. 34.

OPEN STRUCTURE

Close structure is slightly more frequent than open structure.

FIGURED BASS SYMBOLS

Beginning in the late 16th century and extending through the 17th century, there existed a practice of using symbols in connection with the bass voice to indicate the vertical structure and horizontal movement of the voices above the bass. This practice is called Thorough-Bass or Figured Bass.* By the 18th century musicians had worked out a universal system of symbols. The symbol system for the triad is as follows:

* The soprano or some important melodic line, either instrumental or vocal, is usually found with a figured bass.

1. The bass note without any symbol indicates the root position of a triad. The notes of the chord will be in relation to the signature of the key in which the bass is found.

Ex. 35.

2. The flat, sharp, or natural sign is used to obtain chord spellings which would otherwise be impossible to get due to the key signature. When the sign appears directly beneath the bass, the note a third or tenth above the bass note is altered accordingly. Sometimes an arabic number three with a line through it, ₃, is used. This indicates that the note a third or tenth above the bass note is to be raised one-half step.

Ex. 36.

3. The ♭5, ♮5, or ♯5 indicates lowering or raising the note a fifth or an octave and a fifth above the bass note.

Ex. 37.

4. If the pitch of both the third and fifth above the bass note is to be altered chromatically, two symbols are used below the bass note, the lower symbol referring to the third and the upper symbol to the fifth.

Ex. 38.

Part 1

The Chorale Style

Chapter 1

Two Triads with their Roots a Fifth Apart
(First Principle); Repeated Triads
(First Principle)

A. ROOTS A FIFTH APART

FIRST CONVENTIONAL METHOD

When one triad progresses to another which has its root a fifth * above or below the first, keep the common tone in the same voice and move the remaining voices stepwise to the next triad tones.

Ex. 39.

*PRE–BACH EXAMPLES ***

This method of partwriting was used conventionally by pre-Bach composers as early as the late 15th century. Analyze the following examples:

> Locate 21 examples of the first conventional
> method.

---

* The melodic leap of a fourth in the bass is considered an inversion of the principle of two triads with their roots a fifth apart.

** Play or preferably sing each example before analyzing.

Locate 15 examples where the progression of two triads having their roots a fifth apart does not illustrate the first conventional method of partwriting.

Ex. 40.   Lamentationes Jeremiae   *Gaspar van Werbecke (c. 1440–1520)*

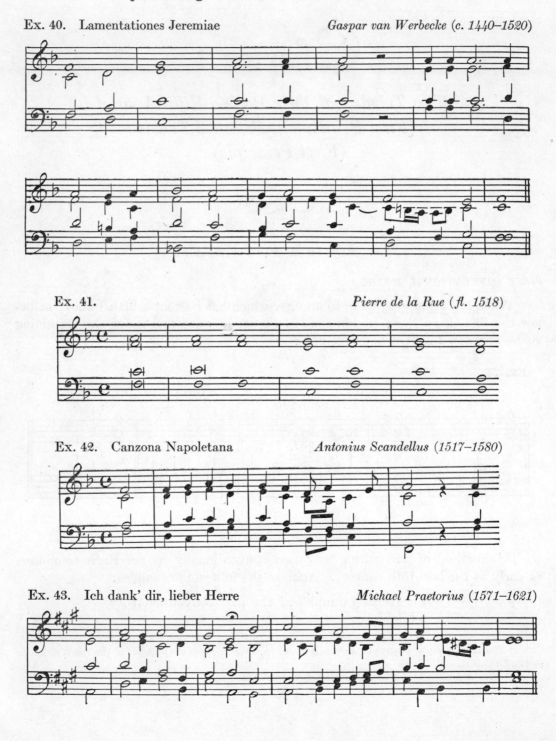

Ex. 41.   *Pierre de la Rue (fl. 1518)*

Ex. 42.   Canzona Napoletana   *Antonius Scandellus (1517–1580)*

Ex. 43.   Ich dank' dir, lieber Herre   *Michael Praetorius (1571–1621)*

Ex. 44.   Von Himmel hoch   *J. H. Schein (1586–1630)*

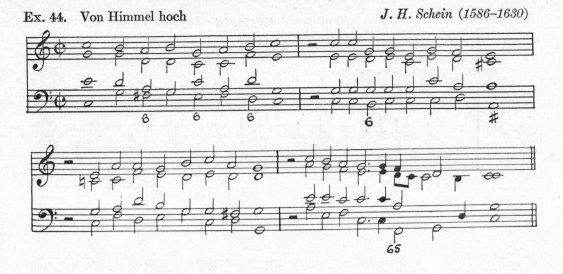

BACH EXAMPLES

Ex. 45.   Herr Christ, der ein'ge Gott'ssohn   **Ex. 46.**   Christus, der ist mein Leben

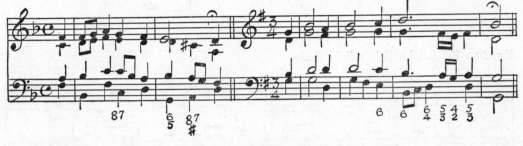

B. REPEATED TRIADS

FIRST CONVENTIONAL METHOD

When a triad is repeated with a new position in the soprano, move the three upper voices in similar motion and retain the open or close structure of the first triad.

Ex. 47.

CLOSE STRUCTURE   OPEN STRUCTURE

PRE-BACH EXAMPLE

Ex. 48. From the Motet "Ecce quo modo moritur"

Jacob Gallus (1550–1591)

EXAMPLE BY A CONTEMPORARY OF BACH

Ex. 49. Christ lag in Todesbanden

Johann Gottfried Walther (1684–1748)

BACH EXAMPLES

Ex. 50. Schmücke dich, o liebe Seele

Ex. 51. Gott lebet noch

PARTWRITING EXERCISES

Partwrite the following exercises, using the following methods:

1) Every triad must have two roots, one third, and one fifth.

2) Each exercise must be in either close or open structure.

3) When two triads have their roots a fifth apart, use the first conventional method.

4) When a triad is repeated having a new soprano tone, use the first conventional method.

A harmonic analysis of the exercise indicating the name of each triad (Roman numeral) should always accompany the solution of the exercise.

Chapter 2

Two Triads with their Roots a Fifth Apart
(Second Principle); Repeated Triads
(Second Principle)

A. ROOTS A FIFTH APART

SECOND CONVENTIONAL METHOD

When one triad progresses to another which has its root a fifth above or below the first, the three upper voices move in similar motion to the next triad tones.

PERFECT AUTHENTIC CADENCE

Ex. 52.

PRE–BACH EXAMPLES

This method of partwriting was used conventionally by pre-Bach composers during the 16th and 17th centuries. Analyze the following examples, locating eleven triad progressions having their roots a fifth apart, using the second conventional method.

Ex. 53. "Salterello" for Four Instruments

attributed to Tylman Susato (16th century)

Ex. 54.   Student Song   Erasmus Widmann (1572–1634)

1st and 2nd Tenor

1st and 2nd Bass

Ex. 55.   Psalm 92   Heinrich Schütz (1585–1672)

Ex. 56.   Psalm 121   Heinrich Schütz

PRE–BACH CHORALE HARMONIZATIONS

Ex. 57.   Christ lag in Todesbanden   Hans Leo Hassler (1564–1612)

Ex. 58.   Es woll' uns Gott genädig sein   Lucas Osiander (1534–1604)

BACH EXAMPLES

Ex. 59. Ach liebe Christen, seid getrost   Ex. 60. Freu' dich sehr, o meine Seele

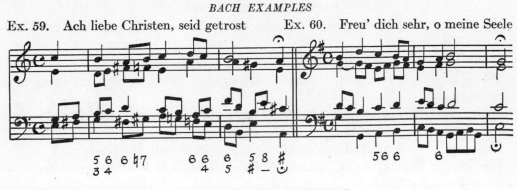

B. REPEATED TRIADS

SECOND CONVENTIONAL METHOD

The change from close to open structure or the reverse may take place when a chord is repeated.

Ex. 61.

PRE–BACH EXAMPLES

This partwriting device is found during the 16th and 17th centuries.

Ex. 62. From "Christmus Song"   *Michael Praetorius*

Analyze example 55.

BACH EXAMPLES

Ex. 63. Aus meines Herzens Grunde   Ex. 64. Valet will ich dir geben

PARTWRITING EXERCISES

Partwrite the following exercises, observing the methods presented in Chapter 1 and Chapter 2.

1) Every triad must have two roots, one third and one fifth.
2) When a triad is repeated, the two conventional methods of partwriting may be used.
3) When two triads progress so that their roots are a fifth apart, use either the first or second conventional method of voice leading.
4) The exercises may have open and close structure during the phrase.
5) The largest leap any upper voice may have when there is a change of harmony is the leap of a third.
6) The largest leap an upper voice may have when a triad is repeated is the leap of a sixth. It is preferable to have the leap of a sixth in the soprano.

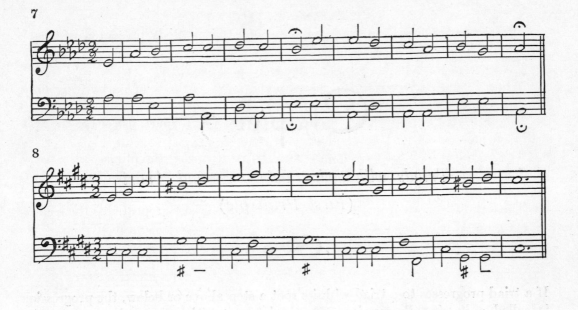

Chapter 3

Triads with their Roots a Second Apart
(First Principle)

If a triad progresses to a triad with its root a step above or below, the progression is called a *Foreign Progression*. Four-voice partwriting research, on examples dating from the late 15th century, reveals that there are basically two common partwriting procedures and a variety of rare exceptional methods used by composers. This chapter deals with the procedure which has the highest frequency.

FIRST CONVENTIONAL METHOD

When a triad progresses to a triad which has its root a second above or below, the three upper parts move contrary to the bass.

Ex. 65.

PRE–BACH EXAMPLES

Ex. 66.   From the Mass on "La sol fa re mi"

Josquin des Prés (c. 1450–1521)

Ex. 67.   From a "Christe Eleison"   *Pierre de la Rue*

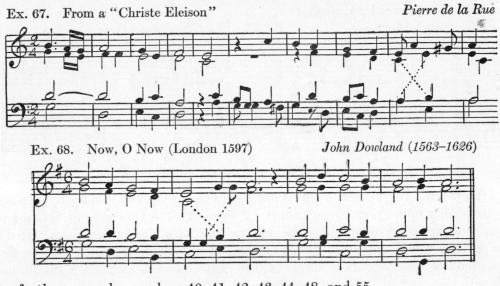

Ex. 68.   Now, O Now (London 1597)   *John Dowland (1563–1626)*

For further examples, analyze 40, 41, 42, 43, 44, 48, and 55.

PRE-BACH CHORALE HARMONIZATIONS

Ex. 69.   Christ lag in Todesbanden   *Lucas Osiander*

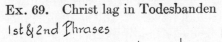

1st & 2nd Phrases

Ex. 70.   Ein' feste Burg   *Daniel Speer (late 17th century)*

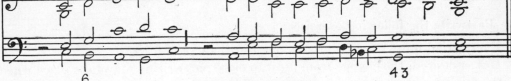

BACH EXAMPLES

Ex. 71.   Wie schön leuchtet der Morgenstern

Ex. 72.   Christ, unser Herr, zum
        Jordan kam   Ex. 73.   Wach' auf, mein Herz

When this foreign progression occurs, two of the upper voices move by step and the remaining upper part leaps a third. Frequently Bach introduces a non-harmonic tone (passing tone) where the interval leap of a third takes place. If this passing tone would cause two voices to move in similar perfect fifths the passing tone would be avoided. In example 72, the passing tone b produces a diminished fifth with the soprano f. These imperfect similar fifths (diminished fifth to a perfect fifth) are not avoided by Bach unless they appear between the soprano and bass.

From time to time in these earlier chapters, devices are pointed out which will be studied later in the text. Special attention is called, however, to the importance of learning the partwriting procedures presented in early chapters, because all exceptional partwriting devices are intrinsically related to them.

PARTWRITING EXERCISES

The partwriting principle of this chapter, together with the principles learned in Chapters 1 and 2, makes it possible to use practically the entire triad harmonic equipment in major and minor keys. The three forms of minor and modulation to the closely related keys have been presented in dictation. In the following exercises, a complete harmonic analysis should accompany the solution. Each chapter from this point on will attempt to approximate the basic harmonic style used by Bach and his contemporaries.

Partwrite the following exercises:

1) Every triad must have two roots, one third, and one fifth.
2) If it is desired, the change from open to close partwriting may take place when the triad is repeated.
3) All principles of partwriting explained previously will be utilized.

Chapter 4

Triads with their Roots a Third Apart (First Principle);
Triads with their Roots a Third Apart
as a Chromatic Progression

When two triads in a progression have two common tones, they are known as *related triads.* If the second triad has its root a third below the first triad, it is known as the *inferior related triad*; if the second triad has its root a third above, it is known as the *superior related triad*; finally, if the root of the second triad is the same, it is known as the *parallel related triad.* A major triad has three related minor triads, and a minor triad has three related major triads.

egb (Superior)   E♭GB♭ (Superior)

CEG — ce♭g (Parallel)   ce♭g — CEG (Parallel)

(Inferior) ace   (Inferior) A♭CE♭

A. ROOTS A THIRD APART

FIRST CONVENTIONAL METHOD

When one triad progresses to another which has its root a third above or below the first, keep the common tones in the same voices and move the remaining voice step-wise to next triad tone.

Ex. 74.

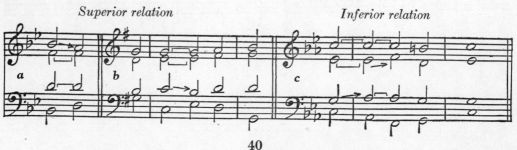

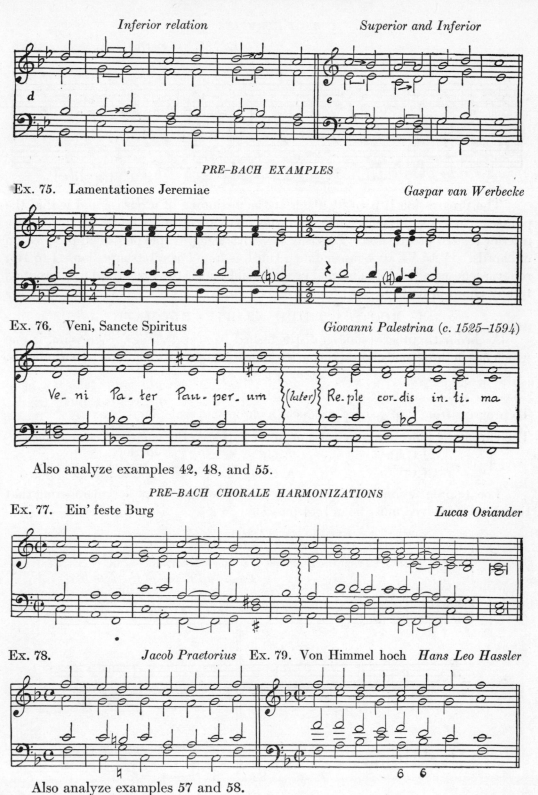

Inferior relation *Superior and Inferior*

PRE–BACH EXAMPLES

Ex. 75. Lamentationes Jeremiae *Gaspar van Werbecke*

Ex. 76. Veni, Sancte Spiritus *Giovanni Palestrina (c. 1525–1594)*

Ve_ni Pa_ter Pau_per_um (later) Re_ple cor_dis in_ti_ma

Also analyze examples 42, 48, and 55.

PRE–BACH CHORALE HARMONIZATIONS

Ex. 77. Ein' feste Burg *Lucas Osiander*

Ex. 78. *Jacob Praetorius* Ex. 79. Von Himmel hoch *Hans Leo Hassler*

Also analyze examples 57 and 58.

Ex. 80.   In dulci jubilo

Ex. 81.   O Herre Gott, dein göttlich Wort

The progression is used by Bach at the beginning of a phrase and within the phrase.   Analysis of Bach's harmonizations reveals a stronger tendency toward the inferior related progression.   This is in line with the principle of normal progression of chords.   IV to VI, roots ascending a third, is found as a retrogression.   I to III, roots ascending a third, is a normal progression because the tonic triad may progress to any chord in its key.

B.   ROOTS A THIRD APART, CHROMATIC

A chromatic progression, as distinguished from a diatonic progression, is one which has in the second chord a chromatic inflection of a note common to both chords.

$$EG\sharp B$$
$$CEG$$

To progress from g to g-sharp produces a chromatic scale line.

The chromatic inflection may raise or lower half-step the common letter name.

EG♯B	CE G	c e♭g
CEG	A♭CE♭	C E G

Locate progressions of this nature in the following examples, remembering that the chords involved must be in root position.

Ex. 82.   From "La rappresentazione di anima e di corpo"

Emilio di' Cavalieri (c. 1550–1602)

Ex. 83.   From a solo Madrigal "Amarilla mia bella"   *Giulio Caccini (c. 1550–1618)*

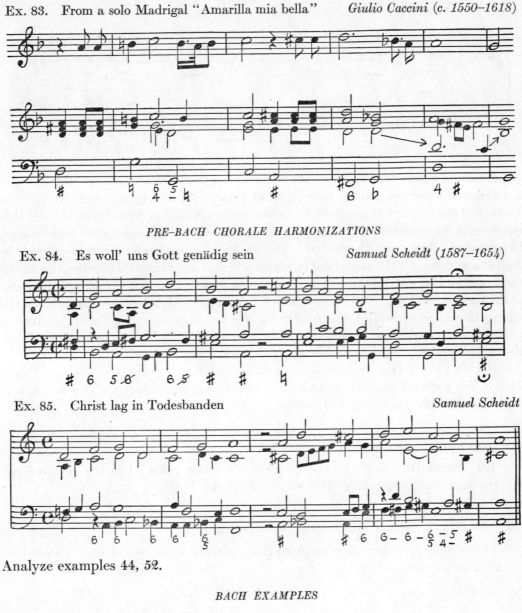

PRE–BACH CHORALE HARMONIZATIONS

Ex. 84.   Es woll' uns Gott genädig sein   *Samuel Scheidt (1587–1654)*

Ex. 85.   Christ lag in Todesbanden   *Samuel Scheidt*

Analyze examples 44, 52.

BACH EXAMPLES

Ex. 86.   Es ist das Heil uns kommen her

Ex. 87.   Wo soll ich fliehen hin

Analysis shows that this progression appears between phrases, or between the last chord of a section and the first chord of a new section.   Composers dating from the early 16th century through Bach to our contemporary composers have used this progression conventionally.   The progression, however, is used under certain conditions, depending upon the period.   The progression is found within the phrase in the 16th and early 17th centuries, in madrigals and instrumental compositions.   In vocal works the outstanding composer to use this device within the phrase was Carlo Gesualdo (1560–1613).   Beethoven has been credited with definitely establishing this type of progression within the phrase, and the progression is given a special name, Third-Relationship.   This Third-Relationship becomes one of the distinguishing characteristics of Wagner's (1813–1883) style.

Bach's use of this progression is definitely for one purpose — to establish a related key without the process of modulation by common chord.   The new key is established at the beginning of the phrase.

THE CONVENTIONAL CHROMATIC PROGRESSION

The chromatic inflection takes place in the same voice when the chords have the same root or a root a third above or below.

THE LESS CONVENTIONAL CHROMATIC PROGRESSION

The chromatic inflection sometimes takes place in another voice.   This method creates a *cross relation*.

BACH EXAMPLES

CONVENTIONAL METHOD

Ex. 88.

Ex. 89.

LESS CONVENTIONAL METHOD

Ex. 90.

cross relation

Ex. 91.

PARTWRITING EXERCISES

Analyze and partwrite the following exercises:

1) Every triad must have two roots, one third, and one fifth.
2) Use all methods of partwriting presented in this and preceding chapters.

Ach Gott und Herr

1

THE CHORALE STYLE

2

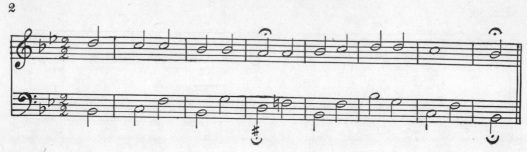

3

4

5

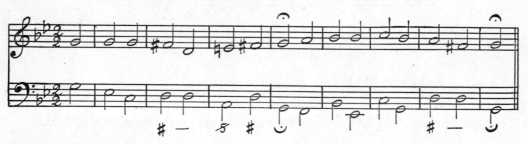

6

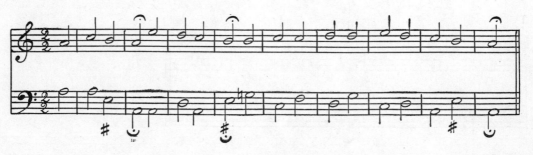

7

8

Chapter 5

Triads with their Roots a Fifth Apart (Conventional Exception); The Triad with a Tripled Root as a Final Chord in the Cadence

A. ROOTS A FIFTH APART, EXCEPTION

THE CONVENTIONAL EXCEPTION

When one triad progresses to another which has its root a fifth above or below the first triad, keep the common tone in the same voice, move the third of the first triad to the third of the second triad, and move the remaining upper voice by step to the next triad tone.

Ex. 92.   Perfect authentic cadence

Any change from close to open structure or the reverse was limited in earlier chapters to repetition of a chord.   The above examples now show that this change may take place when two triads have their roots a fifth apart.

PRE–BACH EXAMPLE

Ex. 93.   Saltarello   Ronde and Saltarello for Four Instruments *Tylman Susato (16th cent.)*

PRE–BACH CHORALE HARMONIZATIONS

Ex. 94.   Vater unser im Himmelreich

M. G. Ernthräus (early 17th cent.)

Ex. 95.   Es woll' uns Gott genädig sein   *Samuel Scheidt*

Ex. 96.   Vom Himmel hoch   *Samuel Scheidt*

BACH EXAMPLES

Ex. 97.   Meinem Jesum las' ich nicht

Ex. 98.   Weg, mein Herz, mit den Gedanken

Ex. 99.   O Haupt voll Blut und Wunden   Ex. 100.   Du, o schönes Weltgebaüde

Bach seems to prefer this method as a conventional exception when V–I or reverse and I–IV or occasionally the reverse occur. The interval of a perfect fourth and a diminished fourth is more frequent than that of the perfect fifth, when the third progresses to the third of the second triad.

The leap of the augmented fourth prohibits use of this method of partwriting in the progression II–V.

Ex. 101.

At this point it is necessary to stress an important theory concerning partwriting exceptions. Bach's exceptional voice leading occurs in tonic, first classification and second classification harmonies. When the exception takes place, he is careful to surround it with conventional procedures. The practice of carefully interlocking exceptions with convention should be applied at all times.

B. TRIAD WITH A TRIPLED ROOT IN THE CADENCE

In Bach's harmonizations of chorales, 1% of the root positions of major triads and 1% of the root positions of minor triads are found with a tripled root. Of these triads, over 95% are found as the last chord in the authentic cadence. The movement of the soprano is supertonic to tonic. Of these authentic cadences about 10% have the tonic triad with a tripled root. This holds for the tonic minor triad as well as the tonic major triad.

Method of partwriting used leading to the tonic triad with the tripled root:

When a triad in the position of the fifth progresses to the octave position of a triad with a tripled root, the third and fifth of the first triad move diatonically to the root of the second triad, and the root of the first triad descends a third to the third of the second triad.

Ex. 102.

PRE–BACH EXAMPLES

Ex. 103.   Motet "O Magnum Mysterium"   *T. L. Vittoria (1540–1611)*

In the technique of Bach, the partwriting illustrated in Vittoria's cadence is extremely rare. He preferred the partwriting method taught in Chapter 1.

Ex. 104.   Now, O now I needs must part   *John Dowland*

PRE-BACH CHORALE HARMONIZATIONS

Ex. 105.   Christ lag in Todesbanden   *Hans Leo Hassler*

Ex. 106.   Ein' feste Burg   *Samuel Scheidt*

BACH EXAMPLES

Ex. 107.   Freu' dich sehr, o meine Seele   Ex. 108.   Von Gott will ich nicht lassen

Note that a non-harmonic tone (passing tone) constantly appears when the upper voice progresses from the doubled root of the dominant triad to the third of the tonic triad.

Further examples may be found in:

Bach-Riemenschneider: 1, 7, 8, 22, 96, 100, 181, 239, 250.
Wonderlich: 12, 34, 55, 61, 91, 116, 129, 154, 156.

Bach's authentic cadence with the soprano line, supertonic to tonic, has the final triad 90% complete and only 10% incomplete (tripled root). In this 10% the leading tone ascends to the tonic. A careful analysis of Bach's cadences unquestionably shows that in his style the leading tone ascends to the tonic or descends to the dominant only because he chooses to have it so. Consequently, a rule formulated to drive the leading tone to the tonic when it is approached from below is questionable, in view of Bach's treatment of the perfect authentic cadence.

PARTWRITING EXERCISES

Phrygian Chorale Melody

Chapter 6

Major and Minor Triads Containing a Doubled Third in Progressions in which the Roots of the Triads are a Second or Third Apart (Conventional Exception)

Of all the major triads used by Bach in fundamental position, about 8% have the third doubled. His minor triads in fundamental position are found about 13% of the time with the doubled third. Partwriting progressions involving major or minor triads with the doubled third become conventional exceptions when the roots of the triads are a second or third apart.

Triads with roots in the bass containing the doubled third are found in either the position of the third or fifth. Bach prefers the position of the third. Approximately 70% of the major triads containing the doubled third are found in the position of the third. About 83% of the minor triads containing the doubled third are found in the position of the third. The triad with the doubled third containing a fifth in four-voice partwriting cannot exist in the position of the octave.

A. ROOTS MOVING UP A SECOND

THE CONVENTIONAL EXCEPTION

When one triad progresses to another which has its root a second above the first, move the third of the first triad in thirds or tenths with the bass, and move the remaining upper voices to the next chord tones contrary to the bass. The second triad in this progression will have one root, two thirds, and one fifth.

Ex. 109.

Definite practical applications of this method of partwriting are as follows:

a) To avoid the augmented second at times in the progression V–VI in minor.
b) To change from open to close structure or the reverse.
c) In the deceptive cadence.

Illustrations of the preceding are as follows:

a) The melodic use of the augmented second is avoided in Bach's style when diatonic chord progressions occur.

Ex. 110.

Bad   *Good*

aug. 2nd

b) The triad with the doubled third may be used to pivot from open to close structure or the reverse.

Ex. 111.

c) The retrogression V–VI in the cadence is known as the *deceptive cadence.* Frequently the VI triad appears with the doubled third.

Ex. 112.

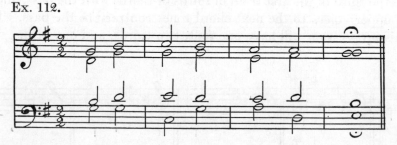

* The voice leading from a triad with a doubled third will be discussed in Section C of this chapter.

This method of partwriting is found as early as the late 15th century. Locate nine examples of it in the following:

Ex. 113. From the Mass "La sol fa re mi" *Josquin des Prés*

Ex. 114. Traverod *Ludwig Senfl (c. 1490–1555)*

For further practice analyze examples 40 and 43.

PRE-BACH CHORALE HARMONIZATIONS

Ex. 115. Ein' feste Burg ist unser Gott Ex. 116. Vom Himmel hoch, da
Lucas Osiander komm' ich her *Lucas Osiander*

Ex. 117. Vater unser im Himmelreich *M. G. Ernthräus*

Ex. 118.   Jesu, nun sei gepreiset

Ex. 119.   Gottes Sohn ist kommen

Ex. 121.   Sanctus, Sanctus Dominus Deus
Sabaoth

Ex. 120.   Christ lag in Todesbanden

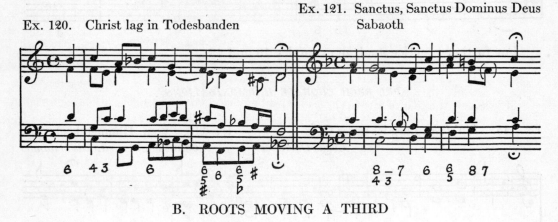

B. ROOTS MOVING A THIRD

THE CONVENTIONAL EXCEPTION

When a triad progresses down a third to another which has a doubled third:

a) Keep two common tones and the remaining upper voice will leap usually a fourth, rarely a fifth.

Ex. 122.

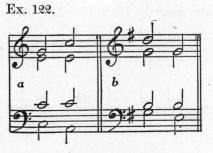

b) Do not keep the common tones; move the third of the first triad in thirds or tenths with the bass and the remaining voices contrary to the bass to the next chord tones.

Ex. 123.

When a triad progresses up a third to another which has a doubled third:

a) Keep the 5th of the first triad and the 3rd of the second triad as a common tone, and the remaining upper voices will move contrary to the bass to the next chord tones.

Ex. 124.

b) Keep the 5th of the first triad and the 3rd of the second triad as a common tone, move the 3rd of the first triad in thirds or tenths with the bass, and the remaining voice will move by step to the next chord tone.

Ex. 125.

PRE-BACH EXAMPLES

The methods of partwriting triads with their roots a third apart just discussed are extremely rare during the 16th and early 17th centuries. It is not until the early 18th century that this becomes a conventional exception.

Locate eleven examples of the progression having two triads with their roots a third apart. The second triad must have the third doubled.

Ex. 126.   Canzona napoletana

Antonius Scandellus

PRE-BACH CHORALE HARMONIZATIONS

Ex. 127.   Christ lag in Todesbanden   Ex. 128.   Es woll' uns Gott genädig sein
         Hans Leo Hassler   *Lucas Osiander*

BACH EXAMPLES

Ex. 129.   Hilf, Herr Jesu, lass gelingen

Ex. 130. Christ, unser Herr, zum Jordan kam

Ex. 131. Gelobet seist du, Jesu Christ

Ex. 132. Zeuch ein zu deinen Toren

Ex. 133. Erstanden ist der heil'ge Christ

Ex. 134.   Herzliebster Jesu, was hast du

Ex. 135.   O grosser Gott von Macht

Bach preferred the root position of a triad progressing down a third to the root position of another. When the second triad of this progression has the doubled third, the chord progression in Bach's style is I–VI. The progression to a triad which has its root a third above is quite rare.

C.   THE PROGRESSION FROM A TRIAD WITH DOUBLED THIRD

A triad with a doubled third may progress to another which has its root, above or below, a fifth, second, or third. Techniques of composition dating from the late 15th century through the 19th century show a vast variety of partwriting procedures for handling this problem. These procedures cannot be organized into simple methods of partwriting like those found in Chapters 1 through 5. There is, however, a common denominator in all progressions leading from a triad with a doubled third. This common denominator is the melodic movement to the next chord of the two voices which double the third.

The horizontal movement of any two parts may be contrary, oblique, or similar. Bach preferred oblique and contrary to similar. In order of frequency, oblique and contrary (about the same percentage for each) overshadow similar motion.

The following examples illustrate the three horizontal resolutions of two voices doubling an interval of a triad:

Ex. 136.

Oblique   Contrary   Similar

The following table lists Bach's melodic preference in order of frequency:

In oblique motion
 (a) the second voice moves a third.
 (b) the second voice moves a fourth or fifth. The scale steps most frequently
   used are tonic to dominant or reverse and tonic to subdominant or reverse.

In contrary motion
 (a) both voices move a step.
 (b) one voice moves a step and the other moves a third.
 (c) one voice moves a step and the other moves a fourth or fifth.
 (d) one voice moves a third and the other a third, fourth, or fifth.

In similar motion (the least frequent)
 (a) one voice moves a step and the other voice a fourth.
 (b) one voice moves a third and the other voice a fifth.

The following examples illustrate resolutions from triads with the doubled third:

Ex. 137.

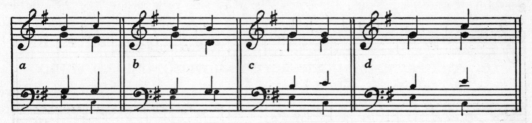

Ex. 138.

Ex. 139.

Locate illustrations of the voice leading from a triad with the doubled third in the following examples: 43, 44, 81, 94, 106, 113, 115, 116, 117, 118, 119, 120, 126, 127, 129, 130, 131, 132, 133, 134, and 135.

PARTWRITING EXERCISES

In solving the exercises one must remember that the frequency of a partwriting device will determine whether it is conventional, a conventional exception, or exceptional. A higher frequency of conventional methods must be used in each exercise. Be sure to follow a conventional exception with convention. The leaps tonic to dominant and tonic to subdominant are always good in the upper voices. The solution of each exercise must be accompanied by a harmonic analysis.

Chapter 7

The Triad in First Inversion:
Tonic, Subdominant, and Dominant Triads

The theory of inversion permits modification of the intervallic structure of a triad without destroying the triad's identity. The first inversion of a triad has the third in the bass. The complete figuration written below the bass tone to indicate the first inversion of a triad is $\frac{6}{3}$. Under normal conditions the 3 is omitted. The following example serves to illustrate the procedure.

Ex. 140.

When a flat, natural, or sharp sign is placed below the 6, the third above the bass tone is affected.

Ex. 141.

VOICE LEADING IN THE BASS INVOLVING FIRST INVERSIONS

The use of an inversion of a triad makes possible better voice leading in the bass. An inverted triad coming between the strong root positions of triads increases the musical interest of a composition. In the following examples, compare the bass

66

voice of the first, which utilizes root positions, with the bass voice of the second, which utilizes triads in root positions as well as first inversion.

Ex. 142.   *J. Sebastian Bach*

PRE–BACH USAGE AND EXAMPLES

The first inversions of major and minor triads may be found as early as the 13th century. It is not the province of this treatise to discuss at length the historical development of inverted triads as they were used chronologically; but it is safe to say that the principles of voice leading into and out of an inverted triad were definitely crystallized by the close of the 16th century. It is also necessary to remember that the principles of chord progression in the 16th century differed from those in the 18th century. Musical treatises of the 16th century do not discuss triads but, rather, explain vertical structures from the intervallic relationship of any upper part to the bass. In short, the bass tone was the foundation of all intervallic relationship above it. Keeping this in mind, the following pre-Bach examples should not be analyzed from a standpoint of fundamental bass; and class discussion should confine itself to the first inversion of a triad, considering the approach and departure, and stressing the melodic movement of the bass voice.

In the following examples, study the triads in first inversion which are introduced by retaining the same bass tone. This is called the *stationary bass introduction of a first inversion of a triad.*

Ex. 144. Credo   *William Byrd (1543–1623)*

Ex. 145.   Motet — Emendem in Melius   *Cristobal Morales (c. 1500–1553)*

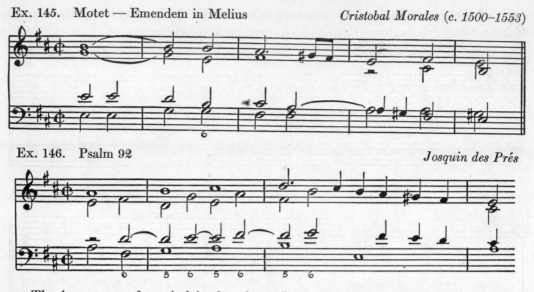

Ex. 146.   Psalm 92   *Josquin des Prés*

The bass tone of a triad in first inversion may be introduced from above or below by step:

Ex. 147.   Uere Languores Nostros
                Thomas Luis De Victoria (c. 1540–1611)

Ex. 148.   Agnus Dei
                Claude Goudimel (c. 1505–1572)

Ex. 149.   Gloria   *William Byrd*

The bass tone of a triad in first inversion may be introduced by leap from above or below. The interval most frequently found is a major or minor third. Which examples have the first inversion of a triad introduced by the root position of the same triad? Which examples have the first inversion of a triad introduced by leap in the bass when two chords are involved?

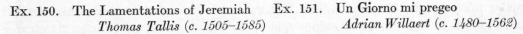

Ex. 150.   The Lamentations of Jeremiah   Ex. 151.   Un Giorno mi pregeo
         Thomas Tallis (c. 1505–1585)   *Adrian Willaert (c. 1480–1562)*

Ex. 152.   Credo   *Claude Goudimel* Ex. 153.   Loquebantur   *Giovanni Palestrina*

Analyze examples 150 through 153 in class discussion, emphasizing the following points:

    a)   Method of doubling used in the triad in first inversion.
        Use the plan discussed in the latter part of this lesson.
    b)   Method of melodic movement in the bass directly after the triad in first inversion.
    c)   Melodic movement from the doubled tones in the triad in first inversion.

The preceding discussion reveals five fundamental procedures used during the 16th century for handling the approach from and departure to a triad in first inversion. They are as follows:

1. The bass tone of a first inversion may be derived from the fundamental position of a triad having the same bass tone. The bass tone of the inverted triad may be left by step or by leap.

2. The bass tone of a first inversion of a triad may be approached by step and left by step.

3. The bass tone of a first inversion of a triad may be approached by leap and left by step.

4. The bass tone of a first inversion of a triad may be approached by step and left by leap.

5. The bass tone of a first inversion of a triad may be approached by leap and left by leap.

BACH'S USAGE

Bach's method of partwriting the first inversion of a triad differs very little from earlier procedures. The controlling factors which helped to organize his method are: 1) much less use of crossing voices, 2) classification of chords, 3) clearer procedure of approach and departure, and 4) crystallization of a method of doubling.

1. CROSSING VOICES

A noticeable decline in the use of crossing voices in four-part vocal writing appears in the latter part of the 17th century among North German composers. Although Bach uses this device in his choral writing as well as instrumental compositions, the number of examples is so slight that little emphasis need be placed upon it. In four-part writing the alto seldom crosses the soprano, and in like manner the bass rarely rises above the tenor. Considering the inner parts, the tenor is found more often crossing the alto. As the number of parts increases, so will the examples of crossing voices increase.

2. CLASSIFICATION OF CHORDS

The following table shows Bach's use of the first inversion of triads in the classification of root movements:

Tonic Triad	I	Most common
First Classification {	V	Very common
	VII	Not as frequent as IV but more frequent than II
Second Classification {	II	Not common (II^7 found more often)
	IV	Quite common
Third Classification	VI	Rare
Fourth Classification	III	Infrequent but found more often than VI

3. PROCEDURE OF APPROACH AND DEPARTURE

The following tables show Bach's method of handling the first inversion of a triad:

Ex. 154.

Bass tone introduced

1) By step — 50%

2) By leap — 23%

3) By implied leap — 22%

4) By chromatic step — 4.5%

5) By same bass tone — .5%

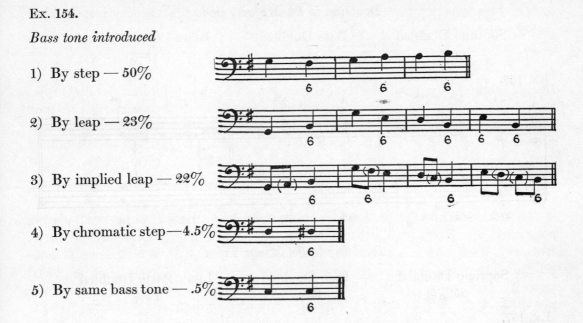

Ex. 155.

Bass tone left

1) By step — 72%

2) By implied leap — 17%

3) By leap — 9.5%

4) By chromatic step — 1.0%

5) By same bass tone — .5%

4. METHOD OF DOUBLING

The following tables show the method of doubling in the first inversions of major and minor triads in chorale harmonizations by Bach:

Doubling in the Major Triad

Soprano Doubled	Bass Doubled	Inner Parts Doubled
66%	19%	15%

Ex. 156.

Doubling in the Minor Triad

Soprano Doubled	Bass Doubled	Inner Parts Doubled
55%	33%	12%

Ex. 157.

Study the preceding tables and answer the following questions:

(a) In the first inversion of a major triad is the soprano, bass, or inner part the best tone to double?

(b) In the first inversion of a minor triad is the soprano, bass, or inner part the best tone to double?

(c) In the major triad find the frequency of the fundamental third and fifth in the soprano.

(d) In the minor triad find the frequency of the fundamental third and fifth in the soprano.

(e) When the inner parts are doubled in major and minor triads, what is the interval of the chord most frequently doubled?

BACH'S USAGE

Of all triads found in first inversion in Bach's chorales the tonic, the first classification dominant, and the second classification subdominant triads have the highest frequency. If we consider these triads by themselves, their respective frequencies are as follows:

Tonic	50%
Dominant	30%
Subdominant	20%

A triad in the first inversion may be introduced in the bass by step from above or below. Analyze the following Bach examples, giving

(1) a. Classification and name of the chord introducing the triad in first inversion.
   b. Classification and name of the triad in first inversion.
   c. Classification and name of the triad following the triad in first inversion.

(2) a. The direction of the bass line into and out of the chord in first inversion.
   b. The doubling in the triad in first inversion.
   c. The movement of the voice leading into and out of the doubled tone of the triad in first inversion.

Ex. 158. Wer weiss, wie nahe mir mein Ende

Ex. 159. Hast du denn, Jesu, dein Angesicht

Ex. 160. O wie selig seid ihr doch, ihr Frommen

Ex. 161. Durch Adams Fall ist ganz verderbt

Ex. 162. Liebster Immanuel, Herzog der Frommen

DEDUCTIONS

1) The soprano is the best tone to double in a first inversion, next the bass, last an inner voice (the inner voice is most often the 5th of the chord).

2) The doubled tone in a first inversion is best left by contrary motion, next oblique motion, and last similar motion.

3) When an inner part leaps a wide interval, the best tones to use are tonic to dominant or tonic to subdominant (the reverse is also good in both cases).

A triad in first inversion may be introduced in the bass by leap from above or below. Analyze the following Bach examples, giving

  (1) a. Classification and name of the chord introducing the triad in first inversion.

       b. Classification and name of the triad in first inversion.

       c. Classification and name of the triad following the triad in first inversion.

  (2) a. The direction of the bass line into and out of the chord in first inversion.

       b. The doubling in the triad in first inversion.

       c. The movement of the voice leading into and out of the doubled tone of the triad in first inversion.

Ex. 163.   Christus, der ist mein Leben

Ex. 164.   Gottlob, es geht nunmehr zu Ende

Ex. 165.   Valet will ich dir geben   Ex. 166.   Vater unser im Himmelreich

DEDUCTIONS

1) In the bass the most common interval used in approaching a triad in first inversion is a third, next a fourth, and last a larger interval.
2) The soprano is the best tone to double in a first inversion. The bass is the next best tone to double, and last the inner part.
3) The doubled tone in a first inversion is best left by contrary motion, next by oblique motion, and last by similar motion.

A triad in first inversion may be introduced from above **or below by implied** leap. If the interval of a third (and sometimes a fourth) in the bass, **introducing a** triad in first inversion, is filled in by a non-harmonic tone, an implied leap **is created.** The voice-leading of the upper parts will retain the same characteristics **found in** the principle of the leap in the bass. Although the device will not be utilized until Chapter 11, it is a conventional characteristic of Bach's style.

Ex. 167. Herzliebster Jesu, was hast du verbrochen

Ex. 168. Wenn wir in höchsten Nöten sein

A triad in first inversion may be introduced in the bass by chromatic stepwise motion. Analyze the following Bach examples, giving

(1) a. Classification and name of the chord introducing the triad in first inversion.
   b. Classification and name of the triad in first inversion.
   c. Classification and name of the triad following the triad in first inversion.

(2) a. The direction of the bass tone into and out of the chord in first inversion.
   b. The doubling in the triad in first inversion.
   c. The movement of the voice leading into and out of the doubled tone of the triad in first inversion.

Ex. 169.   Uns ist ein Kindlein heut' gebor'n

Ex. 170.   Das walt' Gott Vater und Gott Sohn

Ex. 171.   Nun ruhen alle Wälder

DEDUCTIONS

1) When a triad in first inversion is introduced by chromatic step-wise motion, the bass line usually ascends.
2) The rules of doubling in the first inversion remain the same.
3) Movement into and out of the doubled tone is based on the previous deductions.
4) The triad in first inversion introduced by chromatic step-wise motion is usually a first classification dominant triad in a related key. For the present the modulation is to be recognized. In Chapter 22 a slightly different analysis will be discussed in connection with this use of chromatic chord progression.

An exceptional progression involves a first inversion of a triad between phrases. In Chapter 4, the cross relation between the last chord of a phrase and the first chord of the new phrase was explained as a conventional exception in Bach's style. The following examples illustrate this practice when the second triad is in first inversion.

Ex. 172.   Verleih' uns Frieden gnädiglich

Ex. 173.   Christus, der ist mein Leben

The following example illustrates one of the few introductions of a first inversion by the principle of the stationary bass. The progression is chromatic, and it occurs occasionally between phrases.

Ex. 174. Freu' dich sehr, o meine Seele

PARTWRITING SUGGESTIONS

DOUBLING

   (a) Soprano tone is the best to double.

   (b) Bass tone is the next best to double.

   (c) An inner part may be doubled, and the 5th of the chord is preferable.

   (d) Do not double the leading tone or the raised 6th degree of the minor scale.

MELODIC MOVEMENT TO AND FROM A TRIAD IN FIRST INVERSION

   (a) Try to keep the common tone in the same voice.

   (b) Try to make the upper parts move by step into and out of the triad in first inversion.

   (c) The leap of a third in one of the upper voices is possible. Avoid too many leaps in succession.

   (d) The best large interval leap in an upper part is tonic to dominant or the reverse and tonic to subdominant or the reverse.

   (e) The following melodic movement of two upper voices should be encouraged when partwriting:

Ex. 175.

MELODIC MOVEMENT LEADING FROM THE DOUBLED TONE IN THE TRIAD IN FIRST IN-VERSION

   (a) Contrary motion is best.

   (b) Oblique motion is next best.

   (c) Similar motion is possible but infrequent.

Chapter 8

The Triad in First Inversion: Leading-Tone, Supertonic, Submediant, and Mediant Triads

The following table shows the remaining possible triads used in the first inversion in **major and minor** keys:

	FIRST CLASSIFICATION	SECOND CLASSIFICATION	THIRD CLASSIFICATION	FOURTH CLASSIFICATION
Major Key	VII	II	VI	III
Minor Key	VII	II	(VI)	III
	♯			♯
	7			7
	(VII)	$\left(\begin{smallmatrix} \text{II} \\ \# \\ 6 \end{smallmatrix}\right)$	$\left(\begin{smallmatrix} \text{VI} \\ \# \\ 6 \end{smallmatrix}\right)$	(III)

The triads in parentheses are extremely rare. The other triads will be discussed in their order of classification here.

A. FIRST CLASSIFICATION: THE DIMINISHED TRIAD ON THE LEADING TONE

Bach uses the diminished triad in major and minor on the leading tone in two ways: first, as a contrapuntal chord between two positions of the tonic triad, and, second, as a first classification chord preceded by the second classification subdominant triad.

A contrapuntal use of an inverted triad stresses smooth voice leading in all parts. Each voice takes on the characteristics of non-harmonic tones, such as passing tones, neighboring tones, etc. This use of an inverted triad is usually found between two positions of the same triad (no change of classification), and is also found between a chord of one classification and a chord of another classification. The following examples illustrate the contrapuntal use of the inverted triad:

79

Ex. 176.

The first inversion of the leading-tone triad may follow the root position of the second classification subdominant triad. Bach also liked to use the triad originating on the same bass tone of the supertonic triad. In most cases the fifth of the supertonic triad is a passing tone. The following examples show the leading-tone triad following the triads of the second classification.

Ex. 177.

BACH EXAMPLES

Ex. 178. Vater unser im Himmelreich   Ex. 179. Aus meines Herzens Grunde

Ex. 180. Ach Gott, vom Himmel sieh'
darein   Ex. 181. Wach' auf, mein Herz, und singe

Ex. 182. Ach Gott und Herr,
wie gross und schwer   Ex. 183.   O Haupt voll Blut und Wunden

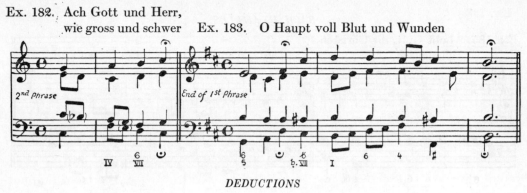

DEDUCTIONS

DOUBLING

(a) The third of the triad is the best tone to double.

(b) The fifth is the next best tone to double.

(c) Never double the root, because it is the leading tone.

INTERVALS FOUND IN THE SOPRANO

In order of frequency, the intervals found in the soprano of a diminished triad are third, fifth, and root.

PARTWRITING

In the majority of examples cited, the three upper parts move by step through the leading-tone triad.

UNEQUAL SIMILAR FIFTHS

Bach does not hesitate to write a perfect fifth to a diminished fifth or the reverse when it occurs between two upper voices, namely soprano and alto, alto and tenor, or tenor and soprano.

B. SECOND CLASSIFICATION: THE SUPERTONIC TRIAD

In a major key the supertonic triad is minor. In a minor key two forms of the supertonic triad are found. The most frequent is the diminished triad. The less frequent is the minor triad with the raised sixth degree of the scale.

Bach does not use the major or minor supertonic triad in first inversion as often as one might be led to believe. A study of his compositions will show that he prefers the first inversion of the supertonic seventh chord.

The following examples show how the triad may be introduced in a major key:

Ex. 184.

BACH EXAMPLES

Ex. 185.   Lobt Gott, ihr Christen,
                allzugleich   Ex. 186.   Wenn wir in höchsten Nöten sein

Ex. 187.   Es ist gewisslich an der Zeit

DEDUCTIONS

CHORD PRECEDING THE SUPERTONIC

(a) Tonic, usually approached by step

(b) Submediant, approached by leap or implied leap

DOUBLING

(a) The third is the best tone to double.

(b) The root may be doubled if one of the roots is in the soprano.

(c) Do not double the fifth.

PARTWRITING

Follow the rules established in Chapter 7. When the triad is preceded or followed by the tonic, keep the fifth of the triad below the root. This rule will help to avoid parallel fifths. Keep the triad in close structure.

The following examples show how the diminished and minor supertonic triad may be used in a minor key:

Ex. 188.

BACH EXAMPLES

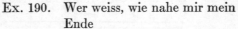

Ex. 189. Das neugeborne Kindelein

Ex. 190. Wer weiss, wie nahe mir mein Ende

Ex. 191. Wer nur den lieben Gott lässt

Ex. 192. Ist Gott mein Schild und Helfersmann

DEDUCTIONS

CHORD PRECEDING THE SUPERTONIC

   (a) The supertonic may be approached by leap or step by tonic.

   (b) The supertonic may be approached by leap or implied leap by the third classification submediant triad.

DOUBLING

   (a) The third is the best tone to double.

   (b) The root is the next best tone to double.

   (c) Avoid doubling the fifth.

INTERVALS FOUND IN THE SOPRANO

   The root or third are found in the soprano; the fifth is rarely found.

PARTWRITING

   The voice leading into the diminished triad is the same as in Chapter 7.

C. THIRD CLASSIFICATION: THE SUBMEDIANT TRIAD

In a major key, Bach occasionally used the first inversion of the submediant triad as common chord between two keys. The triad becomes a second classification supertonic triad in the new key. In all instances the third is doubled. The following examples serve to illustrate Bach's procedure:

BACH EXAMPLES

Ex. 193.   Nun ruhen alle Wälder

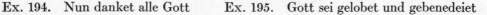

Ex. 194.   Nun danket alle Gott   Ex. 195.   Gott sei gelobet und gebenedeiet

Ex. 196.   Liebster Gott, wann werd' ich sterben

Use of the submediant as a major or diminished triad in minor in first inversion is practically non-existent in the works of Bach.

D. FOURTH CLASSIFICATION: THE MEDIANT MINOR TRIAD IN A MAJOR KEY

Use of this triad in first inversion by Bach is restricted to a few progressions. The triad is preceded by either the dominant or the subdominant triad. In both instances a retrogression occurs in the classification of chords. The triad is followed by either a subdominant or a submediant triad before it progresses to the first classification chord. The following examples show typical progressions involving the first inversion of the mediant triad:

Ex. 197.

BACH EXAMPLES

Ex. 198. Jesu, nun sei gepreiset

Ex. 199. Ich freue mich in dir

Ex. 200. Jesu Leiden, Pein und
Tod

Ex. 201. Ich ruf' zu dir, Herr Jesu Christ

The other typical appearance of the mediant triad in Bach's style is found in the cadence formula. The initial effect of the triad is mediant, because it appears on a strong beat; but this effect is immediately lost, because the sixth above the bass progresses to a fifth above the same bass. The resulting sonority is nothing more than a dominant triad. If the sixth is prepared as a common tone, it is a suspension. If the sixth is approached by step from above, it is an accented passing tone.* Bach inherited the progression from his predecessors. The following examples illustrate the device:

Ex. 202.

BACH EXAMPLE

Ex. 203. Wie schön leuchtet der Morgenstern

DEDUCTIONS

DOUBLING

The third of the mediant triad is always doubled.

INTERVAL FOUND IN THE SOPRANO

The fundamental is most often found in the soprano.

PARTWRITING

Voice leading is the same as described in Chapter 7.

THE MEDIANT TRIAD IN A MINOR KEY

The major mediant triad formed by the descending melodic minor scale is not used in first inversion enough to warrant any consideration. The augmented mediant triad, however, has a fairly high frequency in its first inversion. Use of this triad in minor, as is the case in major, is limited to certain typical progressions. The triad is preceded by a second classification chord (most often a subdominant

* See Chapter 11, page 109.

triad) and then progresses to a submediant triad. The following example illustrates the typical progression involving the first inversion of the mediant triad.

Ex. 204.

BACH EXAMPLES

Ex. 205. Vater unser im Himmelreich Ex. 206. Herr Jesu Christ, du höchstes Gut

Ex. 207. O Ewigkeit, du Donnerwort

As in a major key, Bach uses the augmented mediant triad in minor keys in the cadence formula. The progression comes from his predecessors, and in many ways it retains the 17th century flavor more than it does when in a major key. The following examples illustrate use of the augmented triad in first inversion in the cadence formula:

BACH EXAMPLES

Ex. 208. Christ lag in Todesbanden   Ex. 209. Durch Adams Fall ist
                                                        ganz verderbt

C is an accented upper neighboring tone.

f is an accented passing tone

DEDUCTIONS

DOUBLING

The third of the chord is always doubled.

INTERVAL FOUND IN THE SOPRANO

The fundamental is most often found in the soprano, but sometimes the third is found.

PARTWRITING

The voice leading is the same as described in Chapter 7.

EXERCISES

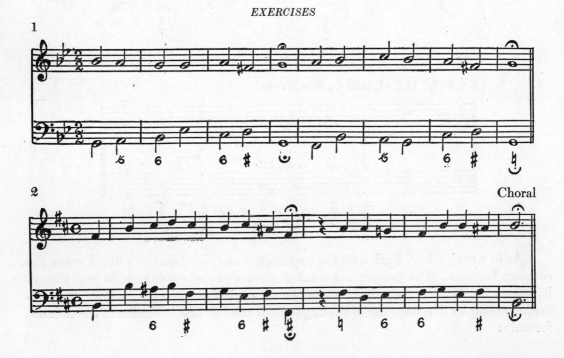

3
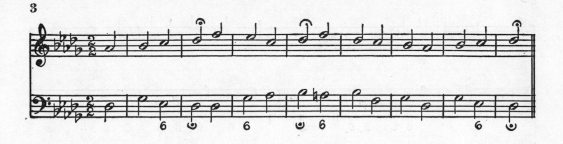

4
Choral

5
Choral

6
Phrygian Melody

7

Chapter 9

The Triad in Second Inversion

The second inversion of a triad, or the 6-4 chord, has the fifth in the bass. The figured bass for the second inversion of a triad is $^6_4$.

Ex. 210.

The triad in second inversion is a non-functional chord.* It plays no part in the classification of chords, and its use in musical texture is non-harmonic. For this reason the voice leading to and from the $^6_4$ chord is essentially controlled by procedures used in the domain of non-harmonic tones.

Examples of the $^6_4$ chord date back as far as the late 13th century. As in the case of the first inversion of a triad, the 16th and 17th centuries provide the best examples clearly defining the conventional use of the $^6_4$ chord. The examples will be classified according to the approach and departure in the bass.

PRE–BACH EXAMPLES

THE PEDAL OR STATIONARY $^6_4$

Ex. 211.   Madrigal — Moro lasso   Ex. 212.   O Bone Jesu
   Carlo Gesualdo (c. 1560–1613)   *Orlando di Lasso (c. 1530–1594)*

* This point of view takes the $^6_4$ chord through the period of Bach.

91

In the previous examples the triad in second inversion has the bass (fifth of the chord) doubled. The upper voices move into the $^6_4$ chord by step and leave either by step or sustained as a common tone.

THE ARPEGGIATED $^6_4$

This is approached by leap or implied leap from a triad of the same spelling.

Ex. 213. Ave Regina
   Orlando di Lasso Ex. 214. Ricercare Gerolamo Cavazzoni (fl. 1542)

Ex. 215. "Gloria," from Missa Brevis   Giovanni Palestrina

Again the bass tone is doubled in the $^6_4$ chord. In the first and third examples, the three upper voices are sustained when the inversion appears. In the resolution on the same bass tone, the two upper parts resolve by step and the remaining voice is sustained as the common tone. The second example differs little from the others. Note that the upper parts move through different positions of the triad by the use of passing tones. In the resolution the common tone is sustained, and the tenor and alto create an ornamental resolution of the b and g to a and f respectively.

THE STEP-WISE $^6_4$

This is approached by step from above or below.

Ex. 216. Sotto due negri e sottilis-
  simi archi Orlando di Lasso Ex. 217. Domine Jesu Christe Orlando di Lasso

Ex. 218.　Benedictus　　　　　　　　　　　　*Orlando Gibbons (1583–1625)*

Again the bass tone is doubled in the $^6_4$ chord. In the first example, the soprano is sustained as a common tone, the alto and tenor move from the essential tones c and a by passing tones to the e and c. In reality these are implied leaps. In the resolution the a in the soprano is a suspension resolving to g-sharp. The c in the tenor is an appoggiatura resolving to b. The alto e is sustained as the doubled root of the EG♯B chord, which is the essential harmony at this point. In the second example note how the $^6_4$ structure is delayed by the suspended b in the soprano to the a, which eventually resolves ornamentally to g-sharp. In the tenor c is a passing tone resolving to b. In the second $^6_4$ chord in the third example, the soprano e is approached by leap from the essential tone a.

THE PASSING $^6_4$

This type apparently does not appear until the 17th century.

DEDUCTIONS

DOUBLING

The conventional interval to double is the fifth of the chord, which is the bass tone.

INTERVAL OF THE CHORD IN THE SOPRANO

The fundamental, third, and the fifth are all good in the soprano.

PARTWRITING

Approach

Keep the common tone or tones if possible in the same voice.
Move the remaining voice or voices by step.

Departure

In the majority of cases the triad in second inversion has a stationary resolution.
The fifth remains in the same voice, becoming the root.
The remaining voices progress down a step. The figuration describes the voice leading as follows: $^6_4$ $^5_3$

BACH'S USAGE

Bach uses the $^6_4$ chord less often than one would expect. He utilizes the types found in the 16th and 17th centuries, but the emphasis placed upon them is radically changed. The following table illustrates the comparative stress placed upon types:

	Pre-Bach	*Bach*
Pedal or stationary $^6_4$ chord	common	rare
Arpeggiated $^6_4$ chord	common	less common
Step-wise $^6_4$ chord	common	common
Passing $^6_4$ chord	rare	quite common
Accented cadential $^6_4$ chord *	rare	common

Bach retains the conventional doubling in the $^6_4$ chord established by his predecessors. The bass tone (the fifth of the chord) is doubled 98% of the time.

BACH EXAMPLES

THE PEDAL OR STATIONARY $^6_4$

Ex. 219.   Beschränkt, ihr Weisen dieser Welt

PASSING $^6_4$ CHORD

Ex. 220.   Komm, Gott Schöpfer, heiliger Geist

The $^6_4$ chord coming between two positions of the same triad is extremely rare. The next example is the most characteristic use of the passing $^6_4$ chord.

Ex. 221.   Valet will ich dir geben

* A complete $^6_4$ chord on a strong beat without delaying 6 or 4: $^7_4$ $^6_-$ or $^6_3$$^-_4$ etc.

ACCENTED CADENTIAL $\frac{6}{4}$ CHORD

This use of the $\frac{6}{4}$ chord is the most common. It may be introduced by step-wise motion from above or below and by the implied leap.

Introduced by step-wise motion:

Ex. 222.   Vater unser im Himmelreich   Ex. 223.   Von Gott will ich nicht lassen

Ex. 224.   Das neugeborne Kindelein

In example 189, which is in triple meter, the $\frac{6}{4}$ chord falls on the second beat. This is more often found than the $\frac{6}{4}$ chord on the first beat.

Introduced by implied leap:

Ex. 225.   Ermuntre dich, mein schwacher Geist

DEDUCTIONS

DOUBLING

Double the bass tone, which is the fifth of the chord.

MELODIC MOVEMENT TO AND FROM A TRIAD IN SECOND INVERSION

(a) Try to retain the common tone.

(b) Try to move the upper voices into the $\frac{6}{4}$ chord by step-wise motion.

INTERVAL OF CHORD IN SOPRANO

(a) The fundamental, third, or fifth of the triad may be found in the soprano.

EXERCISES

Chapter 10

Non-Harmonic Tones: Introduction

∞

In the preceding chapters emphasis has been placed upon the use and partwriting of the fundamental harmonies. In certain instances, however, the vertical sonorities have seemed to be dependent upon stronger vertical sonorities. Use of the $\frac{6}{4}$ chord and certain first inversions of triads have been explained by assuming a horizontal point of view. This introduction and the next three chapters will concentrate upon the relation of the horizontal movement of the four individual voices to the vertical implied harmony.

In the early part of the 17th century there appeared a new conception of handling the relation between the essential and unessential elements in music. By the time of Bach and his contemporaries one finds clarification of these elements. In this period the essential sonorities are those which make up the harmonic fabric that are in turn controlled by the theory of inversion and the theory of fundamental bass. The remaining sounds which appear horizontally in any of the voices but are not in the harmony become, because of their very nature, unessential tones. The majority of unessential tones are dissonant.

A *non-harmonic tone* is a tone which appears in a vertical sonority but plays no part in the theory of inversion of that sonority. The non-harmonic tone does not have the spelling of any of the intervals which make up the implied harmony. The non-harmonic tone is related melodically to one of the members of the chord.

The correct use of essential and unessential tones is dependent upon the style of a period. Without a thorough knowledge of the early 18th century style, one can hardly grasp the trends which these elements took on as musical thought developed toward the Wagnerian style.

THE THEORY OF NON–HARMONIC TONES

The essential sonority of the 18th century is the triad. From a theoretical standpoint the triad can control within its own octave a vast number of unessential tones. Notice the possible unessential tones which belong to the c-major triad:

98

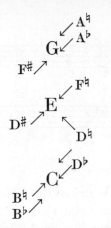

If the three tones of the triad are added to the nine unessential tones related to the triad, the sum is the twelve tones which comprise the equal division of an octave.* When the c-major triad becomes a tonic triad, it loses most of its unessential tones, in the early 18th century style. This is due to the fact that conventional harmonies used to establish the key center present horizontal procedures which conform to the scale. Tones which do not belong to the harmony, but which have the spelling of a scale tone, are *diatonic non-harmonic tones*. In the compositions of Bach one finds non-harmonic tones which have an accidental spelling foreign to the key scale. These non-harmonic tones are chromatic or altered non-harmonic tones.

A non-harmonic tone is found in the musical fabric surrounded by harmonic tones.

Ex. 226.

The manner in which the non-harmonic tone is derived and resolved will classify it. Because of this, it is necessary to emphasize the importance of the classification of non-harmonic tones; for this is the basis of the concept of preparation and resolution of dissonance.

THE CLASSIFICATION OF NON–HARMONIC TONES

1. PASSING TONE

When a non-harmonic tone is interpolated step-wise between two harmonic tones of different pitch, it is called a *passing tone*.

* By the late 19th century, composers and theorists accepted these tones on a closer basis of equality and formed the theory of the duo-decuple scale. This scale was in its formative state in the early 18th century.

Ex. 227.

2. SUSPENSION

If in a progression of two chords any of the tones of the first chord are delayed from their normal step-wise melodic movement at the moment the second chord appears, the non-harmonic dissonant effect is called a *suspension.**

Ex. 228.

3. NEIGHBORING TONE

When a non-harmonic tone is interpolated step-wise between two harmonic tones of the same pitch, it is called a *neighboring tone.*

Ex. 229.

4. ANTICIPATION

If in a progression of two chords any of the tones of the first chord move step-wise to forecast the consonant intervals of the second chord, the dissonance is called an *anticipation.*

* If the resolution of the suspension note ascends, it is frequently referred to as a *retardation.*

Ex. 230.

5. ESCAPE TONE

If a non-harmonic tone is derived step-wise and leaps to a harmonic tone, it is called an *escape tone*.

Ex. 231.

6. APPOGGIATURA

If a non-harmonic tone is derived by leap and resolved step-wise, it is called an *appoggiatura*.

Ex. 232.

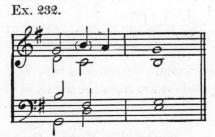

7. PEDAL POINT

If a series of chord progressions occurs over a sustained bass tone, the sustained tone is called *pedal point*.

Ex. 233.

8. CHANGING TONE

If a non-harmonic tone is derived step-wise and leaps an interval of a third in opposite direction to another non-harmonic tone which is resolved step-wise, the dissonant tones are called *changing tones*.

Ex. 234.

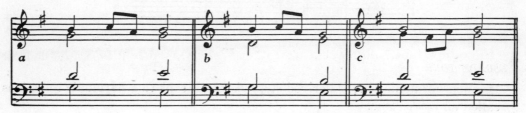

PRE–BACH USE OF UNESSENTIAL TONES

In the sixteenth century, passing tones, suspensions, neighboring tones, anticipations, and escape tones are employed in the musical texture in varying frequency. Passing tones, ascending or descending, are common.   The following examples from the works of Orlandus Lassus illustrate the use of passing tones:

Ex. 235.   Magnum Opus Musicum No. 75   Ex. 236. Magnum Opus Musicum No. 139

Suspensions are also common.   Suspensions may be found in any voice.   The following examples of suspensions are from the works of Orlandus Lassus:

                                                        Ex. 238. Magnum Opus   Ex.   239.   Magnum
Ex. 237.   4th Penitential Psalm   Musicum No. 183   Opus Musicum No. 197

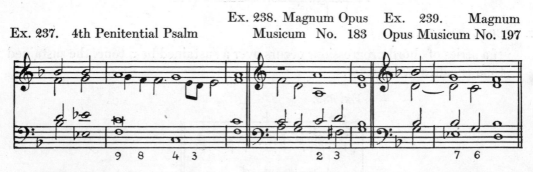

Neighboring tones are less frequent, and the sixteenth century technique uses only the lower neighboring tone.   The following example is found in the works of Orlandus Lassus:

Ex. 240.   Magnum Opus Musicum No. 307

The escape tone is infrequent, and its use is restricted to a four-note melodic figure called the cambiata.

CAMBIATA

Ex. 241.   "Agnus Dei" from Missa Brevis
Giovanni Palestrina

INTERRUPTED CAMBIATA

Ex. 242.   Magnum Opus Musicum No. 259
Orlando di Lasso

The anticipation is less frequent.   The following example is found in the works of Orlandus Lassus:

Ex. 243.   Magnum Opus Musicum No. 173

The following table illustrates the relative frequencies of unessential tones, comparing sixteenth century style with Bach's style:

TYPE	16TH CENTURY	BACH
Passing tone	very frequent	very frequent
Suspension	quite frequent	quite frequent
Neighboring tone	less frequent (lower only)	frequent (upper and lower)
Anticipation	not too frequent	not too frequent
Escape tone	not too frequent (only in cambiata figure)	not too frequent

TYPE	16TH CENTURY	BACH
Appoggiatura	none	rare in chorales
Changing tone	none	rare in chorales (not too frequent in other compositions)
Pedal point	rare	rare in chorales (not too frequent in other compositions)

Chapter 11

The Passing Tone

Passing tones appear in the chorales according to the following table:

Single	unaccented	ascending	
		descending	
	accented	ascending	
		descending	
Double	similar motion	unaccented	ascending
			descending
		accented	ascending
			descending
	contrary motion	unaccented	
		accented	
Triple	similar motion	unaccented	
		accented	
	two similar and one contrary	unaccented	
		accented	
Quadruple	two similar and two contrary		
	three similar and one contrary		

A. UNACCENTED SINGLE PASSING TONE

The unaccented passing tone is the most frequent non-harmonic tone. It appears ascending or descending in any voice.

Ex. 244. Mach's mit mir, Gott   *J. Sebastian Bach*

The passing tones at 1, 2, 4, and 5 move to the next chord in similar motion with either one or two voices. In each case the interval in the second chord, approached by the similar motion of the passing tone and the harmonic tone of the first chord, is either a third or a sixth.

The passing tone at 3 moves contrary to the remaining three voices.

The passing tone at 6 moves in oblique motion to the tenor and in contrary motion to the remaining voices.

Apply the same analytical procedure to the passing tones found in the following chorales:

BASS VOICE

> Wonderlich: 7, 8, 34, 64, 80, 111.
> Bach-Riemenschneider: 39, 313, 100, 164, 368, 32.

TENOR VOICE

> Wonderlich: 57, 143, 9, 16, 21.
> Bach-Riemenschneider: 160, 293, 13, 261, 81.

ALTO VOICE

> Wonderlich: 58, 103, 87, 89, 26.
> Bach-Riemenschneider: 288, 44, 122, 106, 36.

SOPRANO VOICE

> Wonderlich: 6, 136, 148, 44, 25.
> Bach-Riemenschneider: 217, 47, 94, 335, 53.

DEDUCTIONS

The melodic interval of a third formed by two harmonic tones in a progression of two chords is frequently filled in by a passing tone. An exception is found in the authentic cadence, or within the phrase when the three upper voices of the dominant triad progress downwards to the next chord tones of the tonic triad. The possible passing tones between leading tone and dominant are not in the style.

Ex. 245.

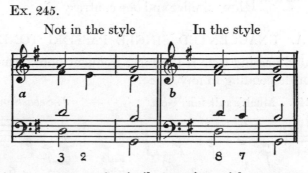

A single passing tone moves in similar motion with one or two other voices to the next harmonic tone. The intervals found most often progressing in similar motion under these conditions are the third, sixth, and perfect or augmented fourth.

Between any combination of four voices with the exception of soprano and bass, a perfect fourth followed by an augmented fourth, or the reverse, is good. Octaves and fifths in similar motion, between the passing tone and any one of the remaining voices, do not appear.

A single passing tone moves contrary to the remaining voices as they progress to the next harmonic tones.

A single passing tone moves obliquely to the remaining voices to the next harmonic tone.

A single passing tone moves obliquely to one voice and contrary to the remaining voices as they progress to the next harmonic tones.

In the following exercises fill in the interval leap of a third in each voice according to the style:

ACCENTED SINGLE PASSING TONE

When a non-harmonic tone which is interpolated step-wise between two harmonic tones of different pitch appears on a beat, it is called an *accented passing tone*. Descending accented passing tones are more frequent than ascending ones.

Ex. 246. An Wasserflüssen Babylon

The accented passing tone at 1 in the alto moves in similar fourths with the bass.

The accented passing tone at 2 in the soprano moves in similar fourths with the bass.

The accented passing tone at 3 in the soprano progresses in contrary motion to the tenor and bass and in oblique motion to the alto.

Apply the same analytical procedure to the accented passing tones found in the following chorales:

BASS VOICE

> Wonderlich: 7, 25, 47, 84, 133.
> Bach-Riemenschneider: 39, 53, 27, 161, 24.

TENOR VOICE

> Wonderlich: 66(4th), 38(4th), 147(4th), 31(5th).
> Bach-Riemenschneider: 266(4th), 90(4th), 322(4th), 70(1st).

ALTO VOICE

> Wonderlich: 21, 31, 17(5th), 21(2nd).
> Bach-Riemenschneider: 81, 119(5th), 167(1st).

SOPRANO VOICE

> Wonderlich: 15(2nd), 46(5th), 109(4th).
> Bach-Riemenschneider: 90(2nd), 58(1st), 48(6th).

DEDUCTIONS

Descending single accented passing tones are the most frequent.

Single accented passing tones are used much less than unaccented passing tones.

The most common single accented passing tone is found in the bass.

Single accented passing tones found in the upper voices are best analyzed from the bass tone of the chord in which they occur. The 4-3 accented passing tone is the most frequent. The other important ones are the 7-6, 9-8, 2-3, and 7-8.

Occasionally two harmonic tones a fourth apart are diatonically connected by interpolating two passing tones. Quite often the second passing tone is accented. This device may be found in other voices, as well as in the bass.

Ex. 247.

In the following exercises select at least one place in each where an accented passing tone may be used effectively, and in addition use unaccented passing tones:

ACCENTED 6-5 PASSING TONE AND ACCENTED 6-7 PASSING TONE

Under certain conditions what appears to be a first inversion of a triad on a strong beat is in reality an accented passing tone, a 6th progressing to a 5th above the bass, forming the root position of a triad. This is frequently encountered in the cadence formulas.

Study the following example:

Ex. 248. Ach Gott, vom Himmel sieh' darein

The g♯ in the tenor is approached by leap and establishes the third of the dominant harmony. The c in the soprano is an accented passing tone. See Chapter 8, page 86. The example is an illustration of an ornamental cadence formula.

B. UNACCENTED DOUBLE PASSING TONES

Unaccented double passing tones appear in similar motion ascending and descending, and in contrary motion.

Ex. 249.   Aus tiefer Not schrei' ich zu dir

Ex. 250.   Erhalt' uns, Herr, bei deinem Wort

Ex. 251.   An Wasserflüssen Babylon

The double passing tones at 1 and 2 moving in similar motion are a third apart (the tenth is an octave and a third). The bass and tenor move in contrary motion to the soprano and alto. At 3, the double passing tones move in sixths. All voices move in similar motion. At 4, the double passing tones moving in sixths progress in similar motion with the alto and in contrary motion to the bass. At 5, the double passing tones move in contrary motion from a tenth to a sixth.

Apply the same analytical procedure to the double passing tones found in the following chorales:

Unaccented double passing tones in similar motion

Wonderlich: 17, 22(4th), 34(3rd), 37(1st), 87, 139(3rd).
Bach-Riemenschneider: 119, 200(4th), 100(3rd), 72(1st), 122, 179(3rd).

Unaccented double passing tones in contrary motion

Wonderlich: 13, 15(3rd, 4th), 18(3rd), 34(4th), 40(2nd).
Bach-Riemenschneider: 10, 245(3rd), 100(4th), 263(5th), 26(2nd), 265(3rd).

Unaccented double passing tones are frequent.

Any combination of two voices may be employed for double passing tones.

The percentage of ascending double passing tones is slightly higher than that of the descending type.

About 16% of the unaccented double passing tones are found to be in contrary motion.

The unaccented double passing tones in similar motion progress in thirds and sixths.

The unaccented double passing tones moving in contrary motion usually have the following interval patterns:

        (1) sixth-octave-tenth

        (2) tenth-octave-sixth

        (3) twelfth-tenth-octave

        (4) octave-tenth-twelfth

        (5) unison-third-fifth

In the following exercises use single and unaccented double passing tones according to the style:

ACCENTED DOUBLE PASSING TONES

Accented double passing tones are infrequent. They are found in similar and contrary motion.

Ex. 252.   Nun lob', mein' Seel', den Herren

Ex. 253.   Herr Jesu Christ, mein's Lebens Licht

At 1 the accented doubled passing tones are in thirds rising to the first inversion of the eg#bd seventh chord. On the first beat of the measure the dominant triad is established, and on the second beat the d in the soprano is a passing seventh which converts the triad into a seventh chord.

At 2 the d and a-sharp in the soprano and alto appear on the second half of the beat and create the feeling of double accented passing tones in contrary motion, because the first inversion of the C#EG# triad is established on the beat. Accented contrary double passing tones are extremely rare.

Study the accented double passing tones in the following chorales:

Wonderlich: 22(8th), 69(1st), 87(1st), 93(5th), 98(1st), 85(1st).
Bach-Riemenschneider: 63(3rd), 69(9th), 110(3rd), 116(4th, 6th, 9th), 92(4th).

DEDUCTIONS

Accented double passing tones in similar motion are not common. They are found ascending and descending in thirds and sixths. Any combination of two voices may contain the double passing tones.

Accented double passing tones in contrary motion are extremely rare. The 4-3 and 7-8 interval relationship above the bass tone is one of the most practical forms to use.

In the following exercises use single and double passing tones, with at least one double passing tone for each exercise:

C. TRIPLE PASSING TONES AND THE PASSING CHORD

Triple passing tones appear, having two voices moving contrary to the third voice.

Ex. 254. O wir armen Sünder

Ex. 255. Ach Gott, vom Himmel sieh' darein

A passing chord results if the vertical sonority caused by three voices moving step-wise and the fourth remaining stationary is non-functional.*

Ex. 256.   Christus, der uns selig macht   Ex. 257.   Schwing' dich auf zu deinem Gott

At 1 and 2 the voices moving in similar motion progress respectively in thirds and sixths. The voice moving in contrary motion progresses according to the principles explained in section B dealing with contrary motion double passing tones.

At 3 the voices moving in similar motion progress in tenths. The tenor voice moving in contrary motion uses the following intervals with the bass: unison, third, and fifth; and with the soprano: tenth, octave, and sixth.

At 4 the bass, alto, and soprano progress as if they were first inversions of triads on consecutive scale steps.

Continue the analysis in the following chorales:

Wonderlich: 3(4th), 6(3rd), 12(5th), 34(3rd), 81(6th), 22(5th, 7th), 28(2nd), 33(6th), 45(3rd).

Bach-Riemenschneider: 88(1st), 100(3rd), 198(7th), 285(3rd, 5th), 305(1st), 307(7th).

DEDUCTIONS

Passing chords in the form of triple passing tones are more frequent than triple passing tones.

Three voices moving in similar motion progress in the shape of a first inversion of a triad.

Two voices moving contrary to the third progress according to the principle of double passing tones in contrary motion.

Accented triple passing tones are rare. Three examples may be cited:

Bach-Riemenschneider: 33(4th), 259(1st, 12th).

D. QUADRUPLE PASSING TONES

Occasionally quadruple passing tones appear in the chorales. Since they are so seldom used, two examples will suffice:

---

* Passing chords may also result from combinations of passing tones and neighboring tones.

Ex. 258. Nun bitten wir den heiligen
Geist   Ex. 259. Ach Gott, wie manches Herzeleid

E. UNCONVENTIONAL DOUBLING IN THE ROOT POSITION OF TRIADS INFLUENCED BY PASSING TONES

Only 3% of the major triads in root position, and 2% of the minor triads, have the 5th doubled. Practically all triads with the doubled 5th are involved in progressions containing dissonance, i.e., unessential tones or discords.

Another unusual vertical structure of a triad appears in connection with the unessential tones. It is composed of two roots and two thirds.

Ex. 260.

This structure is found either as a tonic chord or, infrequently, as a subdominant chord.

The following examples illustrate some unconventional doubling in triads influenced by passing tones:

5TH DOUBLED IN ROOT POSITION OF A TRIAD

Ex. 261. An Wasserflüssen Babylon   Ex. 262. Wo soll ich fliehen hin

3RD DOUBLED IN ROOT POSITION OF A TRIAD WHICH DOES NOT NORMALLY HAVE THE THIRD DOUBLED

Ex. 263.   Nun lob', mein' Seel', den Herren

THE TRIAD WITH TWO ROOTS AND TWO THIRDS

Ex. 264. Herzlich lieb hab' ich dich, o Herr   Ex. 265. Befiehl du deine Wege

PARTWRITING EXERCISES

1

2

Chapter 12

The Suspension

An analysis of the 371 chorales * reveals that Bach used 1,661 suspensions of various types. According to these figures an average of over four suspensions for each chorale could be expected. In reality, there are 21 chorales without suspensions, 61 containing one suspension, 56 containing two, 43 containing three, and so on. There are a few chorales which contain as many as 19 suspensions. The longest chorale, No. 205, "Herr Gott, dich loben wir," which is really a combination of a number of chorales, contains 45 suspensions. The majority of chorales, however, have from one to four suspensions.

There are two kinds of suspensions, the single and the double. A little over 90% are single suspensions. These are found distributed throughout the phrase; but the double suspension is localized in the cadence formula.

All suspensions are figured from the bass, and they are named according to the interval formed between the bass and suspension note. The following examples illustrate a number of common suspensions:

Ex. 266.

* The data on frequencies is taken from a thesis, "The Suspension in the Chorales by Bach" by Wayne Dunlap, written under the author's guidance.

118

A. THE SINGLE SUSPENSION

The single suspension may be found in any voice, but Bach has a definite preference. The following table shows the percentage frequency for each voice.

Soprano	2%
Alto	71%
Tenor	23%
Bass	4%

The voice in which the suspension occurs is divided into three elements, all of which contribute to the correct partwriting of the device. These three elements are the preparation note, the suspension note, and the resolution note.

Ex. 267.

Preparation note   Suspension note   Resolution note

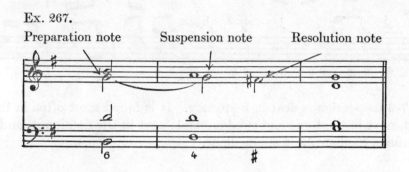

The most common single suspension is the 4-3 suspension. It is found most often in the dominant harmony, next in the tonic, rarely in supertonic, submediant, and mediant, and never in the leading tone.

Ex. 268.   Wie schön leuchtet der
           Morgenstern   Ex. 269.   Seelen-Bräutigam

The next most common single suspension is the 9-8. This is found most often in the tonic harmony, next in the subdominant, next in the dominant and submediant, rarely in the supertonic and mediant, and never in the dominant seventh chord or the leading tone triad.

Ex. 270. Nun sich der Tag geendet hat

Ex. 271. Es wird schier der letzte Tag

The 7-6 suspension is next in frequency. It is found most often in the leading tone triad, next in the tonic and subdominant, next in the dominant, and rarely in the supertonic, mediant, and submediant.

Ex. 272. Wenn mein Stündlein vorhanden ist

Ex. 273. O Haupt voll Blut und Wunden

The single suspension in the bass, based on the frequency indicated earlier in this chapter, may be reduced to two types: the $\frac{5}{2}$, which is the most frequent, and the $\frac{7}{4}$, which is rare. Both types are sometimes referred to as the 2-3 suspension. In the first type the resolution of the bass tone will create the first inversion of a triad; in the second type the resolution of the bass tone will create the fundamental position of a triad. The $\frac{5}{2}$ suspension is found most often in the dominant harmony, next in the tonic, rarely in the leading tone and subdominant, and never in the supertonic, mediant, and submediant. The $\frac{7}{4}$ is found in the tonic harmony and not in any of the remaining harmonies.

Ex. 274.   Es wird schier der letzte Tag   Ex. 275.   Liebster Jesu, wir sind hier

The 2-1 suspension found in the tenor voice is rare.   The following example illustrates Bach's use of this suspension:

Ex. 276.   Christ, der du bist der helle Tag

One of the most important factors in connection with the suspension is the time value assigned the preparation note and the suspension note.   The time value assigned to the preparation note is never less than the time value of the suspension note.   Normally the time value assigned the preparation is the same as, or twice, that of the suspension note.

Ex. 277.

CORRECT   INCORRECT

The preparation note may be tied to the suspension note, or the suspension note may repeat the preparation note.

Ex. 278.   Wenn wir in höchsten Nöten sein   Ex. 279.   Freu' dich sehr, o meine Seele

Locate and analyze the suspensions in the following chorales, keeping in mind location in the phrase, harmonic background, and time value assigned to the preparation note and suspension note:

4-3 SUSPENSION

Soprano

> Wonderlich: 38(1st), 14(4th), 17(5th), 48(6th), 39(1st).
> Bach-Riemenschneider: 9(1st), 340(4th), 119(5th), 166(6th), 43(2nd).

Alto

> Wonderlich: 38(2nd), 6(2nd), 8(1st), 10(4th), 11(6th).
> Bach-Riemenschneider: 9(2nd), 217(2nd), 313(1st), 180(4th), 304(6th).

Tenor

> Wonderlich: 7(4th), 47(2nd), 48(1st), 51(7th), 143(6th).
> Bach-Riemenschneider: 39(4th), 27(2nd), 166(1st), 333(7th), 293(6th).

9-8 SUSPENSION

Soprano

> Wonderlich: 39(2nd).
> Bach-Riemenschneider: 343(2nd).

Alto

> Wonderlich: 10(1st), 15(5th), 24(2nd), 19(3rd), 31(3rd).
> Bach-Riemenschneider: 180(1st), 184(5th), 162(2nd), 210(3rd), 167(3rd).

Tenor

> Wonderlich: 49(3rd), 50(6th), 98(1st), 53(2nd), 106(4th).
> Bach-Riemenschneider: 238(3rd), 16(6th), 338(1st), 282(2nd), 348(4th).

7-6 SUSPENSION

Soprano

> Wonderlich: 90(7th).
> Bach-Riemenschneider: 83(7th).

Alto

> Wonderlich: 1(2nd), 11(2nd), 10(1st), 12(4th), 14(6th).
> Bach-Riemenschneider: 40(2nd), 304(2nd), 180(1st), 1(4th), 340(6th).

Tenor

> Wonderlich: 47(1st), 106(5th).
> Bach-Riemenschneider: 27(1st), 348(5th).

5-2 SUSPENSION IN THE BASS

> Wonderlich: 23(1st), 12(6th), 51(3rd), 96(1st), 101(1st).
> Bach-Riemenschneider: 228(1st), 1(6th), 333(3rd), 30(1st), 131(1st).

DEDUCTIONS

Every suspension demands a preparation note, a suspension note, and a resolution note.

The preparation note is a harmonic tone of the same pitch as the suspension note.

The suspension note is a dissonant tone.

The resolution note is a harmonic tone.

The suspension note descends either a half step or a whole step to the resolution note.

The following table illustrates the time values that may be assigned to the preparation and suspension notes:

PREPARATION NOTE	SUSPENSION NOTE
2 beats	1 beat
1 beat	1 beat
1 beat	$\frac{1}{2}$ beat
$\frac{1}{2}$ beat	$\frac{1}{2}$ beat

The suspension note should not have a time value greater than that of the preparation note. There is one exception to this rule, in the first phrase, second measure, third and fourth beats of:

> Wonderlich: 23.
> Bach-Riemenschneider: 228.

In the 4-3 and 7-6 suspensions the resolution note is rarely doubled in another voice.

In the 9-8 suspension the resolution note is doubled by the bass.

Under certain conditions parallel fifths may be avoided by use of a suspension.

Partwrite the following exercises, using passing tones and single suspensions:

B. RESOLUTION OF THE SINGLE SUSPENSION IN CONNECTION WITH CHANGE OF THE BASS TONE

Occasionally, when the suspended note resolves, the vertical structure may be **a** different inversion of the harmony or a new harmony. In both instances the normal resolution note is not disturbed. The figured bass under these circumstances normally contains one number, namely, 9, 4, 7. This occurs most frequently in the **9** suspension, next in the 7 suspension, and rarely in the 4 (never when the 4 suspension occurs in the dominant harmony). When the harmony changes at the place of resolution, the second chord usually has its root a third below the first chord; occasionally the root of the second chord may be a fifth below the first; the bass tone may be either a third or a fifth below.

THE 9, 7, AND 4 SINGLE SUSPENSIONS

Ex. 280.   Nun sich der Tag geendet
            hat   Ex. 281.   Für Freuden lasst uns springen

Ex. 282.   Ermuntre dich, mein schwacher Geist

Locate and analyze Bach's method of handling the 9, 7, and 4 type single suspensions:

9 SUSPENSION

Wonderlich: 7(5th), 12(5th), 14(5th), 23(1st), 96(4th).
Bach-Riemenschneider: 39(5th), 1(5th), 340(5th), 228(1st), 30(4th).

7 SUSPENSION

Wonderlich: 17(4th), 46(3rd).
Bach-Riemenschneider: 119(4th), 362(3rd).

4 SUSPENSION

Wonderlich: 24(2nd), 46(3rd), 57(4th).
Bach-Riemenschneider: 162(2nd), 362(3rd), 160(4th).

DEDUCTIONS

The 9, 7, and 4 suspensions are treated in the same way as the 9-8, 7-6, and 4-3 suspensions. They have the preparation note, suspension note, and resolution note.

Partwrite the following exercises, using passing tones and suspensions:

(accented Passing tone)

C. THE ORNAMENTAL SINGLE SUSPENSION

Occasionally the suspension of the 4th and 9th are given a decorative melodic line at the time of resolution. In all instances the effect of the legitimate resolution is consummated. The melodic ornament may contain step-wise motion or leaps as large as a fifth. Practically all the ornamental resolutions are located in either the dominant or tonic chords in the cadence. They may be found infrequently within the phrase in tonic or dominant harmonies. Sometimes passing tones may be found in another voice concurrent with the ornamental resolution of a suspension.

Ex. 283.

Ex. 284.   Liebster Jesu, wir sind hier

Locate and analyze Bach's method of handling the ornamental single suspension in the following chorales:

>Wonderlich: 15, 24, 27, 55, 90, 106, 2, 22, 23, 47, 98, 32, 57, 91, 23.
>Bach-Riemenschneider: 184, 162, 232, 8, 83, 348, 279, 200, 228, 27, 187, 87, 160, 283, 228.

D. CHAIN SUSPENSIONS

A succession of two or more single suspensions is called a *chain suspension*.

In a study of 200 chorales, 109 chains of single suspensions were found. Ninety-three were groups of two suspensions, 13 were groups of three suspensions, one contained four suspensions and two contained five suspensions.

Chain suspensions occur on successive beats and allow for the preparation note and resolution note. The preparation note and suspension note are always $\frac{1}{2}$ beat in value. The resolution note of the first suspension will become the preparation note for the next suspension.

Ex. 285.   Heut' ist, o Mensch, ein grosser

Ex. 286.   Komm, Gott Schöpfer, heiliger Geist

Most of the common chains containing two single suspensions are in the following chord progressions:

>9-8 — 4-3   I   V
>9-8 — 7-6   I   VII
>4-3 — 9-8   V   VI
>7-6 — 4-3   IV   I

Chains of more than two suspensions contain the following plan:

9-8 — 4-3 — 9-8 and so on.

4-3 — 9-8 — 4-3

The following combinations are possible:

9-8 — 7-6 — 4-3 and so on.

7-6 — 9-8 — 4-3

It has been pointed out that suspensions rarely appear in the supertonic, mediant, and submediant harmonies. It is usually in a chain of single suspensions that one appears in these harmonies. Chains of double suspensions were not found.

E. THE DOUBLE SUSPENSION

Double suspensions are infrequent. The majority appear in either the tonic or dominant harmonies. A few are found in the subdominant harmony. Although a double suspension may appear within a phrase, the greater majority are found at the cadence. The preparation note, suspension note, and resolution note will be found for each voice involved in the double suspension. The $\frac{6\text{-}5}{4\text{-}3}$ is the most common double suspension, the next is the $\frac{9\text{-}8}{7\text{-}6}$. All other possible double suspensions are rare.

The following excerpts from Bach's harmonizations of the chorales illustrate the double suspension:

Ex. 287.   Was mein Gott will, das g'scheh'

Ex. 288.   Es woll' uns Gott genädig sein

Ex. 289.   Meine Seele erhebet den Herrn

Locate and analyze the double suspensions in the following chorales:

Wonderlich: 48(3rd), 48(4th).
Bach-Riemenschneider: 166(3rd), 166(4th).

PARTWRITING EXERCISES USING PASSING TONES AND SUSPENSIONS

Chapter 13

The Neighboring Tone: Passing Tone
Suspension, Neighboring Tone in Combinations

A. NEIGHBORING TONE

The neighboring tone is next in the order of non-harmonic tone frequency. Single, double, and triple neighboring tones are found in the chorales.

Single neighboring tones are classified into two groups: lower neighboring tone and upper neighboring tone.* The former type is the most frequent. The neighboring tone is in either a half-step or whole-step relation to the harmonic tone. The deciding factor controlling the half-step or whole-step relationship to the harmonic tone is the diatonic scale. The neighboring tone is found in all voices. It is found least often in the soprano in the chorales, because that voice is the cantus, which is seldom ornamented. The following chorales illustrate Bach's use of the single neighboring tone:

Ex. 290. Schaut, ihr Sünder

Ex. 291. Auf, auf, mein Herz, und du mein ganzer Sinn

Ex. 292.

* Accented upper or lower neighboring tones are possible but they are rare. In the bass of Bach-Riemenschneider 143(1st), there is an accented upper neighboring tone.

131

Ex. 293.   Herr Gott, dich loben alle wir

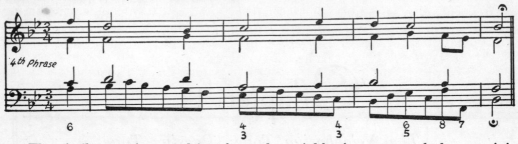

The similar motion resulting from the neighboring tone and the remaining voice or voices as they proceed to the next harmony produces the same interval relationships as those found in the study of passing tones: Thirds, sixths, fourths, imperfect fifths, and sevenths are found, while perfect octaves and perfect fifths are not found.

Analyze the following chorales for neighboring tones:

Wonderlich: 31(4th), 107(1st), 112(4th), 22(5th), 103(4th), 116(5th), 139(2nd).

Bach-Riemenschneider: 167(4th), 49(1st), 330(4th), 200(5th), 44(4th), 7(5th), 179(2nd).

DEDUCTIONS

Lower neighboring tones are most frequent.

The majority of neighboring tones are found in tonic harmony, next in dominant and subdominant, and least of all in the remaining functions.

The similar motion resulting from the neighboring tone and the remaining voice or voices as they proceed to the harmonic tones follows the same deductions made in the study of passing tones.

Occasionally the resolution tone of the neighboring tone is non-harmonic, due to a change of chord. Under these circumstances, the resolution tone usually has the characteristics of an accented passing tone.

Partwrite the following exercises, using passing tones, suspensions, and neighboring tones:

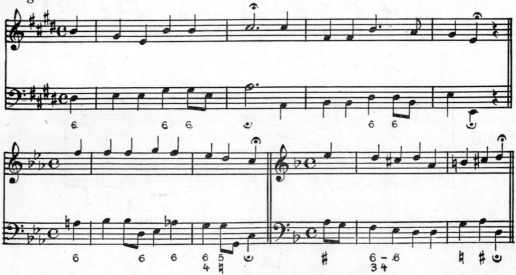

Double neighboring tones are less frequent. The lower neighboring tones are the most frequent.   Upper double neighboring tones and contrary double neighboring tones are rare in comparison to the lower double neighboring tones.

Ex. 294. O Haupt voll Blut und
          Wunden   Ex. 295.   Mit Fried' un Freud' ich fahr' dahin

Ex. 296.   Erschienen ist der herrliche Tag

The double lower neighboring tones in similar motion progress in thirds.   The contrary neighboring tones form a diminished fifth and are derived from harmonic tones a third apart.   They are derived and resolved in tonic harmony.

Analyze the double neighboring tones found in the following chorales:

Lower double neighboring tones

Wonderlich: 80(3rd), 29(2nd), 45(7th), 139(9th), 107(4th, 6th), 112(3rd), 119(5th).

Bach-Riemenschneider: 368(3rd), 209(2nd), 216(7th), 179(9th), 49(4th, 6th), 330(3rd), 85(5th).

Upper double neighboring tones

Wonderlich: 144(3rd), 29(2nd).*
Bach-Riemenschneider: 265(3rd), 209(2nd),* 177(4th), 246(1st), 370(1st), 148(4th).

Contrary double neighboring tones

Wonderlich: 41(2nd), 91(1st), 85(4th).
Bach-Riemenschneider: 17(2nd), 283(1st), 77(4th), 102(3rd).

* Accented double neighboring tones.

DEDUCTIONS

Lower double neighboring tones are the most frequent. The interval between two voices in which double neighboring tones appear is usually a third or a tenth.

Upper double neighboring tones are rare. The interval between two voices in which double neighboring tones appear is most often a third, but a sixth is possible.

Contrary double neighboring tones are less frequent. The intervallic patterns created by two voices in which double neighboring tones appear is as follows:

third	fifth	third
sixth	fourth	sixth
octave	sixth	octave

The majority of double neighboring tones seem to be found in either dominant or tonic harmonies.

Partwrite the following exercises, using passing tones, suspensions, and neighboring tones:

There are a few triple neighboring tones. The following examples illustrate Bach's use of this type of non-harmonic device:

Ex. 297.   Valet will ich dir geben   Ex. 298.   Herzlich tut mich verlangen

B. PASSING TONES IN COMBINATION WITH NEIGHBORING TONES

The following examples illustrate the passing tone in combination with the neighboring tone. Analyze the intervallic relationship between voices which contain non-harmonic tones:

Ex. 299. O Traurigkeit, o Herzeleid   Ex. 300. Erbarm' dich mein, o Herre Gott

Ex. 301. Wer Gott vertraut, hat wohl gebaut

OTHER EXAMPLES

Wonderlich: 34(6th), 16(3rd), 23(1st), 44(1st), 101(4th).
Bach-Riemenschneider: 57(1st), 100(6th), 261(3rd), 228(1st), 335(1st), 131(4th).

DEDUCTIONS

The majority of neighboring tones in combination with passing tones originate in the tonic harmony.

C. SUSPENSIONS IN COMBINATION WITH NEIGHBORING TONES

The following examples illustrate the neighboring tone in combination with the suspension:

Ex. 302. Uns ist ein Kindlein heut' gebor'n   Ex. 303. Jesu, meine Freude

OTHER EXAMPLES

Wonderlich: 80(3rd, 4th), 144(2nd), 133(4th), 129(1st, 2nd, 4th, 6th).
Bach-Riemenschneider: 368(3rd, 4th), 265(2nd), 24(4th), 22(1st, 2nd, 4th, 6th).

DEDUCTIONS

This device is most often found in dominant harmony in the cadence formula.

Partwrite the following exercises, using all types of neighboring tones, passing tones, and suspensions:

Chapter 14

Other Non-Harmonic Tones

A. THE ANTICIPATION

Single and double anticipations are among the least used non-harmonic tones. They are principally located in the cadence formula.

The following examples illustrate common single and double anticipations found in the harmonizations of chorales by Bach:

Ex. 304.   Des heil'gen Geistes reiche Gnad'

Ex. 305.   Werde munter, mein Gemüte

Ex. 306.   Jesu, nun sei gepreiset

Ex. 307.   Freu' dich sehr, o meine Seele

Compare the single anticipations at 1 and 2. By delaying the passing seventh at 1, similar fifths are avoided, but in 2 the passing seventh and the anticipation occur at the same instant. The device at 1 is more frequent. At 3 is an anticipation in combination with a passing tone. At 4 is an anticipation combined with a suspension. The suspension in this

137

device is always resolved before the anticipation takes place. Note the rhythmic groupings used in the voices containing the suspension and anticipation.

Locate and analyze the anticipations in the following chorales:

Wonderlich: 79(4th), 97(4th), 109(4th), 152(6th), 111(5th), 29(3rd, 4th), 55(1st, 2nd, 3rd, 8th).

Bach-Riemenschneider: 59(4th), 175(4th), 149(4th), 121(6th), 32(5th), 209(3rd, 4th), 8(1st, 2nd, 3rd, 8th).

DEDUCTIONS

Anticipations are practically non-existent within the phrase. They are found in the cadence formula, anticipating members of either the tonic harmony or the dominant harmony. Anticipations are frequently used in combination with passing tones or suspensions. In the single anticipation the soprano usually has the device. In the double anticipation the soprano and tenor usually have the device.

B. THE ESCAPE TONE

Single and double escape tones are among the least used non-harmonic tones. They are found within the phrase, usually close to the cadence formula. The following examples illustrate the device:

Ex. 308.   Hast du denn, Jesu, dein Angesicht   Ex. 309.   Ach Gott, wie manches Herzeleid

At 1, the escape tone is derived from the third of the tonic chord. The e^b leaps to the next harmonic tone, changing the direction of the soprano line. At 2, the double escape tones f$^\#$ and a are derived step-wise; they leap, changing the direction of the melodic line to the next harmonic tones.

Locate and analyze the escape tones in the following chorales:

Wonderlich: 38(6th), 109(1st), 111(2nd), 60(4th), 5(2nd).

Bach-Riemenschneider: 9(6th), 149(1st), 32(2nd), 35(4th), 156(2nd), 25(4th), 143(1st), 90(1st).

DEDUCTIONS

The single escape tone is found in the soprano and rarely in other voices. The majority of escape tones are found in tonic harmony.

The melodic contour containing the device is idiomatic for the style.

The escape tone is always derived stepwise ascending from the harmonic tone, and it is left by leap and descends to the next harmonic tone.

Double escape tones are derived and resolved in the same manner as single escape tones.

The interval of a third, and sometimes a sixth, are used between voices containing the double escape tones.

C. THE APPOGGIATURA

The single appoggiatura is among the least used non-harmonic tones. The following example illustrates the appoggiatura in a chorale harmonization:

Ex. 310. Jesu, nun sei gepreiset

At 1, the appoggiatura is approached from the b♭ of the tonic triad and resolves to the root of the supertonic triad.

Locate and analyze the appoggiaturas in the following chorales:

Wonderlich: 152(5th), 3(5th), 64(4th), 126(2nd).
Bach-Riemenschneider: 121(5th), 3(5th), 164(4th), 63(2nd).

DEDUCTIONS

Single appoggiaturas are rare * and double appoggiaturas are practically non-existent.

The single appoggiatura may be found in any voice.

It is approached from below by a leap of a third and resolved downwards by step.

It is found often on the beat and less often on the weak part of a beat.

Similar fifths and octaves are avoided between other voices and the appoggiatura when it is approached and resolved.

D. THE PEDAL POINT

Pedal point is not a characteristic device in chorales. There are a few examples of the device in some chorales. In many instances the pedal point is inverted. If the sustained tone is in an upper part, the device is called an *inverted pedal point.*

* Further study of the appoggiatura will be found in Part 1, Chapter 15.

Inverted pedal points may be the tonic, dominant, or mediant tones of the key. If two tones are sustained, the device is called *double pedal point*. Pedal points of all kinds may be found in Bach's works for organ and orchestra.*   The following examples illustrate the use of pedal point in the chorale:

Ex. 311.   Verleih' uns Frieden gnädiglich

Ex. 312.   Auf dich hoffen wir

PARTWRITING EXERCISES

Partwrite the following exercises using all the non-harmonic tones:

* See Part 3, Chapter 38.

Chapter 15

Seventh Chords: Introduction

A seventh chord is formed by adding a third above the 5th of any type of triad. The interval of the third above the 5th of the triad may be major or minor. Seventh chords are classified as dissonant sonorities. The identification of type of seventh chords depends upon two factors: first, the tonal structure of the triad, and, second, the interval between the root and seventh. The name of the GBDF seventh chord is determined in the following manner:

First factor	GBD	major triad
Second factor	G——F	minor seventh

GBDF is called a *major-minor seventh chord*.

The types of seventh chords used during the 18th and 19th centuries are as follows:

Ex. 313.

Structural name		*Usually called*
major-minor seventh chord	 a	major-minor seventh chord
minor-minor seventh chord	 b	minor seventh chord
diminished-minor seventh chord	c	half-diminished seventh chord
major-major seventh chord	 d	major seventh chord

142

Structural name		*Usually called*
diminished-diminished seventh chord	e	diminished seventh chord
minor-major seventh chord	f	minor-major seventh chord
augmented-major seventh chord	g	augmented-major seventh chord

FIGURATION OF THE SEVENTH CHORD

Figurations for the root position of a seventh chord may be:

7, 7, 7, 7
♮ ♯ 5
♯

Ex. 314.

Figurations for the first inversion may be:

6, 6
5 5
3

Ex. 315.

Figurations for the second inversion may be:

6, 6, 6, 4
4 4 4 3
3 ♭ 3

Ex. 316.

Figurations for the third inversion may be:

$$\begin{array}{c} 6 \\ 4, \ 4, \ 2, \ 4, \\ 2 \ \ 2 \ \ \ 2 \end{array}$$

Ex. 317.

THE DEVELOPMENT OF THE SEVENTH CHORD

16TH CENTURY

Triads appear conventionally as a vertical sonority during the 15th and 16th centuries. These sonorities, it must be remembered, were not recognized as complete chords, but, rather, as vertical sonorities which were a natural outgrowth of three or more voices controlled by the rules of the period. Unessential tones appearing in this period were for the most part dissonant. A study of any music of this period will reveal occasional vertical seventh chord sonorities. Observe the unessential character of the two seventh chords in the following 16th century example: *

Ex. 318.   Versillo de Cuarto Tono   *Antonio de Cabezón (1510–1566)*

* Lute tablature of the 16th century contains seventh chords.

The bdfa sonority appears through the double passing tones a and f in the conventional progression of a first inversion of a triad, GBD to CEG.* The second inversion of the bdfa sonority appears through the double passing tones a and f, the progression being GBD to EG#B. Note that, in both cases, the passing tone exists at the moment the pseudo seventh chord appears.

The 7-6 suspension is likewise a forerunner of the root position of a seventh chord. Observe the unessential tone (suspension) foreshadowing a seventh chord in the following example of 16th century organ music:

Ex. 319.   Versillo de Septimo   *Antonio de Cabezón*

The pseudo incomplete B♭DFA appears through the ornamental 7-6 suspension beginning with b♭ in the bass and a in the soprano.

17TH CENTURY

During the first half of the 17th century, classification of chords was in a state of crystallization. Along with this development of stronger feeling for key center, a feeling for a larger harmonic vocabulary is apparent. Legitimate seventh chords begin to appear. Composers used them sparingly.

Frequently accented complete seventh chords appear in the cadence formula as follows:

Ex. 320.   Nun lob', mein' Seel', den Herren   *Samuel Scheidt*

In the cadence two seventh chords appear in succession. The seventh chord built on g has its seventh prepared in the tenor. The f in the tenor in the first beat is the root of the FAC triad. The e in the tenor on the last beat is the resolution

---

* Remember that 16th century theorists did not recognize chord progression.

tone of the dissonant f in the gb♭(d)f (incomplete) seventh chord. On the second beat in the alto the b♭ is the third of the gb♭df; on the third beat it becomes the dissonant 7th of the CEGB♭ seventh chord. The b♭ resolves to a on the first beat of the last measure. The harmonic progression of the last two measures is I–II⁷–V⁷–I in the key of f-major.

The following example from a chorale setting by Samuel Scheidt shows two seventh chords in first inversion introduced chromatically:

Ex. 321. Nun komm, der Heiden Heiland   *Samuel Scheidt*

At 1, the b♭ in the tenor is a consonance in the e♭-major triad, then a dissonant 7th in the CEGB♭ seventh chord. The b♭ resolves to a in the f-major triad.

At 2, the consonant c in the soprano is the fifth of the f-major triad, then a dissonant 7th in the DF#AC seventh chord. The c resolves to b♭ in the g-minor triad.

By the close of the 17th century the classification of chords was established. Frequently accented complete seventh chords appear in the dominant in an ornamental cadence formula as follows:

Ex. 322.   Erster Ton (Dorian)   *Wegweiser (1692)**

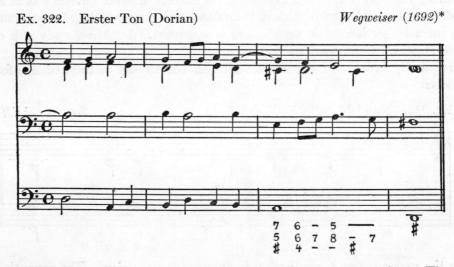

The g in the soprano appears in the form of a 7-6 suspension. The entire penultimate measure is first class harmony in the dominant of the key of d-major.

In the same manner is this second example:

* An anonymous *Method of Organ Playing* with examples of music.

Ex. 323. Dritter Ton *Wegweiser*

Coming from the close of the century, the following example illustrates a seventh chord:

Ex. 324. Vorspiel zu: Dies sind die heil'gen zehn Gebot' *Johann Christian Bach (1643–1703)*

The harmonic tone d in the alto progresses downwards to the dissonant tone c, the seventh, which in turn is given an ornamental resolution. The V⁷ chord DF♯AC contains a 4-3 suspension.

The following example illustrates two seventh chords in first inversion:

Ex. 325. Sechster Ton *Wegweiser*

In the second measure the gb♭d triad progresses to the CEGB♭ seventh chord. The b♭ in the tenor of the g-minor triad becomes the 7th of the CEGB♭ major-minor seventh chord. First b♭ is a consonance, next, it is a dissonance (7th of a chord), and finally it descends to a consonant a. This two-note melodic figure is similar to the suspension figure. In the third measure, the c triad progresses to the GBDF seventh chord. In the soprano voice, the dissonant 7th half note f is approached by step from below and it returns to e. This melodic figure is similar to the neighboring tone figure. This example establishes the fact that the 7th of a chord is an essential harmonic entity. Note that before the f resolves to e, the harmonic background changes to the c-major triad, changing f into a suspended 4th. The f to e becomes a 4-3 suspension. This GBDF chord is an altered 7th chord; its name is II^7, supertonic seventh with the raised 4th degree of the scale.*

$$\begin{array}{c} \# \\ 4 \end{array}$$

THE PREPARED SEVENTH

The 7th of a chord is not only an essential tone of the chord, but it is also in dissonant relationship to the root of the seventh chord. The study of non-harmonic tones establishes the manner in which dissonance may be created in relation to the simple triad harmonic background. It is, therefore, quite logical that the idea of preparing the 7th of seventh chords ought to have its roots in the theory of non-harmonic tones, that an unessential tone must be surrounded by essential tones. In most cases, the unessential tone is dissonant. The 7th of a seventh chord is an essential dissonance. A careful re-examination of pre-Bach examples of seventh chords shows that, in every case, the 7th is preceded by a consonance and is resolved downwards to a consonance. The dissonant 7th must be preceded and followed by a consonance.

With this in mind, carefully observe the three-note melodic line of the voice which contains the 7th, keeping the 7th as the middle tone of the melodic figure. The following melodic figures illustrate the concept:

CHARACTER OF MELODIC FIGURE	NAME	USE IN THE PROGRESSION CONTAINING THE SEVENTH CHORD
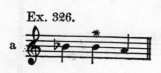 Ex. 326.	*Suspension*	

* See Chapter 24.

CHARACTER OF MELODIC FIGURE	NAME	USE IN THE PROGRESSION CONTAINING THE SEVENTH CHORD
Ex. 327.	*Passing tone*	
Ex. 328.	*Upper neighboring tones*	
Ex. 329.	*Appoggiatura*	

The procedures just illustrated define the term *prepared seventh*. The manner in which the seventh is prepared plays an important part in a style. The following chapters will be based upon this discussion.

BACH'S USE OF SEVENTH CHORDS

The following table illustrates Bach's use of diatonic seventh chords in relation to the complete harmonic equipment:

> Diatonic triads: 83.7%
>
> Diatonic seventh chords: 14.8%
>
> Altered triads and seventh chords: 1.5%

The following table shows the classification frequency of seventh chords as used by Bach:

1st classification: 51.5% $\begin{cases} V^7 & 39\% \\ VII^7 & 12.5\% \text{ (most in minor)} \end{cases}$

2nd classification: 45.5% $\begin{cases} II^7 & 37\% \\ IV^7 & 8.5\% \end{cases}$

3rd classification: 2.5% $\begin{cases} VI^7 & 2.3\% \text{ (most in major)} \\ I^7 & .2\% \text{ (major only)} \end{cases}$

4th classification: .5%   III⁷   (major only)

BACH'S USE OF THE ROOT POSITION AND INVERSIONS OF SEVENTH CHORDS

Contrary to usual textbook presentations, analysis of Bach's procedures reveals that inversions of the seventh chord are the more frequent. The following table illustrates the position in the bass and proves this statement:

Root position   26%

First inversion   58.5%

Second inversion   3%

Third inversion   12.5%

Chapter 16

The Dominant Seventh Chord

The most frequent seventh chord is found in the first classification with its root on the dominant. The following table shows the type of chord and symbol used in major and minor keys.

Major	*Minor*
V^7 (major-minor seventh chord)	V^7 (major-minor seventh chord)
	$\overset{\#}{V^7}$
	V^7 (minor seventh chord)
	This chord is infrequent.

A. THE ROOT POSITION

THE SUSPENSION FIGURE

Ex. 330.

In the soprano the consonant $b^\flat$ in the II becomes the dissonant 7th in the V^7. The dissonant $b^\flat$ resolves downward by scale step to the consonant a in the tonic chord.

Analyze the following Bach examples from two standpoints:

1. (a) Classification and name of chord introducing the V^7.
   (b) Classification and name of chord following the V^7.

2. Character of the voice leading, in each voice, from the preparation chord through the resolution chord.

Ex. 331.   O Herre Gott, dein göttlich
            Wort   Ex. 332.   Ach lieben Christen, seid getrost

Ex. 333.   Nun preiset alle Gottes Barmher-   Ex. 334.   Ermuntre dich, mein
            zigkeit   schwacher Geist

At 1 and 3, the dominant seventh chord follows the subdominant triad and progresses to the submediant triad. The 7th of the V^7 resolves downward by step. In both instances the V^7 is incomplete, having the root doubled and the fifth omitted.

At 2, the V^7 follows the supertonic triad and progresses to the tonic. Notice the ornamental figuration of the 7th; the sixteenth note d is a lower neighboring tone.

At 4, the incomplete V^7 follows the subdominant triad and progresses to the tonic. The 7th is given an ornamental introduction and resolution. The f# is a lower neighboring tone to the preparation tone g, which becomes the 7th of this V^7. Although the g progresses to e, a harmonic tone in V chord, the e rises to the f-sharp, which is the normal resolution tone of the 7th of the V^7.

At 5, the 7th c of the V^7 ascends to the root and then leaps down a third to the normal resolution tone. This is a type of ornamental resolution.

For further study, analyze the root position of the V^7 in the following chorales:

Wonderlich: 127(1st), 153(2nd), 24(6th), 106(2nd, 4th).
Bach-Riemenschneider: 219(1st), 299(1st), 323(2nd), 334(4th), 162(6th).

DEDUCTIONS

1. When the 7th of the V^7 is prepared by the suspension figure, the V^7 is introduced by chords of the second classification, namely II and IV.

2. The 7th of the V^7 descends one half step in a major key to its resolution tone.

3. The 7th of the V^7 descends a whole step in a minor key to its resolution tone.

4. The 7th of the V^7 may be ornamented in its resolution. Under all conditions of ornamentation, the basic resolution of the dissonant 7th must be consummated.

5. The V⁷ may progress to either tonic or submediant, within the phrase or at the cadence.

6. Occasionally a complete V⁷ may progress to an incomplete tonic.

THE PASSING TONE FIGURE

Ex. 335.

In example a, the d-c-b in the alto, the three note descending melodic line illustrates the passing tone figure. The harmonic progression is I–V⁷–I. In example b, the d-c-b in the soprano line illustrates the passing tone figure. The harmonic progression is V–V⁷–I.

Analyze the following Bach examples from two standpoints:

1. (a) Classification and name of the chord introducing the V⁷.

   (b) Classification and name of the chord following the V⁷.

2. Character of the voice leading, in each voice, from the preparation chord through the resolution chord.

Ex. 336.   Schmücke dich, o liebe Seele   Ex. 337.   Dank sei Gott in der Höhe

Ex. 338.   Wenn wir in höchsten Nöten sein   Ex. 339.   O Gott, du frommer Gott

At 1, the V⁷ follows the first inversion of the tonic and progresses to the tonic. The passing tone figure b-a-g is in the soprano. When the V appears, the alto voice contains a suspension note e♭, and the tenor harmonic tone f is followed by a lower neighboring tone e♭. The complete 7th chord sounds on the fourth beat and resolves to an incomplete tonic.

At 2, the V⁷ follows the V triad containing a suspension. The passing tone figure c-b♭-a is in the tenor. The V⁷ resolves to a complete tonic triad.

At 3, the harmonic progression is the same as at 1. Notice the ornamentation of the 7th in the tenor voice.

At 4, the V⁷ follows the $\frac{6}{4}$ structure on the dominant. The tenor has the passing tone figure. Notice the anticipation in the soprano voice on the fourth beat.

For further study, analyze the root position of the V⁷ in the following chorales:

Wonderlich: 29(4th), 34(2nd), 48(2nd), 51(2nd, 7th), 82(5th), 120(1st), 90(8th), 109(4th), 111(2nd).

Bach-Riemenschneider: 60(5th), 100(2nd), 166(2nd), 251(2nd, 5th), 271(5th), 272(6th), 333(2nd, 7th), 337(1st, 5th), 350(3rd).

DEDUCTIONS

1. When the 7th of the V⁷ is prepared by the passing tone figure, the V⁷ is introduced by either the tonic and its inversions, or by the V triad in root position or first inversion, but not by chords of the second classification.
2. The 7th of the V⁷ always descends by scale step to its resolution tone.
3. The 7th may be ornamented in its resolution.
4. The progressions, including the passing tone figure, are usually found in the cadence formula.

THE APPOGGIATURA FIGURE

Ex. 340.

The appoggiatura figure is in the tenor, a-c-b♭. The seventh chord is formed on the last part of the beat. When this type of preparation occurs in the root position of the V⁷, the V triad always precedes the V⁷.

Analyze the following Bach examples from two standpoints:

1. (a) Classification and name of the chord introducing the V⁷.
   (b) Classification and name of the chord following the V⁷.
2. Character of the voice leading, in each voice, from the preparation chord through the resolution chord.

Ex. 341. Nun preiset alle
Gottes Barmherzigkeit   Ex. 342. Ich dank' dir schon durch deinen Sohn

Ex. 343.   Lobet den Herren, denn
er ist sehr freundlich

At 1, the appoggiatura figure appears in the tenor. The 5th of the V leaps to the 7th of the V^7, which in turn has a normal resolution.

At 2, the appoggiatura figure in the tenor is interrupted by an ornamental resolution of the 7th, e^b. The essentially dissonant e^b prepares the ornamental 4-3 suspension in the tonic.

At 3, the appoggiatura figure is altered by the passing tone $f^\sharp$. Bach frequently fills in the leap of a third by use of a passing tone.

For further study, analyze the root position of the V^7 in the following chorales:

Wonderlich: 48(7th), 108(2nd), 110(6th), 112(6th), 113(1st), 45(5th).

Bach-Riemenschneider: 294(3rd), 289(6th), 314(3rd), 166(7th), 216(5th), 127(1st).

DEDUCTIONS

1. When the appoggiatura figure prepares the 7th of the V^7, the dominant triad always precedes the V^7.
2. The 7th of the V^7 is usually approached from the 5th of the V triad. Occasionally the 3rd of the V triad may leap a 5th to the 7th of the V.
3. The resolution of the 7th may be normal or ornamental.
4. The preparation of the 7th by the appoggiatura figure is not too frequent.

THE NEIGHBORING TONE FIGURE

Ex. 344.

The neighboring tone figure in the tenor, a-b^b-a, prepares and resolves the b^b 7th. This device is infrequent for the root position of the V^7.

Analyze the following Bach examples from two standpoints:

1. (a) Classification and name of the chord introducing the V^7.
   (b) Classification and name of the chord following the V^7.
2. Character of the voice leading, in each voice, from the preparation chord through the resolution chord.

Ex. 345.   Christ ist erstanden

At 1, the V⁷ is preceded by the submediant triad. The 7th is approached by step from below and given an ornamental resolution.

DEDUCTIONS

1. The V⁷ in root position is preceded by the VI (a chord of the third classification) when the preparation of the 7th reveals the neighboring tone figure. This part-writing method is rare when the root position of the V⁷ is used.

2. The resolution of the 7th may be normal or ornamental.

PARTWRITING THE ROOT POSITION OF THE V⁷

1) Before partwriting, make a harmonic analysis of the exercise below the figured bass.

2) The harmonic analysis will often help in selecting the preparation and resolution figure.

3) The style does not reveal parallel perfect fifths and octaves in the voice leading. Avoid doubling active tones, and in the voice leading avoid wide leaps if possible.

B. THE FIRST INVERSION

THE SUSPENSION FIGURE

Analyze the following Bach examples, giving

1. (a) Classification and name of chord introducing the V⁷.
   (b) Classification and name of chord following the V⁷.
2. The character of the voice leading to and from the V⁷. Careful attention must be given the bass line.

Ex. 346.   Meine Seele erhebet den Herrn   Ex. 347.   Jesu, meine Freude

Ex. 348. O Mensch, bewein' dein' Sünde gross   Ex. 349. Dies sind die heil'gen zehn Gebot'

Ex. 350.   Sei gegrüsset, Jesu gütig

Ex. 351.   Was Gott tut, das ist wohlgetan

At 1 and 2, the $^6_5$ inversion at the V⁷ is approached from below by step from the first inversion of the subdominant triad. In a major key, the bass note of the IV is frequently doubled in an upper part. In a minor key, this doubling does not occur in the IV because the raised 6th is an active tone. Note the smooth voice leading to and from the V⁷. Note that in both examples the resolution of the 7th is downwards.

At 3 and 4, the $^6_5$ inversion of the V⁷ follows the supertonic triad. The root of the II chord progresses by means of a passing tone to the first inversion of the V⁷.

At 4, the d in the tenor of the V⁷ is approached by leap to the irregular doubling in the fundamental position of the supertonic triad.

At 5, Bach introduces the first inversion of the V⁷ by a leap of a diminished 5th in the bass.

At 6, the first inversion of the V⁷ is used in a chromatic modulation to the key of d-major.

For further study, analyze the first inversion of the V⁷ in the following chorales:

Wonderlich: 33(2nd), 106(3rd), 80(2nd), 11(5th).

Bach-Riemenschneider: 134(2nd), 152(3rd), 155(2nd), 304(5th).

DEDUCTIONS

1. When the 7th of the V⁷ is prepared by the suspension figure, the first inversion of the V⁷ is introduced by chords of the second classification.
2. The 7th resolves downwards.
3. All tones are present in the first inversion of the V⁷.
4. The bass note of the first inversion of the V⁷ may be approached by step or leap.
5. The chord following the first inversion of the V⁷ is usually the tonic. Sometimes the first inversion of the V⁷ may be followed by the root position of the V⁷.

THE PASSING TONE FIGURE

Examples of the first inversion of the V⁷ with its 7th prepared by the passing tone figure are not too frequent.

Analyze the following Bach examples, giving

1. (a) Classification and name of chord introducing the V⁷.

(b) Classification and name of chord following the V⁷.

2. The character of the voice leading to and from the V⁷. Careful attention must be given the bass line.

Ex. 352. Jesu, Jesu, du bist mein   Ex. 353. Du grosser Schmerzensmann

At 1, the $\frac{6}{5}$ inversion of the V⁷ follows the first inversion of the tonic. The f and e♭ are passing tones, filling in the interval of a fourth, g down to d. Notice how unequal fifths are avoided in the outer parts in the progression I$_{(6)}$ to V⁷$_{(6)}$.
$\quad\quad\quad$ $_{(5)}$

At 2, the $\frac{6}{5}$ inversion of the V⁷ follows the first inversion of the V.
$\quad\quad$ ♯ $\quad\quad\quad\quad\quad\quad\quad\quad\quad\quad\quad\quad$ ♯
$\quad\quad$ 7 $\quad\quad\quad\quad\quad\quad\quad\quad\quad\quad\quad\quad$ 7

Analyze the unessential tones.

For further study, analyze the first inversion of the V⁷ in the following chorales:

$\quad$ Wonderlich: 139(2nd), 140(1st), 52(6th).
$\quad$ Bach-Riemenschneider: 179(2nd), 94(1st), 298(6th), 203(5th).

DEDUCTIONS

1. The first inversion of the V⁷ follows the tonic in first inversion or root position. The tonic chord has the 5th in the soprano, and the V⁷ has the 7th in soprano.

2. Special use of non-harmonic tones in the bass passing tones or suspensions avoids unequal fifths between soprano and bass.

3. The leap from the bass note of the first inversion of the tonic to the bass note of the 1st inversion of the V⁷ may be either a perfect fourth or a diminished fourth.

4. The V⁷ in first inversion may follow the V triad.

THE NEIGHBORING TONE FIGURE

Analyze the following Bach examples, giving

1. (a) Classification and name of chord introducing the V⁷.
$\quad$ (b) Classification and name of chord following the V⁷.

2. The character of the voice leading to and from the V⁷. Careful attention must be given the bass line.

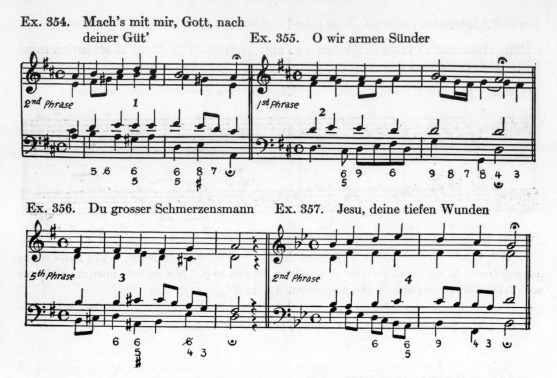

Ex. 354.   Mach's mit mir, Gott, nach
            deiner Güt'   Ex. 355.   O wir armen Sünder

Ex. 356.   Du grosser Schmerzensmann   Ex. 357.   Jesu, deine tiefen Wunden

At 1 and 2, the first inversion of the V⁷ follows the root position of the tonic and is followed by the tonic.   2 is a non-harmonic tone variation of 1.

At 3 and 4, the first inversion of the V⁷ follows the first inversion of the tonic and is followed by the tonic.   At 4, the bass line from the first inversion of the tonic progresses through two passing tones (the second accented) to the first inversion of the V⁷.

For further study, analyze the first inversion of the V⁷ in the following chorales:

Wonderlich: 15(1st), 16(1st), 94(4th), 2(3rd).
Bach-Riemenschneider: 184(1st), 26(1st), 263(4th), 279(3rd).

DEDUCTIONS

1. The first inversion of the V⁷ usually follows the root position of the tonic and progresses to the root position of the tonic.
2. The first inversion of the V⁷ may follow the first inversion of the tonic by leap in the bass or by filled-in leap as at 4.

THE APPOGGIATURA FIGURE

Analyze the following Bach examples, giving

1. (a) Classification and name of chord introducing the V⁷.
   (b) Classification and name of chord following the V⁷.
2. The character of the voice leading to and from the V⁷.   Careful attention must be given the bass line.

Ex. 358.   Was mein Gott will, das g'scheh'   Ex. 359.   Befiehl du deine Wege

At 1, the first inversion of the V⁷ follows the first inversion of the tonic. The bass line in this progression has been encountered before in this chapter.

At 2, between the phrases, the V⁷ in first inversion occasionally appears at the beginning of a new phrase establishing a new key. Note the cross relation.

For further study, analyze the first inversion of the V⁷ in the following chorales:

Wonderlich: 47(2nd), 50(2nd, 5th), 51(2nd, 7th), 70(5th), 72(5th).
Bach-Riemenschneider: 27(2nd), 16(2nd, 5th), 333(2nd, 7th), 21(5th), 367(5th).

DEDUCTIONS

1. When V⁷ in first inversion occurs in the phrase, it follows the first inversion of the tonic and progresses to the tonic in root position. This progression is rare within the phrase.
2. The V⁷ in first inversion occurs occasionally at the beginning of a phrase, using the appoggiatura figure between the last chord of the preceding phrase and its resolution to the tonic. Cross relation occurs frequently in the voice leading in the progression to the V⁷.

PARTWRITING EXERCISES USING THE FIRST INVERSION OF THE V⁷

1) Before partwriting, make a harmonic analysis of the exercise.
2) The harmonic analysis will often help in selecting the preparation and resolution figure.
3) Work for smooth voice leading, and avoid parallel perfect fifths and octaves and doubled active tones.

C. THE SECOND INVERSION

The second inversion of the V⁷ is the least frequent position. This inversion of the chord is practically limited to one use in Bach. The neighboring tone, appoggiatura, and suspension figures are rare. The passing tone figure precedes and resolves the seventh in two ways, ascending and descending.

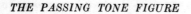

THE PASSING TONE FIGURE

Ex. 360.

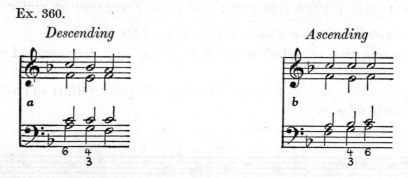

When the ascending passing tone figure is used, the 7th of the V⁷ rises to the dominant. A study of Bach's use of this figure will reveal that 7th of the V⁷ does not resolve down in the conventional manner. Bach and his contemporaries apparently considered the second inversion of the V⁷ under these conditions from a horizontal standpoint (a passing chord). Unequal fifths between two voices are frequent in this use of the V⁷.

Analyze the following Bach examples, giving

1. (a) Classification and name of the chord introducing the V⁷.
   (b) Classification and name of the chord following the V⁷.
2. The character of the voice leading to and from the V⁷. Careful attention must be given the bass line.

Ex. 361. Aus meines Herzens Grunde   Ex. 362. Gott lebet noch

Ex. 363. Gott, der du selber bist das Licht Ex. 364. Keinen hat Gott verlassen

At 1, the second inversion of the V⁷ follows the first inversion of the I and progresses to the root position of the I. The passing tone preparation and resolution figure is in the soprano. Unequal fifths between the soprano and alto are correct in this style.

At 2, the harmonic progression is the same as at 1. Notice the appoggiatura d in the alto, which reduces the effect of unequal fifths.

At 3, the harmonic progression is the reverse of 1 and 2. The ascending passing tone preparation and resolution figure is in the tenor. In this progression the 7th may rise. The bass and tenor move in thirds at 3 and 4. In this progression the second inversion of the V⁷ may be considered non-functional, and the chord a passing chord. This opinion holds for chords having durations of a beat or a half beat.

DEDUCTIONS

1. The second inversion of the V⁷ may be used between the 1st inversion of the tonic and the root position of the tonic. Imperfect fifths may appear between the upper voices.
2. The second inversion of the V⁷ may be used between the root position of the tonic and the first inversion of the tonic. The 7th of the V⁷ may ascend to the 5th of the tonic. Imperfect fifths may appear between the upper voices.

THE NEIGHBORING TONE AND SUSPENSION FIGURES

The following Bach examples illustrate the way in which the second inversion occasionally appears:

Ex. 365.   Puer natus in Bethlehem   Ex. 366.   Befiehl du deine Wege

At 1, the neighboring tone figure prepares and resolves the 7th of the V⁷ while a chromatic modulation to a minor takes place. Notice the smooth voice leading in alto and bass.

At 2, the suspension figure is found in the progression II⁷–V⁷–I. This progression will not be used until Chapter 17.

PARTWRITING EXERCISES USING THE SECOND INVERSION OF THE V⁷

1) Before partwriting, make a harmonic analysis of the exercise.
2) Work for smooth voice leading, and avoid parallel perfect fifths and octaves and doubled active tones.
3) Unequal fifths are permissible when partwriting the VII and the second inversion of V⁷.

D. THE THIRD INVERSION

THE SUSPENSION FIGURE

Analyze the following Bach examples, giving

1. (a) Classification and name of chord introducing the V⁷.
   (b) Classification and name of chord following the V⁷.

2. The character of the voice leading to and from the V⁷. Careful attention must be given the bass line.

Ex. 367. Puer natus in
          Bethlehem   Ex. 368. Es spricht der Unweisen Mund

Ex. 369. Es spricht der Unweisen Mund

Ex. 370. Schwing' dich auf zu deinem Gott

In all the examples, the suspension, preparation, and resolution figures are in the bass.

At 1, the third inversion of the V⁷ follows the first inversion of the II and progresses to the first inversion of the I, which becomes a IV in g-major. The remaining voices progress smoothly through the V⁷.

At 2, the third inversion of the V⁷ follows the IV and progresses to the first inversion of the I. The remaining voices progress smoothly through the V⁷.

At 3, the third inversion establishes the key of b-flat major at the beginning of a phrase. The familiar leaps of dominant to tonic and supertonic to dominant are found in the soprano and alto as the V⁷ resolves to the tonic.

At 4, the third inversion of the V⁷ has the unusual position of the final chord in the cadence. This is rare. The octave leap g to g in the bass is considered a suspension preparation. The V⁷ follows the second classification II in first inversion.

For further study, analyze the third inversion of the V⁷ in the following chorales:

Wonderlich: 47(2nd, 3rd), 55(6th), 110(1st, 6th), 112(4th), 6(1st).
Bach-Riemenschneider: 27(2nd, 3rd), 8(6th), 84(1st, 6th), 330(4th), 217(1st).

DEDUCTIONS

1. The third inversion of the V⁷ controlled by the suspension figure follows the second classification chords II or IV, and progresses to the first inversion of the tonic.
2. All intervals of the chord are present in the third inversion.
3. The third inversion of the V⁷ may be at the beginning of a phrase or within the phrase. It is rarely found as the final chord in a half cadence.

THE PASSING TONE FIGURE

Analyze the following Bach examples, giving

1. (a) Classification and name of chord introducing the V⁷.
   (b) Classification and name of chord following the V⁷.
2. The character of the bass line to and from the V⁷.

Ex. 371. Wenn mein Stündlein vorhanden ist   Ex. 372. O Gott, du frommer Gott

Ex. 373. Ich freue mich in dir   Ex. 374. O Gott, du frommer Gott

At 1, the third inversion of the V⁷ follows the second inversion of the tonic and progresses to the first inversion of the tonic. All voices progress smoothly into the V⁷.

At 2, the third inversion of the V⁷ follows the root position of the V⁷ triad.

At 3, the third inversion of the V⁷ follows the root position of the AG#E triad. At the end of the phrase the AC#E triad was tonic. The third inversion of the V⁷ at the beginning of the phrase is in the key of d-major. The AC#E triad became a V in the key of d-major.

At 4, the third inversion of the V⁷ is controlled by the chromatic passing tone figure. The V⁷ follows the IV⁷ in c-minor. This progression will be discussed in Chapter 23.

$$\sharp\sharp$$
46

For further study, analyze the third inversion of the V⁷ in the following chorales:

Wonderlich: 63(3rd), 67(6th), 95(5th).
Bach-Riemenschneider: 303(3rd), 284(6th), 327(5th).

DEDUCTIONS

1. The use of the passing tone preparation and resolution figure in connection with the third inversion of the V⁷ is not so frequent as the use of the suspension figure.
2. The V⁷ controlled by this figure appears at the beginning or within the phrase.
3. When the chromatic passing tone figure is used, a modulation takes place.
4. Leaps in the voice leading occur when the chord is at the beginning of a phrase. Within the phrase the approach to the third inversion of the V⁷ is smooth in all voices.
5. The third inversion of the V⁷ progresses to the first inversion of the I.

THE NEIGHBORING TONE FIGURE

Analyze the following Bach examples, giving

1. (a) Classification and name of chord introducing the V⁷.
   (b) Classification and name of chord following the V⁷.
2. The character of the voice leading to and from the V⁷. Careful attention must be given the bass line.

Ex. 375.   Dir, dir, Jehovah, will ich
                singen   Ex. 376.   Nun ruhen alle Wälder

At 1, the third inversion of the V⁷ follows the first inversion of the tonic and progresses to the tonic. The tenor could have been a b-flat in the tonic chord. Bach likes the leap of the 5th in the tenor, especially supertonic to dominant, subdominant to leading tone, and dominant to tonic.

At **2,** the new phrase begins immediately in the key of a. The c-sharp minor triad in the preceding phrase is a tonic triad. The c-sharp minor triad has the effect of a mediant triad in a-major.

Analyze the third inversion of the V^7 in the following chorales:

Wonderlich: 85(2nd).
Bach-Riemenschneider: 77(2nd).

DEDUCTIONS

1. Use of the partwriting of the third inversion of the V^7 controlled by the neighboring tone figure is rare.
2. The third inversion of the V^7 both follows and progresses to the tonic in first inversion.
3. The progression is most useful within the phrase.

THE APPOGGIATURA FIGURE

Analyze the following Bach examples, giving

1. (a) Classification and name of the chord introducing the V^7.
   (b) Classification and name of the chord following the V^7.
2. The character of the voice leading to and from the V^7. Careful attention must be given the bass line.

Ex. 377. Puer natus in Bethlehem   Ex. 378.   Straf' mich nicht in deinem Zorn

Ex. 379.   O grosser Gott von Macht

At **1,** the third inversion of the V^7 follows the V triad. The root of the V leaps to the 5th and then leaps to the 7th of the V^7, which in turn resolves by step to the bass note of the first inversion of the tonic.

At 2, the third inversion of the V⁷ follows the II triad. The a-flat in the bass of the V⁷ is approached by the filled-in appoggiatura figure. The bass note of the V⁷ resolves ornamentally to the g, the bass note of the first inversion of the tonic.

At 3, the third inversion of the V⁷ follows chromatically the g-minor triad. The phrase begins in the key of c-minor. The f of the V⁷ chord is approached by the ascending leap of a minor 7th, and resolves downwards to the e-flat of the tonic c-minor triad in first inversion.

Analyze the third inversion of the V⁷ in the following chorales:

Wonderlich: 45(8th), 63(2nd).
Bach-Riemenschneider: 216(8th), 303(2nd).

DEDUCTIONS

1. The use of the third inversion of the V⁷ controlled by the appoggiatura figure is not frequently encountered.
2. The device is found between phrases and within the phrase:

   (a) Between phrases a change of key takes place.

   (b) Within the phrase the third inversion of the V⁷ follows either the V or II.

3. The third inversion of the V⁷ progresses to the tonic in first inversion.

PARTWRITING THE ROOT POSITION OF THE V⁷

1) Before partwriting, make a harmonic analysis of each exercise.
2) Avoid parallel perfect fifths and octaves and doubled active tones.
3) Try to maintain smooth voice leading.

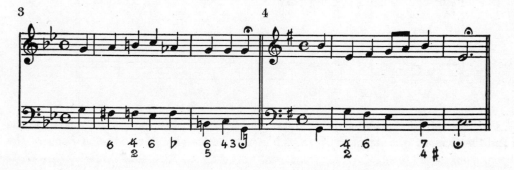

Chapter 17

The Supertonic Seventh Chord

The next most common seventh chord is found in the second classification with its root on the supertonic. The following table shows the type chord and the symbol used in major and minor keys:

Major
II⁷ (minor seventh chord)

Minor
II⁷ (half-diminished seventh chord)
II⁷ (minor seventh chord). In the 18th
♯ century this chord is practically non-
6 existent.

Before studying the partwriting and use of the supertonic seventh in major or minor keys, note that the 7th of the supertonic seventh is practically limited to the suspension figure. The chord is found most often in first inversion, next in root position, occasionally in third inversion, and practically never in second inversion.

One more fact concerning analysis must be established. An ambiguous sonority frequently appears with its bass note on the supertonic. Carefully examine, and follow the analysis of, the following example:

Ex. 380.   Gottlob, es geht nunmehr zu Ende

At 1 and 2, the vertical sonorities are the same. Each sonority contains a seventh and two thirds above the bass. In each case the 7th is prepared and resolved in the suspension figure. The difference between 1 and 2 is in the movement of the bass. The bass note progresses by leap at 1 and by step at 2. After study of many examples, it is evident that the

171

sonority has two definite and distinct functions: a second classification II⁷ or a first classification VII with a 7-6 suspension.

To decide the function of the sonority, examine the movement of the bass note into and out of the sonority.

The following examples illustrate this conclusion:

FIRST CLASSIFICATION, VII

Ex. 381.   Meine Augen schliess' ich jetzt

The bass moves by step.

SECOND CLASSIFICATION, II⁷

Ex. 382.   Ach was soll ich Sünder machen   Ex. 383.   O Ewigkeit, du Donnerwort

The bass moves by leap either before or after * the vertical sonority under consideration.

* The author does not consider at this point, in view of the many examples analyzed, the practice established in suspensions where a suspension may resolve with change of bass (Chapter 12).

A. THE ROOT POSITION

THE SUSPENSION FIGURE

Analyze the following Bach examples, giving

1. (a) Classification and name of chord introducing the II⁷.
   (b) Classification and name of chord following the II⁷.
2. Character of the voice leading in each voice. Special attention should be given to the bass line.

Ex. 384. Herr Christ, der ein'ge
Gott'ssohn

Ex. 385. Du grosser Schmerzensmann

Ex. 386. Wie schön leuchtet der
Morgenstern

Ex. 387. Wach' auf, mein Herz, und singe

At 1, the II⁷ follows the VI (chord of the third classification). The root of the VI leaps a fifth to the root of the II⁷. The 7th is controlled by the suspension figure preparation. One of the remaining upper voices remains the same, and the other progresses by step. The II⁷ progresses to the V with normal doubling.

At 2, the II⁷ follows the first inversion of the tonic. The suspension figure is in the alto. The remaining voices move step-wise into the II⁷. The complete II⁷ progresses to an incomplete V⁷ (two roots, one third, and one seventh). The third of the II⁷ generates the preparation figure for the 7th of the V⁷.

At 3, the II⁷ follows the first inversion of the tonic. The suspension figure is in the alto. The II⁷ progresses to the first inversion of the leading tone triad on the second part of the beat.

At 4, the II⁷ follows the first inversion of the tonic. The suspension figure is in the alto. The II⁷ progresses to an ornamentation of a first classification harmony as part of the cadence. The progression is as follows: II⁷–V⁷–VII–I.

For further study, analyze the following chorales:

Wonderlich: 24(6th), 65(3rd), 139(3rd).
Bach-Riemenschneider: 162(6th), 287(3rd), 179(3rd).

DEDUCTIONS

1. The II⁷ may follow VI or I or occasionally IV.
2. The II⁷ may progress to V or sometimes to V⁷ or occasionally to VII in first inversion.
3. The II⁷ is found in root position more often in a major key.
4. The upper voices which do not have the suspension figure progress most often without leap through the II⁷.
5. The seventh of the II⁷ resolves in the same manner as the 7th of the V⁷.
6. The root of the II⁷ may be approached and left by leap.
7. The II⁷ may appear at any point of the phrase.

THE PASSING TONE FIGURE

Analyze the following Bach examples, giving

1. (a) Classification and name of chord introducing the II⁷.
   (b) Classification and name of chord following the II⁷.

2. Character of the voice leading, in each voice, from the preparation chord through the resolution chord.

Ex. 388.   Von Gott will ich nicht lassen

The II⁷ is introduced through the first inversion of the II. The passing tone figure is in the soprano. Notice that the resolution of the 7th is momentarily retarded to form the 6-5 melodic line over the dominant g in the bass. The same progression is found in the chorale:

Wonderlich: 134(2nd).
Bach-Riemenschneider: 108(2nd).

DEDUCTIONS

1. When the 7th of the II⁷ is controlled by the passing tone figure, the II⁷ follows the first inversion of the II.

2. Small leaps may occur in the upper voices between II and II⁷, since the supertonic sonority is established by the first inversion of the triad.

3. The II⁷ may be followed by the dominant triad or seventh chord. The tonic triad in inversion may appear between the II⁷ and the dominant harmonies.

THE NEIGHBORING TONE AND APPOGGIATURA FIGURES

There are no examples of these melodic figures used in connection with the II⁷.

SUMMARY OF BACH'S USE OF THE ROOT POSITION OF THE II⁷

PREPARATION OF THE 7TH

1) *Suspension Figure*

    (a) The II⁷ follows VI, IV, or I.

    (b) The II⁷ may progress to V or V⁷. The I in inversions may appear between the II⁷ and V or V⁷.

    (c) The complete II⁷ progresses to an incomplete V⁷.

Ex. 389.

2) *Passing Tone Figure*

    (a) The II⁷ follows II in the first inversion.

    (b) This use of the II⁷ is rare.

    (c) The II⁷ may progress to V, V⁷, or an inversion of the tonic on the way to V or V⁷.

3) *Neighboring Tone and Appoggiatura Figures*

There are no examples of the 7th of the II⁷ introduced by these figures.

4) Bach rarely uses the root position of the II⁷ in a minor key. The II⁷ was not found in the chorales.*

PARTWRITING EXERCISES

1) Make a harmonic analysis of each exercise before filling in the alto and tenor.

* Bach raises the 6th degree of the scale, however, in connection with the raised 4th degree (Chapter 23).

2) The harmonic analysis will help in selecting the preparation and resolution figure of the 7th of the V⁷ and II⁷.

3) Work for smooth voice leading, and avoid parallel perfect fifths and octaves and doubled active tones.

B. THE FIRST INVERSION

THE SUSPENSION FIGURE

Analyze the following Bach examples, giving

1. (a) Classification and name of chord introducing the II⁷.
   (b) Classification and name of chord following the II⁷.

2. Character of the voice leading, in each voice, from the preparation chord through the resolution chord.

Ex. 390. Jesu Leiden, Pein und Tod   Ex. 391.   Jesu, der du meine Seele

Ex. 392.   Ich dank' dir, lieber Herre   **Ex. 393.   Herzlich tut mich verlangen**

Ex. 394.   Vater unser im Himmelreich   **Ex. 395.   An Wasserflüssen Babylon**

Ex. 396.   Meine Seele erhebet den Herrn

At 1, the II⁷ in first inversion in the key of e-major follows the I. Notice the leap in the bass to the first inversion of the II⁷. The remaining voices move by step, except the soprano, which contains the preparation figure.

At 2, the same progression appears in a minor key.

At 3, and 4, the II⁷ follows the subdominant triad in first inversion. At 3, passing tones, and at 4, the passing tonic $^6_4$, appear between the IV and the II⁷. Notice the smooth voice leading into the II⁷.

At 5, the II⁷ follows the submediant triad. Observe the rhythm of the chord progression in the last measure: VI–II⁷–V–I. Quite often II⁷ and V are found progressing in the time duration of one beat.

At 6, the II⁷ is located in a digression as part of an ornamental cadence.

At 7, observe the bass line c-a-d. Notice that on the last half of the first beat the root position of the II⁷ does not have the third. This is a Bach mannerism. The tempo, being moderately fast, carries the II⁷ in first inversion over to the V, without stressing the II⁷ in root position.

At 1, 2, 4, 5, 6, and 7, the first inversion of the II⁷ is followed by the V triad.

For further study, analyze the following chorales:

Wonderlich: 25(4th), 26(4th), 30(4th), 48(1st), 7(2nd), 116(2nd), 63(1st).
Bach-Riemenschneider: 53(4th), 154(4th), 42(4th), 166(1st), 39(2nd), 7(2nd), 73(4th, 5th).

DEDUCTIONS

1. The II^7 in first inversion may follow IV in first inversion, VI, or I in root position or inversion.
2. The II^7 in first inversion progresses normally to the dominant triad. Occasionally the tonic $^6_4$ may come before the V.
3. All members are present in the first inversion of the II^7.
4. The progression II^7–V may occur during the time duration of one beat.
5. The first inversion of the II^7 may occur at any point within the phrase. The majority, however, are found as part of the cadence formula.
6. The bass note of the first inversion of the II^7 may be approached by leap.

THE PASSING TONE, NEIGHBORING TONE AND APPOGGIATURA FIGURES

These are not used.

SUMMARY OF BACH'S USE OF THE II^7 IN FIRST INVERSION

1. The II^7 in first inversion is controlled by one preparation only, the suspension figure.
2. The first inversion of the II^7 may follow I in fundamental position or its inversions, IV in first inversion, VI in root position.
3. Voices which do not have the preparation figure progress smoothly into the first inversion of the II^7. The bass line may leap a 3rd, a perfect 4th or a 5th to the bass note of the II^7 in first inversion.

PARTWRITING EXERCISES

1) Make a harmonic analysis of each exercise before filling in the alto and tenor.
2) Work for smooth voice leading, and avoid parallel perfect fifths and octaves and doubled active tones.

C. THE SECOND INVERSION

No satisfactory diatonic examples of the second inversion of the II⁷ in either major or minor keys have been found. The following Bach examples reveal the unessential characteristics of the sonority.

Ex. 397.　O Traurigkeit,
　　　　　　o Herzeleid　Ex. 398.　Herzliebster Jesu, was hast du

Ex. 399.　Warum betrübst du dich, mein Herz

At 1 and 2, the tenor b and a are accented passing tones.
At 3, the soprano a is a passing tone.

These examples, which are typical, give no evidence of a strong second inversion of the II⁷. It is also interesting to observe that this progression was not found in a major key.

D. THE THIRD INVERSION

Analyze the following Bach examples, giving

1. (a) Classification and name of chord introducing the II⁷.
　　(b) Classification and name of chord following the II⁷.

2. Character of the voice leading, in each voice, from the preparation chord through the resolution chord.

Ex. 400. Was willst du dich, o meine Seele

Ex. 401. Ach Gott, erhör' mein Seufzen

At 1, the third inversion of the II[7] is prepared by the suspension figure originating in the tonic triad. Notice the descending melodic minor scale generated by the passing tone c. The remaining voices move by step into the II[7]. The II[7] is followed by the V[7] in first inversion.

At 2, the third inversion of the II[7] follows the first inversion of the VI. This progression is rare. The II[7] progresses to the V in first inversion. The c in the alto is a lower neighboring tone.

For further study, analyze the following chorales:

Wonderlich: 25(3rd), 87(2nd).
Bach-Riemenschneider: 53(3rd), 61(5th), 122(2nd), 144(3rd), 196(6th).

DEDUCTIONS

1. The third inversion of the II[7] follows the root position of the tonic.
2. In similar motion the soprano, alto, and bass may descend or ascend from the tonic triad into the third inversion of the II[7].
3. The third inversion of the II[7] progresses into the V or V[7] in first inversion.
4. This progression seems to occur most often at the beginning of a phrase.

THE PASSING TONE FIGURE

This preparation of the II[7] in third inversion is extremely rare. One example is given:

Ex. 402. Schwing' dich auf zu deinem Gott

At 1, the third inversion of the II[7] follows the a-minor triad. Notice the cross relation.

At 2, the a in the tenor is an accented passing tone. The harmony is the first inversion of the IV.

NEIGHBORING TONE AND APPOGGIATURA FIGURES

These are not used.

SUMMARY OF BACH'S USE OF THE II[7] IN THIRD INVERSION

1. The II[7] in third inversion is controlled by one preparation only, the suspension figure.
2. The II[7] in third inversion follows the tonic in root position and rarely the VI in first inversion.
3. The II[7] in third inversion progresses normally into either the V or V[7] in first inversion.
4. The three upper voices move smoothly into the II[7] in third inversion.

PARTWRITING EXERCISES

1) Make a harmonic analysis of each exercise before filling in the alto and tenor.
2) Work for smooth voice leading, and avoid parallel perfect fifths and octaves and doubled active tones.

Chapter 18

The Leading Tone Seventh Chord in Minor

Following the supertonic seventh chord in major and minor keys is the leading tone seventh chord in minor. It is a diminished seventh chord and its symbol is VII$^{\sharp}_{7}$.

A. THE ROOT POSITION

THE SUSPENSION FIGURE

Analyze the following Bach examples, giving

1. (a) Classification and name of chord introducing the VII$^{\sharp}_{7}$.

   (b) Classification and name of chord following the VII$^{\sharp}_{7}$.

2. Character of the voice leading in each voice, especially the bass.

Ex. 403.   Christ, der du bist der helle Tag

Ex. 404. Herr Jesu Christ, du hast bereit

5th Phrase

Ex. 405. Hilf, Herr Jesu, lass gelingen

3rd Phrase

At 1, the VII⁷ follows the g-minor triad, which is a second classification IV in d-minor.

The b-flat becomes the 7th of the VII⁷ and resolves to the root of the V in first inversion.

Notice the leap of a diminished fifth to the root of the VII⁷ in the bass.

At 2, the VII⁷ follows the first inversion of the second classification IV in the key of g-minor. The suspension figure is in the alto. Notice the leap of the diminished seventh to the root of the VII⁷ in the bass. The VII⁷ progresses into the I, which contains a 9-sus-pension. This device delays the unequal fifths between the tenor and alto, a-e♭ and g-d.

At 3, the VII⁷ follows an ornamental resolution of the II⁷. The suspension figure is in the tenor. Notice how the d in the tenor on the last half of the beat anticipates the fifth of the tonic triad in the next measure. Again the tonic triad has 9-8 suspension.

For further study, analyze the following chorales:

Wonderlich: 21(2nd), 22(3rd), 126(2nd).
Bach-Riemenschneider: 81(2nd), 200(3rd), 63(2nd), 201(6th).

DEDUCTIONS

1. The VII^7 frequently follows IV in root position or first inversion.
   ♯
   7

2. The VII^7 occasionally follows the root position of the II^7.
   ♯
   7

3. The root of the VII^7 may be approached in the bass by step or leap. Bach likes
   ♯
   7

   to leap a diminished fifth, subdominant down to leading tone.   Occasionally the leap of a diminished seventh occurs from the submediant down to the leading tone.

4. The upper voices progress smoothly.

5. The VII^7 usually resolves directly into the tonic in root position.   If the 3rd is
   ♯
   7

   below the 7th in the VII^7 it is usually held over into the tonic becoming a 9-sus-
   ♯
   7

   pension.   This avoids unequal fifths.   Sometimes the 3rd may rise to the third of the tonic triad.

THE PASSING TONE FIGURE

When this figure is used in connection with the root position of VII^7, the pro-
   ♯
   7

gression leading into the VII^7 is always chromatic, either direct or concealed, and a modulation occurs.   ♯
   7

Analyze the following Bach examples, giving

1. (a) The root movement of the chromatic progression into the VII^7.
   ♯
   7

   (b) Classification and name of the chord following the VII^7.
   ♯
   7

2. Character of the voice leading, especially in the bass.

Ex. 406. Herzliebster Jesu, was hast du Ex. 407. Von Gott will ich nicht lassen

Ex. 408. Warum betrübst du dich, mein Herz Ex. 409. Herzlich tut mich verlangen

At 1, the VII⁷ is introduced by a triad in fundamental position, its root being a dimin-

$$\overset{\sharp}{7}$$

ished 4th above. The passing tone figure is in the tenor. Notice the cross relation between the tenor and the bass.

At 2, the VII⁷ is introduced by a triad in first inversion which has its root a third below.

$$\overset{\sharp}{7}$$

The d diminished triad is VII in e-flat major. The key of e-flat major is destroyed by the chromatic progression, and the diminished seventh chord establishes the key of g-minor. Here the VII⁷ is used in the authentic cadence.

$$\overset{\sharp}{7}$$

At 3, the chromatic passing tone figure appears in the tenor. The e-major triad, which has its root a third above the root of the VII⁷ of d-minor, is a V in a-minor. The chromatic

$$\overset{\sharp}{7} \qquad \overset{\sharp}{7}$$

chord progressions destroy the feeling for the key of a-minor.

At 4, the chromatic modulation is from d-major to e-minor. The g-major triad progresses to the d-sharp diminished seventh chord. In the bass, the f-sharp and e are passing tones. Notice the aural effect of this progression in relation to the progression at 1, where the passing tones do not appear in the bass. At 4, the cross relation is not noticeable.

For further study, analyze the following chorales:

Wonderlich: 26(3rd), 127(4th), 90(3rd), 63(4th), 156(5th), 133(2nd).
Bach-Riemenschneider: 154(3rd), 219(4th), 83(3rd), 303(4th), 285(5th), 24(2nd), 202(9th).

DEDUCTIONS

1. When the VII^7 is controlled by the passing tone figure, a chromatic chord pro-

$$\substack{\sharp \\ 7}$$

gression is involved.

2. When the chromatic inflection does not occur in the same voice, the cross relation is permissible.

3. The root of the VII^7 may be approached by step or leap. The approach is down

$$\substack{\sharp \\ 7}$$

by leap and up by a chromatic half step. The same leap is established in the first
analysis.

4. The VII^7 progresses directly into the tonic. A suspension occurs frequently in

$$\substack{\sharp \\ 7}$$

the tonic.

5. In this progression the passing tone figure usually occurs in the tenor.

6. The VII^7 may be used in the authentic cadence in the same manner as the first

$$\substack{\sharp \\ 7}$$

classification chord: V, V^7, or VII^7 progressing to I.

$$\substack{\sharp \quad \sharp \qquad \sharp \\ 7 \quad 7 \qquad 7}$$

THE NEIGHBORING TONE FIGURE

Under the control of the neighboring tone figure the VII^7 is found in diatonic
as well as chromatic progressions. $\substack{\sharp \\ 7}$

Analyze the following Bach examples, giving

1. (a) The type of progression leading into the VII^7.

$$\substack{\sharp \\ 7}$$

(b) Classification and name of the chord following the VII^7.

$$\substack{\sharp \\ 7}$$

2. Character of the voice leading, especially in the bass.

Ex. 410. Herzliebster Jesu, was hast du   Ex. 411.   Gelobet seist du, Jesu Christ

Ex. 412. Jesus Christus, unser Heiland Ex. 413. Es ist das Heil uns kommen her

At 1, the neighboring tone figure appears in the tenor. The VII⁷ follows the tonic and progresses to the tonic.

At 2, the same progression occurs. Note that the VII⁷ is used in the authentic cadence.

At 3, the VII⁷ follows the tonic in first inversion. In the bass a and g are passing tones.

At 4, a chromatic modulation to f-sharp minor takes place. Note the concealed cross relation, also the leap of a minor 6th in the bass.

For further study, analyze the following chorales:

Wonderlich: 50(6th), 70(1st), 79(1st), 93(1st), 144(5th).

Bach-Riemenschneider: 16(6th), 21(1st), 59(1st), 356(1st), 265(5th).

DEDUCTIONS

1. When the seventh of the VII⁷ is controlled by the neighboring tone figure, the VII⁷ usually follows the tonic in root position and occasionally in the first inversion. The chromatic progression is rare.

2. The neighboring tone figure usually appears in the tenor, sometimes in the alto, and not in the soprano.

3. In the VII⁷ the 3rd appears above the 7th.

4. The VII⁷ may be used as a first classification chord in the authentic cadence.

THE APPOGGIATURA FIGURE

It is to be noted that in connection with the VII⁷ two appoggiatura figures are used.

When the leap is from a third above, the figure may be filled in by a passing tone, creating the filled-in appoggiatura figure.

Analyze the following Bach examples, giving

1. (a) The type of progression leading into the VII⁷.

   $\frac{\sharp}{7}$

   (b) Classification and name of the chord following the VII⁷.

   $\frac{\sharp}{7}$

2. Character of the voice leading, especially in the bass.

Ex. 414.   Puer natus in Bethlehem

Ex. 415.   Du, o schönes Weltgebäude

Ex. 416.   Vater unser im Himmelreich   Ex. 417.   Jesu, meine Freude

Ex. 418.   Wir Christenleut'

At 1, a concealed chromatic progression from the g-major triad into the g-sharp diminished seventh occurs. The appoggiatura figure appears in the tenor. The VII⁷ of a minor progresses to the tonic with a doubled third.
$$\begin{smallmatrix}\sharp\\7\end{smallmatrix}$$

At 2, the VII⁷ follows the first inversion of the VII in g-minor. Notice that the d in
$$\begin{smallmatrix}\sharp\\7\end{smallmatrix}\qquad\qquad\begin{smallmatrix}\sharp\\7\end{smallmatrix}$$
the tenor anticipates the 5th of the tonic triad.

At 3, the appoggiatura figure contains a leap of a fourth in the tenor. This is concealed chromatic modulation to a-minor, by means of the c-major triad to the g-sharp diminished seventh. The passing tones in the bass help to conceal the cross relation between the alto g in the c-major triad and the g-sharp in the bass of the VII⁷ in a-minor.
$$\begin{smallmatrix}\sharp\\7\end{smallmatrix}$$

At 4, the VII⁷ follows the IV in the key of e-minor. The bass line follows the ascend-
$$\begin{smallmatrix}\sharp\\7\end{smallmatrix}\qquad\qquad\begin{smallmatrix}\sharp\\6\end{smallmatrix}$$
ing melodic minor scale. The appoggiatura figure uses the natural 6th found in the harmonic or natural minor scales because of its resolution to the 5th degree of the scale. The cross relation is permissible under these conditions. Bach frequently uses this progression.

At 5, the appoggiatura figure appears in the tenor, containing the leap of a minor third down to the dissonant 7th.

For further study, analyze the following chorales:

Wonderlich: 83(3rd), 91(5th), 100(6th); filled-in appoggiatura: 51(6th), 24(4th), 50(2nd), 107(7th).

Bach-Riemenschneider: 19(3rd), 283(5th), 45(6th); filled-in appoggiatura: 333(6th), 162(4th), 16(2nd), 49(6th).

DEDUCTIONS

1. The leap in the appoggiatura figure usually ascends, but occasionally descends to the 7th of the VII⁷. The leap of the third may be filled in by a passing tone.
$$\begin{smallmatrix}\sharp\\7\end{smallmatrix}$$

2. When the appoggiatura figure controls the VII⁷ the progression introducing the
$$\begin{smallmatrix}\sharp\\7\end{smallmatrix}$$
VII⁷ is occasionally diatonic but more often chromatic.
$$\begin{smallmatrix}\sharp\\7\end{smallmatrix}$$

PARTWRITING EXERCISES

1) Make a harmonic analysis of each exercise before filling in the alto and tenor.
2) Harmonic analysis will assist in determining which preparation and resolution figure to use in connection with the seventh of the seventh chord.
3) Work for smooth voice leading, and avoid parallel perfect fifths and octaves. Avoid doubling active tones.

B. THE FIRST INVERSION

Analyze the following Bach examples, giving

1. (a) Classification and name of chord introducing the VII⁷.

$$\overset{\sharp}{7}$$

(b) Classification and name of chord following the VII⁷.

$$\overset{\sharp}{7}$$

2. (a) Type of preparation figure used in connection with the 7th of the VII⁷.

$$\overset{\sharp}{7}$$

(b) Character of the voice leading in the remaining voices.

Ex. 419. Ist Gott mein Schild und Helfersmann

Ex. 420. Ach Gott, vom Himmel sieh' darein

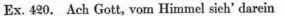

Ex. 421. Freu' dich sehr, o meine Seele

At 1, the second classification supertonic triad in first inversion progresses to the first inversion of the VII⁷, which is in turn followed by the first inversion of the tonic. In the alto the suspension figure controls the seventh of the VII⁷. The outer voices progress through double passing tones to the root and third of the VII⁷.

At 2, the second phrase opens with the first inversion of the VII⁷, which progresses to the first inversion of the tonic. The neighboring tone figure in the tenor begins with the last chord of the phrase.

At 3, the VII⁷ follows the II and progresses to the first inversion of the tonic. The

    ♯   ♯
    7   6

filled-in appoggiatura figure is in the alto.

Analyze the following chorales:

Wonderlich: 54(6th), 80(3rd), 92(5th), 93(5th), 95(7th), 100(1st), 117(3rd), 131(6th), 144(6th).

Bach-Riemenschneider: 67(6th), 368(3rd), 324(5th), 356(5th), 327(8th), 45(1st), 240(3rd), 109(6th), 265(6th).

DEDUCTIONS

THE SUSPENSION FIGURE

The VII⁷ in first inversion follows chords of the second classification, usually

    ♯
    7

the supertonic.

The VII⁷ in first inversion progresses to the first inversion of the tonic triad.

    ♯
    7

THE NEIGHBORING TONE FIGURE

The VII⁷ in first inversion may be introduced by the tonic (first inversion),

    ♯
    7

first classification chords, V or V⁷ or by a chromatic progression.

          ♯   ♯
          7   7

The VII⁷ in first inversion progresses to the first inversion of the tonic triad.

    ♯
    7

THE PASSING TONE FIGURE

No examples found.

THE APPOGGIATURA FIGURE

The VII⁷ in first inversion follows the VII, occasionally the tonic.

    ♯   ♯
    7   7

The VII⁷ in first inversion progresses to the first inversion of the tonic, or oc-

    ♯
    7

casionally to the first inversion of the V⁷.

         ♯
         7

A passing tone usually fills in the leap of the third in the figure.

GENERAL DEDUCTIONS

As in the case of the root position of the VII⁷, the cross relation can appear

$$\overset{\#}{7}$$

when the suspension or neighboring tone figures are not used. In most instances the VII⁷ in first inversion progresses to the first inversion of the tonic.

$$\overset{\#}{7}$$

C. THE SECOND INVERSION

Analyze the following Bach examples, giving

1. (a) Classification and name of chord introducing the VII⁷.

$$\overset{\#}{7}$$

   (b) Classification and name of chord following the VII⁷.

$$\overset{\#}{7}$$

2. (a) Type of preparation figure used in connection with the 7th of the VII⁷.

$$\overset{\#}{7}$$

   (b) Character of the voice leading in the remaining voices.

Ex. 422. Herr Jesu Christ, wahr'r Mensch
und Gott

Ex. 423. Ach Gott und Herr,
wie gross und schwer

Ex. 424.   Das alte Jahr vergangen ist

At 1, the VII⁷ in second inversion follows the subdominant.   The VII⁷ progresses to

$$\overset{\sharp}{7}$$

the tonic in fundamental position.   The suspension figure appears in the soprano.   Note the leap in the bass from the second inversion of the VII⁷ as the remaining voices progress by step to the tonic triad.

$$\overset{\sharp}{7}$$

At 2, the VII⁷ in second inversion is approached by a chromatic progression.   The VII⁷

$$\overset{\sharp}{7}$$

progresses directly to the root position of the tonic.   The appoggiatura figure is in the tenor.

At 3, the VII⁷ in second inversion follows the tonic and progresses to the first inversion

$$\overset{\sharp}{7}$$

of the tonic in the key of b-minor.   The neighboring tone figure appears in the alto.

Analyze the following chorales:

Wonderlich: 10(2nd), 83(5th), 135(6th), 144(4th), 148(3rd).
Bach-Riemenschneider: 180(2nd), 19(5th), 267(6th), 265(4th), 68(3rd).

DEDUCTIONS

THE SUSPENSION FIGURE

The VII⁷ in second inversion follows chords of the second classification.

$$\overset{\sharp}{7}$$

The VII⁷ in second inversion progresses to the tonic in root position or first inversion. $\overset{\sharp}{7}$

THE PASSING TONE FIGURE

No examples were found.

THE NEIGHBORING TONE FIGURE

The VII⁷ in second inversion follows the tonic in root position or first inversion.

$$\overset{\sharp}{7}$$

The VII⁷ in second inversion progresses to tonic in root position or first inversion.   #
      7

THE APPOGGIATURA FIGURE

In a diatonic progression the VII⁷ in second inversion follows tonic in any
position in the bass.   #
         7

VII⁷ in second inversion progresses to the tonic in root position or first inversion. #
    7

VII⁷ may be introduced in a chromatic progression.   The bass note of the VII⁷
  #   #
  7   7

is usually introduced by step from above.

GENERAL DEDUCTIONS

The leap in the bass from a second inversion of a seventh chord is an unused
procedure.   A leap from the bass note of the VII⁷ in second inversion is, however,
                                                   #
                                                   7

an exception.   The bass note of the second inversion of the VII⁷ is the subdominant.
                                                                         #
                                                                           7

The progression VII⁷ in second inversion to tonic in root position gives a plagal
          #
          7

feeling to the progression.   Bach uses this progression not only in the chorales but
also in other works: for instance, the final cadence of Prelude XVIII, Vol. I of the
Well-Tempered Clavichord.

Ex. 425.   Prelude XVIII — Well-Tempered
Clavichord, Bk. I   *J. Sebastian Bach*

IV   VII⁷   I
              #7   #3

D. THE THIRD INVERSION

The third inversion of the VII^7 is rare.

$$\overset{\#}{7}$$

Analyze the following Bach examples, giving

1. (a) Classification and name of chord introducing the VII^7.

$$\overset{\#}{7}$$

   (b) Classification and name of chord following the VII^7.

$$\overset{\#}{7}$$

2. (a) Type of preparation figure used in connection with the 7th of the VII^7.

$$\overset{\#}{7}$$

   (b) Character of voice leading in the remaining voices.

Ex. 426.   Ich hab' mein' Sach' Gott heimgestellt

Ex. 427.   Was mein Gott will,
das g'scheh'

Ex. 428.   Wir Christenleut'

At 1, the e^b in the bass anticipates the bass note of the third inversion of the VII^7.

$$\sharp \atop 7$$

This is an extremely rare method of introducing the 7th of a seventh chord. In the first beat the e-flat progresses to the d, which anticipates the root of the V.

$$\sharp \atop 7$$

At 2, the third inversion of the VII^7 is introduced by chromatic progression. The VII^7

$$\sharp \atop 7 \qquad\qquad\qquad\qquad \sharp \atop 7$$

progresses to the second inversion of the tonic in b-minor, which is a passing chord to the second inversion of the VII^7. The seventh is prepared by the chromatic passing tone figure.

$$\sharp \atop 7$$

At 3, the third inversion of the VII^7 follows the first inversion of the IV in the key of

$$\sharp \atop 7$$

g-minor. The VII^7 progresses to the tonic in second inversion, which is a passing chord to

$$\sharp \atop 7$$

the II^7 (altered chord *). The seventh of the VII^7 is prepared by the suspension figure.

$$\sharp\sharp \atop 46 \qquad\qquad\qquad\qquad \sharp \atop 7$$

DEDUCTIONS

1. The VII^7 in third inversion follows chords of the second classification, usually

$$\sharp \atop 7$$

the first inversion of the IV.

2. The VII^7 in third inversion progresses to either the V^7 or the second inversion

$$\sharp \atop 7 \qquad\qquad\qquad\qquad \sharp \atop 7$$

of the I.

3. The VII^7 in third inversion may be introduced as part of a chromatic chord pro-

$$\sharp \atop 7$$

gression.

4. The 7th may be introduced and resolved by the supension figure and occasionally by the descending chromatic passing tone figure.

PARTWRITING EXERCISES

1) Make a harmonic analysis of each exercise before filling in the alto and tenor.
2) Work for smooth voice leading and avoid parallel perfect fifths and octaves. Avoid doubling active tones.

* See Chapter 23.

Chapter 19

The Subdominant Seventh Chord in Major and Minor

The next prominent seventh chord is found in the second classification on the subdominant in major and minor. The following table shows the type chord and symbol used in major and minor keys:

Major Key	Minor Key
IV⁷ (major seventh chord)	IV⁷ (minor seventh chord)
	IV⁷ (major-minor seventh chord)

Minor Key

IV⁷ (minor seventh chord)
IV⁷ (major-minor seventh chord)
#
6   Fundamental position, rare*
    First inversion, common
    Second inversion, rare
    Third inversion, rare

A. THE ROOT POSITION

THE SUSPENSION FIGURE

Analyze the following Bach examples, giving

1. (a) Name and classification of chord introducing the IV⁷.
   (b) Name and classification of chord following the IV⁷.
2. The character of the voice leading in each part.

Ex. 430. Ermuntre dich, mein schwacher
Geist

Ex. 429. Ein' feste Burg ist unser Gott

* Bach-Riemenschneider: 96(2nd), 314(3rd).

199

Ex. 431.   Vater unser im Himmelreich

Ex. 432.   Nimm von uns, Herr, du treuer Gott

Ex. 433.   Vater unser im Himmelreich

Ex. 434.   Erhalt' uns, Herr, bei deinem Wort

At 1, the IV⁷ follows the tonic and progresses to the dominant triad. The IV⁷ frequently appears on the second part of a beat. The suspension figure is in the tenor. The three upper voices move down to the dominant as the bass rises to the root of the dominant triad.

At 2, the IV⁷ follows the tonic and progresses to the dominant seventh chord in third inversion. The IV⁷ is incomplete, having the conventional two roots, one third and one seventh. The suspension figure is in the soprano.

At 3, the IV⁷ follows the submediant triad (third classification) and progresses to the dominant triad. The suspension figure is in the soprano. The three lower voices move contrary to the soprano. The 5th of the IV⁷ leaps to the root of the dominant in the tenor (the popular leap of tonic to dominant or the reverse is always good).

At 4, the IV⁷ follows the tonic and progresses to the dominant. The suspension figure is in the soprano. As at 3, the third is below the seventh of the IV⁷ when it progresses to V. Under these conditions Bach avoids consecutive fifths by either leaping from the 5th of the IV⁷ to the root of the V or by leaping down from the 3rd of the IV⁷ to the 5th of the V. Watch carefully the many variations of partwriting Bach devises to avoid consecutive fifths from IV⁷ to V.

At 5, the IV⁷ follows the submediant and progresses to the dominant seventh. The suspension figure appears in the soprano. The 7th of the V⁷ is controlled by the filled-in appoggiatura figure. This is the first time that the root position of a seventh chord progresses up a step to the root position of another seventh chord.*

Ex. 435.

(a) Practically non-existent in Bach style.

(b) Bach uses this partwriting.

At 6, the IV⁷ in g-minor follows the tonic and progresses to the V with the doubled

$$\overset{\#}{7}$$

5th. The suspension figure appears in the soprano. The partwriting in the tenor is the same as at 4, but in the V triad the 5th rises to the root. Watch in further examples for variations in the inner voice which double the 5th.

For further study, analyze the root position of the IV⁷ in the following chorales:

Wonderlich: 27(2nd), 81(6th), 37(1st), 128(4th), 149(4th).

Bach-Riemenschneider: 232(2nd), 2(6th), 72(1st), 12(4th), 339(4th).

DEDUCTIONS

1. The IV⁷ follows tonic or the third classification submediant chord.

2. The IV⁷ is most often found in the cadence formula.

3. The seventh of the chord is most often found in the soprano.

4. The IV⁷ is rarely found incomplete.

5. The IV⁷ progresses most often to the dominant triad, and infrequently to the dominant seventh chord.

6. When the 3rd is below the seventh of the IV⁷, it frequently falls a fifth to the 5th of the dominant triad.

7. The IV⁷ is found frequently on the second half of the beat.

THE PASSING TONE FIGURE

Analyze the following Bach examples, giving

1. (a) Name and classification of chord introducing the IV⁷.

   (b) Name and classification of chord following the IV⁷.

2. The character of the voice leading in each part.

* The VII⁷ in root position always progresses to the tonic triad in root position.
$$\overset{\#}{7}$$

Ex. 436. Wenn mein Stündlein vorhanden ist

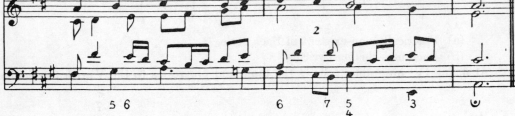

Ex. 437. Christus, der uns selig macht

At 1, the IV⁷ follows the IV in first inversion. The passing tone figure appears in the soprano. The IV⁷ progresses to the V triad containing an ornamental resolution of the 9-8 suspension.

At 2, the IV⁷ follows the IV in first inversion. The e in the bass is an accented passing tone. The 4 suspension detracts one's attention from the doubled fifth in the V. Bach uses the 4-3 suspension frequently in a V triad when it appears with a doubled 5th.

At 3, the IV⁷ follows the IV in first inversion and progresses to the dominant triad in a half cadence. The tenor leap from f to b is a diminished fifth. In this progression, the diminished fifth appears in minor and the perfect fifth in major.

For further study, analyze the following chorales:

Wonderlich: 43(3rd), 44(3rd), 122(2nd), 89(3rd), 90(7th), 92(1st).
Bach-Riemenschneider:290(3rd), 335(3rd), 14(2nd), 106(3rd), 83(7th), 324(1st).

DEDUCTIONS

1. The IV⁷ follows the IV in first inversion.
2. Again the IV⁷ resolves to V and sometimes to V⁷.

3. Again the IV^7 is part of the cadence formula, although it occasionally may appear within the phrase.

THE NEIGHBORING TONE AND APPOGGIATURA FIGURES

Occasionally examples of the IV^7 may be found bound up in the neighboring tone and filled-in appoggiatura figure. The following are the rare examples of these:

Ex. 438. Nun lob', mein' Seel', den Herren

Ex. 439. Mit Fried' und Freud' ich fahr' dahin

Ex. 440. Lobt Gott, ihr Christen, allzugleich

At 1, the IV^7 follows the first inversion of the supertonic triad in a-major. The neighboring tone figure is in the soprano. On the third beat of the measure the root of the IV^7 is raised, forming the IV$^7_{\#4}$. The formation of this chord delays the resolution of the c-sharp one beat.

At 2, the IV^7 follows the FAC triad, which has become a VI triad in a-minor. The appoggiatura figure is in the soprano. The IV^7 progresses to the V in an ornamental cadence formula. The e in the bass is an accented passing tone.

At 3, the IV^7 follows the first inversion of the tonic. The filled-in appoggiatura figure is in the soprano.

PARTWRITING EXERCISES

1) Make a harmonious analysis of each exercise before filling in the alto and tenor.
2) Work for smooth voice leading and avoid parallel fifths and octaves. Avoid doubling active tones.

IV⁷

B. THE FIRST INVERSION

THE SUSPENSION FIGURE

Analyze the following examples, giving

1. (a) Name and classification of chord introducing the first inversion of the IV⁷.
    (b) Name and classification of chord following the first inversion of the IV⁷.

2. The character of the voice leading in each part.

Ex. 441.   Herzlich tut mich verlangen

Ex. 442. Gott des Himmels und der Erden

Ex. 444. Herr Jesu Christ, wahr'r Mensch und Gott

Ex. 443. Mitten wir im Leben sind

Ex. 446. Es ist genug; so nimm, Herr

Ex. 445. Herr, straf mich nicht in deinem Zorn

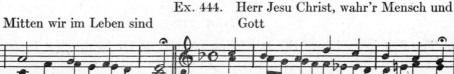

At 1, the IV⁷ in first inversion follows the first inversion of the tonic. The IV⁷ is given an ornamental resolution to the dominant triad, forming a phrygian cadence. The suspension figure is in the alto.

At 2, the I⁷ in first inversion becomes the IV⁷ in the key of e-major. The IV⁷ progresses to the first inversion of the V⁷. The suspension figure is in the alto. Notice the tonic to dominant leap in the tenor, the 5th of IV⁷ to the root of the V⁷ respectively.

At 3, the IV⁷ in first inversion follows the first inversion of the mediant triad. The IV⁷ progresses to the first inversion of the V⁷. The suspension figure is in the alto.

At 4, the IV⁷ in first inversion follows the mediant triad in root position. The IV⁷ progresses to the V⁷ in first inversion. The suspension figure is in the alto.

At 5, the GBDF IV⁷ progresses to the V⁷ in d-minor. The suspension figure is in the alto. The GBDF is the common chord II⁷ in the key of f-major, becoming IV⁷ in d-minor.

At 6, the BD$^\sharp$F$^\sharp$A IV^7 progresses to the VII in f-sharp minor.   The suspension figure

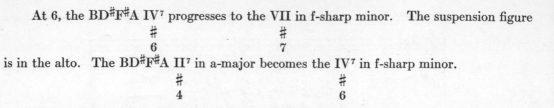

is in the alto. The BD$^\sharp$F$^\sharp$A II^7 in a-major becomes the IV^7 in f-sharp minor.

For further study, analyze the following chorales:

Wonderlich: 38(5th), 39(6th), 110(5th), 1(6th), 61(2nd, 3rd), 130(2nd).
Bach-Riemenschneider: 9(5th), 343(6th), 84(5th), 40(6th), 181(2nd, 3rd), 142(2nd).

DEDUCTIONS

1. The first inversion of the IV^7 follows I, III, or III in the first inversion. It is also the common chord II^7 = IV^7 or II^7 = IV^7 in the process of modulation, the II^7 usually following the tonic of the old key.

2. The first inversion of the IV^7 progresses to the first inversion of the V or V^7 or to the root position of the VII.

3. In most cases the IV^7 in first inversion takes up the first half of a beat and resolves to the first classification chords on the second half of the beat.

4. IV^7 in first inversion progresses to the V in a phrygian cadence.

5. When the IV^7 in first inversion progresses to the V^7 in first inversion, the following partwriting is found:

Ex. 447.   Frequent   Less frequent   Rare

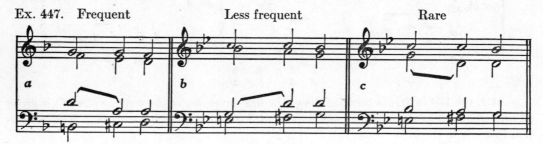

In each of these examples
  (a) the root of the IV^7 becomes the 7th of the V^7.
  (b) the 5th of the IV^7 leaps to the root of the V^7, the tonic to the dominant.
  (c) the remaining voices move step-wise.

6. The four voices progress the same in a major key.

7. The root is usually in the soprano of the IV^7 in first inversion. The suspension figure appears most often in the alto.

THE PASSING TONE, NEIGHBORING TONE, AND APPOGGIATURA FIGURES

There are practically no examples of these figures in connection with the first inversion of the IV^7.

PARTWRITING EXERCISES

1) Make a harmonic analysis of each exercise before filling in the alto and tenor.
2) Work for smooth voice leading and avoid parallel fifths and octaves. Avoid doubling active tones.

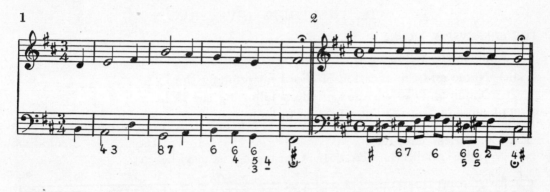

C. THE SECOND INVERSION

There are actually no examples of the second inversion of the IV⁷ in the chorales. However, a few examples are cited here, showing the IV⁷ in second inversion, produced as a vertical sonority caused by non-harmonic tones. These examples are like the examples cited in the discussion on the development of 7th chords in Chapter 25.

Ex. 448. O Welt, ich muss dich lassen   Ex. 449. Ach Gott, vom Himmel sieh' darein

At 1, the second inversion of the IV⁷ vertical sonority is caused by the passing tone a in the alto.

At 2, the second inversion of the IV⁷ vertical sonority in the key of a-minor is the

$$\substack{\sharp \\ 6}$$

result of the double passing tones d-f-sharp in the tenor and alto. The progression is really tonic to dominant.

D.　THE THIRD INVERSION

THE SUSPENSION FIGURE

Analyze the following Bach examples, giving

1. (a) Name and classification of chord introducing the IV⁷.
   (b) Name and classification of chord following the IV⁷.
2. The character of the voice leading in each part.

Ex. 450.　Verleih' uns Frie-
　　　　den gnädiglich　　　Ex. 451.　Christus, der ist mein Leben

Ex. 452.　Herr, nun lass in Frieden　　　Ex. 453.　Was willst du dich, o meine Seele

At 1, the IV⁷ in third inversion follows the fourth classification chord, the mediant. The IV⁷ progresses to the first inversion of the leading tone triad. The suspension figure is in the bass.

At 2, the IV⁷ in third inversion follows the first inversion of the tonic. The IV⁷ progresses to the first inversion of the leading tone triad.

At 3, the IV⁷ in third inversion follows the first inversion of the tonic in the key of

$$\substack{\sharp \\ 6}$$

a-minor. The g-sharp in the tenor is a lower neighboring tone. At 3, the d in the bass is an upper neighboring tone which ornaments the suspension figure. The IV⁷ progresses to the

$$\substack{\sharp \\ 6}$$

leading tone triad in first inversion. The c in the bass is an accented passing tone.

At 4, the GBDF chord is a common chord between f-major and d-minor, II⁷ in f-major

becoming IV⁷ in d-minor. The IV⁷ progresses to the leading tone triad in first inversion.

For further study, analyze the following chorales:

Wonderlich: 36(3rd), 142(8th), 9(7th), 82(2nd), 97(3rd), 131(4th).

Bach-Riemenschneider: 34 (3rd), 139(8th), 13(7th), 60(2nd), 175(3rd), 109(4th).

DEDUCTIONS

1. The IV⁷ in third inversion follows the first inversion of the tonic or the root position of the mediant.

2. The IV⁷ in third inversion is frequently a common chord to two keys in a modulation.

3. In major or minor the IV⁷ of IV⁷ in third inversion progresses to the leading tone triad.

4. The IV⁷ in first inversion appears near the beginning of a phrase or within the phrase.

5. The VII in first inversion usually has two thirds, one root, and one fifth.

6. In the progression IV⁷ to VII the root of the IV⁷ is the common tone and the remaining voices move step-wise as follows:

Ex. 454.

THE PASSING TONE, NEIGHBORING TONE, AND APPOGGIATURA FIGURES

No examples of the neighboring tone figure are found, but there are a few isolated examples of the seventh of the IV⁷ prepared in the bass by the passing tone and appoggiatura figures.

Ex. 455. Nun preiset alle Gottes Barmherzigkeit

Ex. 456.   Jesu Leiden, Pein und Tod   Ex. 457.   Gelobet seist du, Jesu Christ

Ex. 458.   Mit Fried' und Freud' ich fahr' dahin

At 1, the third inversion of the IV⁷ follows the IV in root position in the key of a-minor.

$$\overset{\sharp}{6} \qquad\qquad \overset{\sharp}{6}$$

The IV⁷ progresses to the VII in first inversion.   The passing tone figure is in the bass.

$$\overset{\sharp}{6} \qquad\qquad \overset{\sharp}{7}$$

At 2, the chromatic passing tone figure is in the bass.   The chromatic progression from the first inversion of the tonic in e-major nullifies the key of e-major, and the AC♯EG seventh chord is a IV⁷ in the key of e-minor.   The g in the bass becomes a pedal point for

$$\overset{\sharp}{6}$$

the beat, the chord progression being IV⁷ VII.   The g in the bass moves to an accented

$$\overset{\sharp}{6} \quad \overset{\sharp}{7}$$

passing tone f-sharp on the way to e, which is the root of the e-minor tonic triad.   The entire measure is extremely dissonant and shows how Bach can produce tension by the use of seventh chords and non-harmonic material.

At 3, the filled-in appoggiatura figure appears in the bass.   The key of d-major is nullified by the concealed chromatic chord progression with a cross relation between the c-sharp in the tenor of the a-major triad and the c in the bass of the DF♯AC which is a IV⁷ in the key

$$\overset{\sharp}{6}$$

of a-minor.   The passing tone b fills in the appoggiatura figure in the bass a-c-b.   Again the third inversion of the IV⁷ progresses to the first inversion of VII.

$$\overset{\sharp}{6} \qquad\qquad\qquad \overset{\sharp}{7}$$

At 4, the filled-in appoggiatura figure is in the bass. The d is a passing tone between e-c-b. The e-minor triad is the common chord to d-minor and a-minor, II in d-minor becoming a V in a-minor. The DF#AC seventh chord is IV⁷ in a-minor progressing to the first inversion of the VII.

PARTWRITING EXERCISES

1) Make a harmonic analysis of each exercise before filling in the alto and tenor.
2) Work for smooth voice leading and avoid parallel fifths and octaves. Avoid doubling active tones.

Chapter 20

The Other Diatonic Seventh Chords

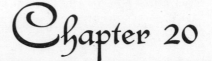

The other diatonic seventh chords are:

VII⁷ in major — First classification

VI⁷ in major and minor ⎫
I⁷ in major ⎭ Third classification

III⁷ in major — Fourth classification

A. THE LEADING TONE SEVENTH CHORD IN MAJOR: ROOT POSITION

The seventh chord built on the leading tone in a major key is a half-diminished seventh chord. The leading tone seventh chord (VII⁷) in major is much less frequent than the VII⁷ in minor. The chord has a limited function in the chorales.

It is found in the progression IV₆–VII⁷–I. If the seventh is above the fifth in the VII⁷, the voices progress to the tonic with a doubled third.

Ex. 459.

It is important to notice that the IV₆ has the bass note doubled. The VII⁷ appears invariably on the second half of the beat. The VII⁷ is formed by double passing tones. The suspension figure controls the seventh of the VII⁷.

Analyze the following chorales for the use and partwriting of the VII⁷ in major:

Wonderlich: 25(3rd), 58(4th), 92(4th), 152(1st).
Bach-Riemenschneider: 53(3rd), 288(4th), 324(4th), 121(1st).

DEDUCTIONS

1. The root position of the VII[7] in major is limited to one progression: IV₆–VII[7]–I.
2. The seventh of the VII[7] is controlled by the suspension figure.
3. The first inversion of the IV has the bass note doubled.
4. The tonic triad following the VII[7] usually has the third doubled.

INVERSIONS

Inversions of the VII[7] in major are rare. The following examples from the chorales illustrate their typical usage:

Ex. 460. Erbarm' dich mein, o Herre Gott

Ex. 461. Freu' dich sehr, o meine Seele

At 1, the 1st inversion of the VII[7] neatly fits into the contrapuntal scheme between the c-major triads. The suspension figure appears in the alto. The a changes the c-major triad into an a-minor triad. The VII[7] is followed by V with an accented passing tone e in the tenor. This progression is a variation of the standard I–VII (with a 7-6 suspension)–I (in first inversion).

At 2, the IV in the key of c-major progresses to the second inversion of the VII[7]. The VII[7] progresses to the first inversion of the I. The suspension figure is in the soprano. This progression is a variation of the IV–VII (in first inversion)–I (either in root or first inversion).

PARTWRITING EXERCISES

1) Make a harmonic analysis of each exercise before filling in the alto and tenor.
2) Work for smooth voice leading and avoid parallel perfect fifths and octaves. Avoid doubling active tones.

B. THE SUBMEDIANT SEVENTH CHORD IN MAJOR AND MINOR: ROOT POSITION

The submediant seventh chord in major and minor keys is found most often in fundamental position. The following table shows the type chord and symbol used in major and minor keys:

Major Key	Minor Key
VI[7] (minor seventh chord)	VI[7] (major seventh chord)
	VI[7] (half-diminished seventh chord)
	$\overset{\sharp}{6}$

THE VI[7] IN MAJOR AND THE NORMAL VI[7] IN MINOR

Analyze the following Bach examples, giving

1. (a) Name and classification of chord introducing the VI[7].
    (b) Name and classification of chord following the VI[7].
2. (a) Type of preparation and resolution figure.
    (b) The movement of the remaining voices.

Ex. 462. Ach was soll ich Sünder machen   Ex. 463.   O Ewigkeit, du Donnerwort

Ex. 464.   Singen wir aus Herzens Grund   Ex. 465.   Meines Lebens letzte Zeit

At 1, the VI⁷ follows the tonic in first inversion and progresses to the supertonic *
seventh in root position. The suspension preparation and resolution figure appears in the
soprano. Note the double third in the II⁷.

At 2, the VI⁷ follows the mediant seventh chord and progresses to the supertonic
seventh. The suspension preparation and resolution figure is in the soprano.

At 3, the VI⁷ follows the mediant triad and progresses to the root position of the leading
tone triad. The suspension preparation and resolution figure is in the soprano. Note that
in root position a diminished triad used in this manner sounds well. Contrary motion between the soprano and bass voices leading to the tonic triad are essential in the progression
of VI⁷–VII–I.

At 4, the VI⁷ follows the tonic and progresses to the first inversion of the subdominant.
This progression is usually found in the half cadence formula.

Analyze the use of the VI⁷ in the following chorale phrases:

Wonderlich: 110(5th), 129(6th), 130(2nd).
Bach-Riemenschneider: 36(5th), 84(5th), 22(6th), 142(2nd), 112(2nd).

DEDUCTIONS

1. VI⁷ follows mediant (triad or seventh) or tonic triads.

2. VI⁷ progresses to (a) chord of the second classification II or IV.

                             (b) chord of the first classification, V⁷ in first inversion or VII
                                  in root position.

                             (c) in a minor key, usually IV in first inversion.

3. The 7th of the VI⁷ is controlled by the suspension preparation and resolution
   figure.

THE VI⁷ IN MINOR

    #
    6

* If the vertical sonority built on the supertonic containing two thirds and a minor 7th is approached by leap
and left by leap or combination of step-leap or leap-step, the sonority will be considered a legitimate II⁷. Refer
to Chapter 17, page 171.

Analyze the following examples, giving

1. (a) Name and classification of chord introducing the VI⁷.

$$\overset{\#}{6}$$

(b) Name and classification of chord following the VI⁷.

$$\overset{\#}{6}$$

2. (a) Type of preparation and resolution figure.
   (b) The melodic character of the remaining voices.

Ex. 466.   Warum betrübst du dich, mein Herz

Ex. 467.   Herr Jesu Christ, du höchstes Gut

Ex. 468.   Verleih' uns Frieden gnädiglich

At 1, the VI⁷ follows the V and progresses to the VII. The suspension figure is in the soprano. The VI⁷ acts as a passing chord between the two chords in the first classification.

At 2, the VI⁷ follows the III in first inversion and progresses to the VII.   The sus-

pension figure is in the soprano. The VI⁷ acts as a passing chord between the III and the VII.

At 3, the EGBᵇD vertical sonority is a doubtful VI⁷. The 7th in the alto is prepared

by the suspension concept but the resolution is irregular. Some theorists call this resolution *passive*. A better idea, perhaps, is that e and g in the bass and tenor are double passing tones, and that, therefore, the d is a consonance in the b-flat major triad and the double passing tones delete the cross relation f and f-sharp in the progression III–V in the key of g-minor. The b-flat major triad is the common chord, I in b-flat major becoming the IV in g-minor.

Analyze the VI⁷ in the following chorales:

Wonderlich: 65(1st), 107(6th), 114(4th), 123(5th), 145(4th).
Bach-Riemenschneider: 287(1st), 49(6th), 28(4th), 57(5th), 115(4th).

DEDUCTIONS

1. The VI⁷ follows V or III in first inversion.

2. The VI⁷ usually progresses to VII in root position.

3. The 7th of the VI⁷ is prepared and resolved by the suspension figure.

4. The remaining voices usually proceed into and out of the VI⁷ by step.

THE INVERSIONS

Examples of the VI⁷ in inversion are extremely rare. When they appear in the musical fabric, they are usually passing chords.

Analyze the following chorale phrases containing the inversion of the VI⁷, stating

1. (a) Name and classification of chord introducing the VI⁷.
    (b) Name and classification of chord following the VI⁷.

2. (a) Type of preparation and resolution figure.
   (b) The melodic character of the remaining voices.

Wonderlich: 12(2nd), 142(5th), 89(8th), 25(2nd), 144(3rd), 43(4th), 130(6th).
Bach-Riemenschneider: 1(2nd), 139(5th), 106(8th), 53(2nd), 265(3rd), 290(4th), 142(6th).

DEDUCTIONS

The VI^7 in major and the VI^7 in minor appear as passing chords in the following progressions:

$$\#$$
$$6$$

Major				*Minor*	
V_6	$VI_{6\atop5}$	VII_6	I	$VI_{6}{\#\atop5}$	$VII_6{\#}$
				6	7
IV_6	$VI_{4\atop2}$	$II^7_{6\atop5}$	V_6	VI_6	VII_6
			$\#\atop7$	$\#\atop6$ ^{5}	$\#\atop7$
			V_4	VI_4	VII_6
			$\#^2\atop7$	$\#^3\atop6$	$\#\atop7$

The VI^7 sometimes is a common chord when it is a minor seventh chord. Its resolution is always to VII_6. The seventh is always approached and resolved in the suspension figure. In the remaining parts, the voice leading through the inversion of the VI^7 is step-wise.

PARTWRITING EXERCISES

1) Make a harmonic analysis of each exercise before filling in the alto and tenor.
2) Work for smooth voice leading and avoid parallel perfect fifths and octaves. Avoid doubling active tones.

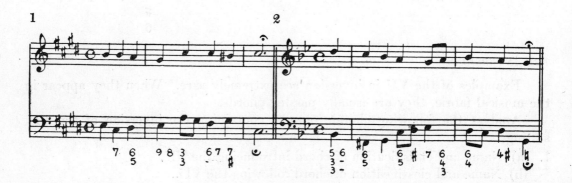

C. THE TONIC SEVENTH CHORD IN MAJOR

The seventh chord built on the tonic in a major key is a major seventh chord. Tonic harmony, when it is dissonant, has a strong tendency to progress to chords with their roots in the second classification. The I^7 and VI^7 progress naturally to roots of the second classification a fourth away, namely, I^7 to IV and VI^7 to II. The I^7 is a chord belonging to the third classification of root movement.

THE ROOT POSITION AND INVERSIONS

The root position and inversions of the I⁷ are quite rare.

Analyze the following Bach examples, giving

1. (a) Name and classification of chord introducing the I⁷.
   (b) Name and classification of chord following the I⁷.
2. (a) Type of preparation and resolution figure.
   (b) The movement of the remaining voices.

Ex. 469.   Es ist gewisslich an der Zeit

Ex. 470.   Puer natus in Bethlehem

Ex. 471.   Allein zu dir, Herr Jesu Christ

At 1, the I⁷ follows the V⁷ and progresses to the II⁷. The suspension figure is in the alto.

At 2, the I⁷ follows the I₆ and progresses to the IV. The passing tone figure is in the soprano.

At 3, the I⁷ follows the V and progresses to the IV. The ornamental suspension figure is in the tenor.

At 4, the third inversion of the I⁷ follows the V and progresses to the first inversion of the IV. The suspension figure is in the bass.

For further study, analyze the following chorales:

Wonderlich: 60(1st), 112(5th), 137(4th), 138(7th).
Bach-Riemenschneider: 35(1st), 330(5th), 191(7th).

DEDUCTIONS

1. The I⁷ in root position or inversion follows the V or V⁷. The 7th is introduced by the suspension figure.
2. When the I⁷ in root position or inversion follows the I (root position or first inversion) the 7th is introduced by the passing tone figure.
3. The I⁷ progresses to chords which have their roots in the second classification. The IV is more frequent than the II.
4. All intervals of the I⁷ are present.

PARTWRITING EXERCISES

1) Make a harmonic analysis of each exercise before filling in the alto and tenor.
2) Work for smooth voice leading and avoid parallel perfect fifths and octaves. Avoid doubling active tones.

D. THE MEDIANT SEVENTH CHORD IN MAJOR

In the fourth classification in a major key, occasionally a minor seventh chord appears on the mediant. In root position the chord is usually incomplete, appearing with one root, two thirds, and one seventh.

Analyze the following Bach examples, giving

1. (a) Name and classification of chord introducing the III⁷.
   (b) Name and classification of chord following the III⁷.

2. (a) Type of preparation and resolution figure.
   (b) The movement of the remaining voices.

Ex. 472.   O Ewigkeit, du Donnerwort   Ex. 473.   Werde munter, mein Gemüte

Ex. 474.   Jesu, meiner Seelen Wonne

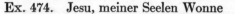

At 1, the III⁷ follows the II. The suspension figure is in the alto. The III⁷ progresses to the VI⁷. The III⁷ contains one root, two thirds, and one seventh.

At 2, the III⁷ follows the II. The ornamental suspension figure is in the tenor. The III⁷ progresses to the VI. The III⁷ contains one root, two thirds, and one seventh.

At 3, the III⁷ follows VII in first inversion in the key of a-major. The III⁷ progresses to the IV⁷. The suspension figure is in the tenor. The IV⁷ contains two roots, one third, and one seventh.

For further study, analyze the following chorales:

Wonderlich: 39(2nd).

Bach-Riemenschneider: 343(2nd), 90(3rd), 213(1st).

DEDUCTIONS

1. The III⁷ in root position or in inversion is rare. The III⁷ is found only in major keys.
2. The chord is found in a digression from either the first classification or the second classification.
3. The III⁷ progresses normally to VI third classification, or by elision to the IV second classification.
4. The suspension figure introduces the seventh of the III⁷ and is the only preparation and resolution figure used.
5. The remaining voices move smoothly according to their respective characteristics. The bass may leap to the root of the VI⁷.

PARTWRITING EXERCISES

1) Make a harmonic analysis of each exercise before filling in the alto and tenor.

2) Work for smooth voice leading and avoid parallel perfect fifths and octaves. Avoid doubling active tones.

Chapter 21

Altered Non-Harmonic Tones

Occasionally tones appear in the voice leading, during a normal progression of diatonic chords, which do not have the same spelling as found in the diatonic scale. Sing the following example before discussing the analysis:

Ex. 475.   Lass, o Herr, dein Ohr sich neigen

Ex. 476.   Wer Gott vertraut, hat wohl gebaut

The first example is in b-flat major. At 1, the a-flat in the alto is a passing tone. Although the a-flat is a foreign tone to the key of b-flat, it in no way disturbs the normal progression of the tonic to the third inversion of the supertonic seventh. The a-flat is considered a lowered seventh degree of the scale of b-flat major.

The second example is in g-major. At 2, the c-sharp in the tenor is one of the double passing tones between the g-major triad and the d-major triad. The c-sharp does not affect the classification of the d-major triad. Sing the chorale phrase and omit the double passing tones; then repeat, singing the double passing tones; you will find that the c-sharp does not disturb the progression of the tonic to the dominant. The c-sharp is the raised fourth degree of the scale of g-major.

DEFINITIONS AND CLASSIFICATIONS

A non-harmonic tone which has a spelling foreign to the diatonic scale, and which does not disturb the classification of the root movement, is called an *altered non-harmonic tone.*

What is the origin of such tones? Dr. Hugo Riemann explains the a-flat in the first example as the mixolydian seventh. Sing the alto from (1) to the end of the phrase; you will find that you have outlined the tones of the mixolydian mode on b-flat except for the c (second degree). It should be noted that, although the a-flat is a chromatic alteration of the seventh degree of the b-flat major scale, it is approached and left diatonically. Students are apt to think and to use altered tones chromatically. As a matter of fact, about half of the altered tones, either non-harmonic or harmonic, are derived by diatonic procedures.

If each mode is generated from the same tone of a major key, the following table illustrates the new chromatic alterations which are introduced:

MODE *	SCALE	1	2	3	4	5	6	7	DIFFERENCE
		ALTERATION OF MAJOR SCALE **							
Dorian	B♭CD♭E♭FGA♭B♭			♭				♭	2
Phrygian	B♭C♭D♭E♭FG♭A♭B♭		♭	♭			♭	♭	4
Lydian	B♭CDEFGAB♭				#				1
Mixolydian	B♭CDE♭FGA♭B♭							♭	1
Aeolian	B♭CD♭E♭FG♭A♭B♭			♭			♭	♭	3

Comparing the modes which have the smallest difference in chromatic alterations with the music of the 17th and 18th centuries, one finds that the common alterations are lowered-seven and raised-four in major. A much less frequent alteration is lowered-six. Rare alterations are lowered-two, lowered-three in major.

If each mode is generated from the same tone of a minor key,*** the following table illustrates the chromatic alterations which are introduced:

MODE	SCALE	1	2	3	4	5	6	6#	7	7#	DIFFERENCE
		ALTERATIONS OF MINOR SCALE									
Dorian	B♭CD♭E♭FGA♭B♭										0
Phrygian	B♭C♭D♭E♭FG♭A♭B♭		♭								1
Lydian	B♭CDEFGAB♭			#	#						2
Mixolydian	B♭CDE♭FGA♭B♭				#						1 ⎫ Same
Ionian	B♭CDE♭FGAB♭				#						1 ⎭

The alterations in minor which have the highest frequency are raised-four, raised-three (in cadence). The lowered-two is infrequent.

BACH'S USAGE

There are slightly over a hundred altered non-harmonic tones in the 371 chodrales. Most of the alterations take place in a major key. There are only three

* See Appendix.

** For raising a scale step use sharp, for lowering a scale step use flat. Although the author disagrees with this established procedure, he sees no reason for further confusion in creating new terminology and symbolization. If e-flat is the fourth degree of the scale of b-flat major and one encounters an e-natural, it must be called raised-four, meaning raising one half-step.

*** The minor scales are pure, harmonic, and melodic. Therefore any new alteration must differ from these three forms of the minor scale.

altered non-harmonic tones in a major key; they are, in order of frequency, lowered-seven, raised-four, and lowered-three. In minor Bach uses only one altered non-harmonic tone, raised-four. These altered non-harmonic tones are introduced and resolved most often diatonically. They are usually passing tones, infrequently lower neighboring tones; they are never suspensions, escape tones, or appoggiaturas.

A. LOWERED–SEVEN IN MAJOR

Analyze the following examples, stating

(1) In which voice the alteration is found.
(2) In which chord the altered tone is found.
(3) The voice leading in and out of the altered tone.

Ex. 477. Schaut, ihr Sünder   Ex. 478. Nun preiset alle Gottes Barmherzigkeit

Ex. 479. Kyrie, Gott Vater in Ewigkeit

At 1, the lowered-seven passing tone appears in the bass, derived from the root of the tonic chord. The harmonic progression is I to IV.

At 2, the lowered-seven passing tone appears in the alto, derived from the root of the tonic chord. The altered non-harmonic tone appears in the half-cadence formula I to IV.

At 3, the lowered-seven passing tone appears in the tenor, derived from the root of the tonic chord. The harmonic progression is I to IV.

For further examples, analyze the following:

Wonderlich: 1(2nd), 22(1st), 47(1st), 102(1st), 130(5th).
Bach-Riemenschneider: 40(2nd), 200(1st), 27(1st), 276(1st), 142(5th).

DEDUCTIONS

1. The lowered-seven passing tone appears in the alto, tenor, and bass. (The tone does not appear in the soprano because it is the cantus. There is no reason, however, why it cannot be used in the soprano in Part III.

2. The lowered-seven passing tone is always found in tonic harmony.

3. The I containing the lowered-seven passing tone usually progresses to IV, occasionally to II and VI.

4. The lowered-seven is found as a descending passing tone, derived and resolved diatonically.

B. RAISED–FOUR IN MAJOR AND MINOR

Analyze the following examples, stating

(1) In which voice the alteration is found.

(2) In which chord the alteration is found and the harmony following.

(3) The voice leading in and out of the altered tone.

Ex. 480. Freu' dich sehr, o meine Seele

Ex. 481. Warum betrübst du dich, mein Herz

Ex. 482. Jesu, meine Freude

At 1, the raised-four appears in the tenor as one of the double passing tones in the progression I to V.

At 2, the raised-four in the alto appears as a single lower neighboring tone in a chromatic progression. The c-minor triad is a tonic, and the c-sharp diminished seventh chord is an altered chord, in the key of g-minor.

At 3, the raised-four appears in the bass in the progression II⁷ to V in the key of g-major.

For further examples, analyze the following chorales:

Wonderlich: 87(2nd), 53(4th), 154(3rd), 50(6th).
Bach-Riemenschneider: 122(2nd), 282(4th), 321(3rd), 352(1st & 5th), 163(3rd), 16(6th).

DEDUCTIONS

1. The raised-four appears most often in the inner voices and occasionally in the bass.

2. It is usually derived diatonically as an ascending passing tone. It may be a lower neighboring tone. It is rarely a chromatic ascending passing tone.

3. The raised-four is usually found in combination with a passing tone in similar or contrary motion.

4. The raised-four appears most often in tonic harmony. It may be derived chromatically in supertonic harmony.

C. OTHER ALTERED NON–HARMONIC TONES

Analyze the following examples, stating

(1) In which voice the alteration is found.

(2) In which chord the altered tone is found.

(3) The voice leading in and out of the altered tone.

Ex. 483. Verleih' uns Frieden gnädiglich   Ex. 484. Herr, ich habe missgehandelt

Ex. 485. Ich dank' dir, lieber Herre

At 1, the a-sharp in the tenor is a raised-three in the key of f-sharp minor. It is a chromatic passing tone, moving in contrary motion to the passing tone e in the alto. The harmonic progression is VI to IV.

At 2, the a-flat in the alto is a lowered-six in the key of c-major. It is a chromatic passing tone, moving in combination with the lower neighboring tone b in the tenor. The harmonic progression is II⁷ to I.

At 3, the g-natural in the tenor is a lowered-three in the key of e-major (second phrase ends in e-major; see B. R. collection, chorale 341). The g-natural is approached and left diatonically. The harmonic progression is IV to IV.

DEDUCTIONS

1. Any altered non-harmonic tone other than the lowered-seven in major and raised-four in major and minor is infrequent. Lowered-six and lowered-three are the infrequent altered non-harmonic tones in major. The raised-three is rare in minor.

2. On the whole, the rare altered non-harmonic tones are found as chromatic passing tones.

PARTWRITING EXERCISES

Before adding the alto and tenor, make a harmonic analysis of each exercise. Avoid parallel fifths and octaves and doubling active tones. Work for smooth voice leading.

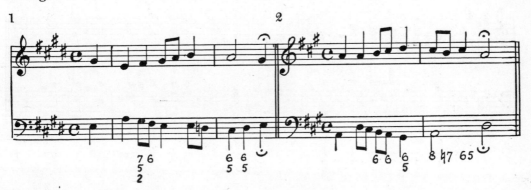

Chapter 22

Altered Chords: Introduction

Sing the following Bach examples:

Ex. 486. Wenn mein Stündlein vorhanden ist

Ex. 487. Jesu, meine Freude

Play example 486 while the class sings the fundamental bass. At 1, the CEGB♭ seventh chord contains a b-flat which is a foreign tone to the key of g-major. This chord, however, does not lose its function in the key of g-major, and it progresses normally as a second classification subdominant function to the first classification leading-tone function. If the example is sung or played using at 1 either CEG or the third inversion CEGB, it will become aurally clear that the CEGB♭ is also a second classification subdominant function. The CEGB♭ chord is called an *altered chord*. The b-flat is a lowered third degree of the scale of g-major.

Play example 487 while the class sings the fundamental bass. At 2, the EG♯BD seventh chord contains a raised-six and a foreign tone g-sharp in the key of d-minor. As in the first example, the EG♯BD seventh chord does not lose its function as a second classification supertonic chord which progresses normally to the first classification dominant triad. The g-sharp is a raised-fourth degree in the key of d-minor.

An altered chord must satisfy two requirements:

(1) Its spelling must contain raised or lowered degrees of the key.

(2) It must retain the function of the basic diatonic chord from which it is derived.

ALTERED CHORDS IN THE 17TH CENTURY

Infrequently examples of altered chords in the formative state are found during the 17th century. In the following examples from the compositions of Samuel Scheidt, notice how the altered chords and the seventh chords are in embryo:

Ex. 488.   Esaia, dem Propheten   *Samuel Scheidt*

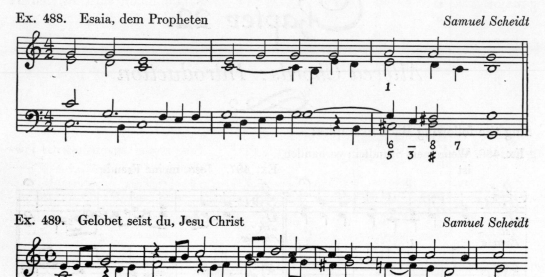

Ex. 489.   Gelobet seist du, Jesu Christ   *Samuel Scheidt*

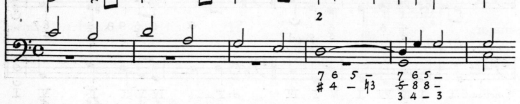

At 1, the root of the altered chord is a. The chord is in first inversion and the g is given an ornamental melodic resolution leading to the f-sharp which is the third of the d-major triad. The root movement a to d to g shows the progression to be second classification, first classification, tonic. The c-sharp is therefore a raised fourth degree in the key of g-major.

At 2, the entire measure is an embryo supertonic function in the key of c-major. The first beat of the measure contains all the elements of a DF#AC seventh chord. Notice the manner in which the horizontal movement of the upper voices forms a six-four, then a four suspension, and finally a root position of the d-minor triad. The next measure also illustrates the early appearance of the seventh chord.

SYMBOLIZATION OF ALTERED CHORDS

The scale degree which is raised or lowered, producing an altered chord, is placed beneath the Roman numeral with a sharp or flat above it. A sharp means the scale degree is raised one-half step, and a flat means the scale degree is lowered one-half step. For example:

KEY	ALTERED CHORD	SYMBOL	NAME

Ex. 490.

g-major  IV ♭ 6 — Subdominant with lowered-six

g-major II⁷ ♭ 6 — Supertonic seventh with lowered-six

g-major  II⁷ ♯ 4 — Supertonic seventh with raised-four

g-minor  II⁷ ♯♯ 46 — Supertonic seventh with raised-four and six

g-minor  II ♭ 6 — Supertonic with lowered-two

Chapter 23

Altered Chords in Minor

Considering the natural and raised-six and seven of the minor key as part of the diatonic minor system, the only alterations found in Bach producing altered chords are the lowered-two and raised-four. Furthermore, the raised-four is used in combination with the raised-six. It is also important to observe that Bach's altered chords in minor are limited to the second classification.

The following table, which enumerates his altered chords, is to be memorized:

SECOND CLASSIFICATION

Symbol	Type Chord	Name	Symbol	Type Chord	Name
II ## 46	Major triad	Supertonic with raised-four and six	IV ## 46	Diminished triad	Subdominant with raised-four and six
II⁷ ## 46	Major-minor seventh chord	Supertonic seventh with raised-four and six	IV⁷ ## 46	Diminished seventh chord	Subdominant seventh with raised-four and six
II ♭ 2	Major triad	Supertonic with lowered-two			

Bach does not use the listed altered chords equally. The following table gives the relative frequency of the five altered chords as they appear in the style:

II⁷ ## 46	frequent	IV⁷ ## 46	frequent
II ## 46	infrequent	IV ## 46	infrequent
II ♭ 6	rare		

234

A. II AND II⁷

Examine the following chorale phrases:

Ex. 491. Jesu, meine Freude

Ex. 492. Wie bist du, Seele, in mir so gar betrübt

Ex. 493. Wir Christenleut'

Ex. 494. Puer natus in Bethlehem

At 1 and 2, the first inversion of the II⁷ follows the tonic and progresses to the dominant triad with raised-seven. The altered tone a-sharp is approached by a diminished fifth leap from the tonic. The remaining tones of the II⁷ are approached and left as if the seventh chord were an ordinary II⁷ in e-minor.

At 3, the first inversion of the II⁷ follows the second inversion of the tonic and progresses to the dominant with raised-seven in g-minor. The altered tone is approached and left by step. This is a variation of the following common progression:

Ex. 495.

At 4, the first inversion of the II follows the subdominant and progresses to the domi-

$$\begin{array}{c} \text{##} \\ \text{46} \end{array}$$

nant with raised-seven in a-minor. The altered tone is introduced chromatically. Note the manner in which the suspended-g in the subdominant is resolved.

Analyze the following Bach examples, giving

(1) (a) Name and classification of the altered chord.
    (b) Name and classification of the chord introducing the altered chord.
    (c) Name and classification of the chord following the altered chord.

(2) The character of the voice leading.
    (a) Analyze the melodic movement in the voice which contains the altered tone.
    (b) Analyze the voice leading of the remaining parts.

(3) Doubling in the altered chord.

$$\begin{array}{c} \text{II} \\ \text{##} \\ \text{46} \end{array}$$

Wonderlich: 128(3rd), 150(2nd).
Bach-Riemenschneider: 12(3rd), 146(2nd), 280(3rd).

$$\begin{array}{c} \text{II}^7 \\ \text{##} \\ \text{46} \end{array}$$

Wonderlich: 50(7th), 70(2nd), 73(6th), 79(Last Ph), 92(6th), 93(6th).
Bach-Reimenschneider: 16(7th), 21(2nd), 89(6th), 59(Last Ph), 324(6th), 356(6th).

DEDUCTIONS

1. The altered tone is never doubled.
2. The altered tone appears most often in the bass.
3. The altered tone is introduced in three ways:
    (a) As a chromatic inflection. The chromatic chord progression occurs within the same classification as follows:

$$\text{IV–II (first inversion):} \quad \text{IV–II}^7 \text{ (first inversion)}$$
$$\begin{array}{cc} \text{##} & \text{##} \\ \text{46} & \text{46} \end{array}$$

    (b) Step-wise. Usually in the bass from above.
    (c) By leap. Usually in the bass. Most often down a diminished fifth from the tonic, the progression is as follows: I–II^7.

$$\begin{array}{c} \text{##} \\ \text{46} \end{array}$$

4. The altered tone, raised-four, ascends a half-step to the dominant.
5. Voice leading of the remaining parts.
 (a) If the altered chord is a triad, the remaining voices are controlled by the rules governing diatonic triads.
 (b) If the altered chord is a seventh chord, the remaining voices are controlled by the rules governing the diatonic seventh chords.
6. Altered supertonic chords usually progress to the dominant triad; occasionally to the first inversion of the mediant; rarely to the second inversion of the tonic.
7. Either II or II⁷ may be used in common chord modulation or chromatic modulation.

PARTWRITING EXERCISES USING II AND II⁷

1) Before partwriting, always make a harmonic analysis of the exercise.
2) Approach the partwriting of the altered chord through the altered tone. The remaining voices are controlled by the diatonic procedures.

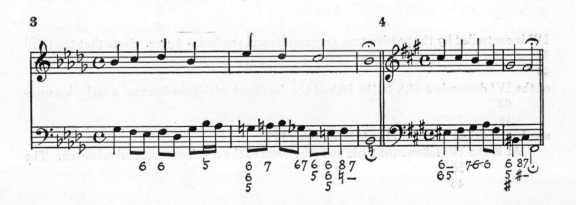

B. IV AND IV⁷

$$\frac{\#\#}{46} \qquad \frac{\#\#}{46}$$

Examine the following chorale phrases:

Ex. 496. Was betrübst du dich, mein
          Herze

Ex. 497. Lebensfürst, Herr Jesu Christ

Ex. 498. Was mein Gott will, das g'scheh'

At 1, the IV⁷ follows the subdominant and progresses to the dominant with raised-

$$\frac{\#\#}{46}$$

seven. The altered c-sharp is derived chromatically. The remaining voices of the IV⁷ are

$$\frac{\#\#}{46}$$

approached and left according to the rules governing the IV⁷ or IV⁷. The seventh of the

$$\frac{\#}{6}$$

IV⁷ is controlled by the passing tone preparation and resolution figure. Note that the third

$$\frac{\#\#}{46}$$

of the IV⁷ descends a fifth to the fifth of the dominant with raised-seven, a melodic move-

$$\frac{\#\#}{46}$$

ment established in the study of the diatonic IV⁷.

At 2, the IV⁷ follows the tonic and progresses to the dominant with raised-seven. The

$$\frac{\#\#}{46}$$

altered d-sharp is approached by a diminished fifth leap in the bass. Again the remaining voices of the IV⁷ are approached and left as if the chord were a diatonic IV⁷ or IV⁷.

$$\overset{\text{\#\#}}{46} \qquad\qquad\qquad\qquad \overset{\text{\#}}{6}$$

At 3, the IV is derived from the tonic and progresses to the dominant with raised-

$$\overset{\text{\#\#}}{46}$$

seven. This is practically the only way in which Bach uses the IV. The chord is found in

$$\overset{\text{\#\#}}{46}$$

second inversion, progressing to the dominant with raised-seven in the cadence formula. The chord is an embellishment of the tonic in a progression which is really a I–V.

$$\overset{\text{\#}}{7}$$

Analyze the following Bach chorales, giving

(1) a. Name and classification of the altered chords.
    b. Name and classification of the chord introducing the altered chord.
    c. Name and classification of the chord following the altered chord.
(2) The character of the voice leading:
    a. Analyze the melodic movement in the voice which contains the altered tone.
    b. Analyze the voice leading of the remaining parts.
(3) Doubling in the altered chord.

$$\text{IV}^7$$
$$\overset{\text{\#\#}}{46}$$

Wonderlich: 24(3rd), 31(4th), 32(2nd, 4th), 79(3rd), 38(3rd, 4th).
Bach-Riemenschneider: 162(3rd), 167(4th), 87(2nd, 4th), 59(3rd), 9(3rd, 4th).

Wonderlich: 118(4th), 113(3rd), 86(2nd), 136(3rd, 6th), 123(1st).
Bach-Riemenschneider: 26(4th), 185(3rd), 118(2nd), 47(3rd, 6th), 57(1st).

Wonderlich: 149(4th), 140(5th).
Bach-Riemenschneider: 339(4th), 94(5th).

$$\text{IV}$$
$$\overset{\text{\#\#}}{46}$$

Wonderlich: 53(3rd), 87(2nd, 5th), 145(4th).
Bach-Riemenschneider: 282(3rd), 122(2nd, 5th), 115(4th).

DEDUCTIONS

$$\text{IV}^7$$
$$\overset{\text{\#\#}}{46}$$

1. The altered tone is never doubled.
2. The altered tone appears most often in the bass.

3. The altered tone is introduced in three ways:
   (a) As a chromatic inflection. The chromatic chord progression occurs within the same classification as follows:

IV–IV⁷
##
46

II (first inv)–IV⁷
##
46

   (b) By half-step from above.
   (c) By leap of a diminished fifth from the tonic, most often in the bass.

4. The raised-four ascends to the dominant. It rarely descends chromatically to the subdominant, which becomes the seventh of the dominant with raised-seven. The remaining voices are approached and left by the rules established by IV or IV⁷.

#
6

5. The IV⁷ may follow I, II, IV, and occasionally VI.

##
46

6. The IV⁷ progresses to dominant with raised-seven. It rarely progresses to a $\frac{6}{4}$

##
46

   or $\frac{6}{\#}$ over the dominant tone in the bass.

7. The IV⁷ is useful in modulation as a common chord as follows:

Tonic key VII⁷ becomes IV⁷ subdominant key
##
7   46

Tonic key IV⁷ becomes VII⁷ dominant key
#
46   7

IV
##
46

1. The IV is found on the second half of a beat.

##
46

2. It is in second inversion and derived from the tonic.

3. The bass note leaps to the dominant.

4. It is invariably found in the half-cadence preceding the dominant with raised-seven.

PARTWRITING EXERCISES ADDING IV AND IV⁷

1) Before partwriting, always make a harmonic analysis of the exercise.

2) Approach the partwriting of the altered chord through the altered tone. The remaining voices are controlled by the diatonic procedures.

The II is found in first inversion and is commonly called the *Neapolitan-sixth*

chord. In the chorales only one II was found.

Ex. 499. Ach Gott, vom Himmel sieh' darein

At 1, the first inversion of the II opens the phrase and progresses chromatically to the IV⁷.

$$\begin{array}{c} \flat \\ 2 \end{array}$$

$$\begin{array}{c} \#\# \\ 46 \end{array}$$

DEDUCTIONS

The II is always found in first inversion with the bass note doubled. In other

$$\begin{array}{c} \flat \\ 2 \end{array}$$

compositions, vocal and instrumental, Bach resolves the first inversion of the II as follows:

$$\begin{array}{c} \flat \\ 2 \end{array}$$

	* VII⁷ (second inversion)
	#
	7
	V
	#
	7
First inversion of II	III (first inversion)
$\flat$	#
2	7
	I (second inversion)
	* IV
	* IV⁷
	##
	46

PARTWRITING EXERCISES ADDING THE II

$$\begin{array}{c} \flat \\ 6 \end{array}$$

1) Before partwriting, always make a harmonic analysis of the exercise.

2) Approach the partwriting of the altered chord through the altered tone. The remaining voices are controlled by the diatonic procedures.

* These functions were found more often than the remaining functions.

Chapter 24

Altered Chords in Major

In a major key the scale steps which are altered in the works of Bach are as follows:

SINGLE ALTERATION	DOUBLE ALTERATIONS
raised-one	raised-one and lowered-seven
raised-four	lowered-three and raised-four
raised-five	lowered-three and six
lowered-three	
lowered-six	
lowered-seven	

The following table enumerates Bach's altered chords in major and is to be memorized:

FIRST CLASSIFICATION

	Symbol	Type Chord	Name
V	VII^7	Diminished seventh	Leading-tone
no altered chords	♭		seventh with
	6		lowered-six

SECOND CLASSIFICATION

Symbol	Type Chord	Name	Symbol	Type Chord	Name
II ♯ 4	Major triad	Supertonic with raised-four	IV ♯ 4	Diminished triad	Subdominant with raised-four
II^7 ♯ 4	Major-minor seventh	Supertonic seventh with raised-four	IV^7 ♯ 4	Half-diminished seventh	Subdominant seventh with raised-four
II ♭ 6	Diminished triad	Supertonic with lowered-six	IV ♭ 6	Minor triad	Subdominant with lowered-six

244

Symbol	Type Chord	Name	Symbol	Type Chord	Name
II⁷ ♭6	Half-diminished seventh	Supertonic seventh with lowered-six	IV⁷ ♭♯34	Diminished seventh	Subdominant seventh with lowered-three and raised-four
			IV⁷ ♭3	Major-minor seventh	Subdominant with lowered-three

THIRD CLASSIFICATION

Symbol	Type Chord	Name	Symbol	Type Chord	Name
VI ♯1	Major triad	Submediant with raised-one	I ♯1	Diminished triad	Tonic with raised-one
VI⁷ ♯1	Major-minor seventh	Submediant seventh with raised-one	I⁷ ♭7	Major-minor seventh	Tonic seventh with lowered-seven
VI ♭♭36	Major triad	Submediant with lowered-three and six	I⁷ ♯♭17	Diminished seventh	Tonic seventh with raised-one and lowered-seven

FOURTH CLASSIFICATION

Symbol	Type Chord	Name	Symbol	Type Chord	Name
III ♯5	Major triad	Mediant with raised-five	V⁷ ♯5	Diminished seventh	Dominant seventh with raised-five
III⁷ ♯5	Major-minor seventh	Mediant seventh with raised-five			

Bach does not make equal use of the altered chords in a major key. Some are extremely rare while others are quite frequent.

The following list contains the rare altered chords:

II, IV⁷, II⁷, VII⁷, I, III⁷, VI
♭6 ♭3 ♭6 ♭6 ♯1 ♯5 ♭♭36

The following list contains the infrequent altered chords:

IV, II, IV, V⁷, IV⁷
♭6 ♯4 ♯4 ♯5 ♭♯34

The following list contains the moderately frequent altered chords:

III, VI, VI⁷, I⁷, IV⁷
♯5 ♯1 ♯1 ♯♭17 ♯4

The following list contains the most frequent altered chords:

II⁷, I⁷
\# ♭
4 7

A. THE ALTERED CHORD OF THE FIRST CLASSIFICATION

VII⁷
♭
6

Examine the following chorale phrase:

Ex. 500.   Mach's mit mir, Gott, nach deiner Güt'

At 1 the VII⁷ is a new function caused by the chromatic modulation.   The c-natural
♭
6

in the alto is introduced and left by the appoggiatura preparation resolution figure containing the passing tone b.   The remaining voices progress to the tonic triad with a doubled
third.

Analyze the following examples which contain the VII⁷ (use the plan established in Chapter 23):   ♭
                                                                          6

Wonderlich: 65(3rd), 150(4th), 156(5th).
Bach-Riemenschneider: 287(3rd), 146(4th), 285(5th), 43(6th).

DEDUCTIONS

1. The lowered-six appears in an inner part.
2. The altered tone appears most often as a chromatic inflection.
3. The lowered-six descends to the dominant.
4. The VII⁷ is usually introduced in a chromatic progression.
   ♭
   6
5. The VII⁷ progresses normally to the tonic.
   ♭
   6

B. ALTERED CHORDS OF THE SECOND CLASSIFICATION
II, II⁷ and IV, IV⁷

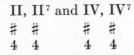

Examine the following chorales:

Ex. 501. Herzlich lieb hab' ich dich, o Herr   Ex. 502.   Puer natus in Bethlehem

Ex. 503.   Christus ist erstanden,
            hat überwunden   Ex. 504.   Herzliebster Jesu, was hast du

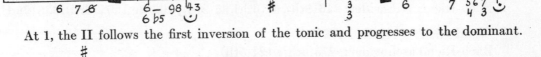

At 1, the II follows the first inversion of the tonic and progresses to the dominant.

$$\overset{\sharp}{4}$$

The raised-four is approached by step and ascends to the dominant.

At 2, the II⁷ follows the submediant and progresses to the dominant. The raised-four

$$\overset{\sharp}{4}$$

is approached by leap and ascends to the dominant. The seventh of the II⁷ is controlled by
the suspension preparation resolution figure. $\overset{\sharp}{4}$

At 3, the first inversion of the IV follows the first inversion of the dominant and pro-

$$\overset{\sharp}{4}$$

gresses to the dominant. The raised-four is approached by half-step as a seven-six suspension in the alto. The raised-four ascends to the dominant.

At 4, the IV⁷ follows the submediant triad and progresses to the dominant. The

$$\overset{\sharp}{4}$$

raised-four is approached by half-step from the accented passing tone a in the bass. The
raised-four ascends to the dominant.

Analyze the following examples which contain second classification chords with raised-four (use the plan established in Chapter 23):

II
#
4

Wonderlich: 42(5th), 143(3rd), 50(5th).
Bach-Riemenschneider: 4(5th), 293(3rd), 16(5th).

II⁷
#
4

Wonderlich: 5(4th), 6(4th), 49(2nd).
Bach-Riemenschneider: 156(4th), 217(4th), 238(2nd).

Wonderlich: 69(10th), 73(1st), 86(6th), 128(2nd), 144(5th), 145(3rd, 5th).
Bach-Riemenschneider: 107(10th), 89(1st), 118(6th), 12(2nd), 265(5th), 115(3rd, 5th).

IV
#
4

Wonderlich: 1(5th), 22(1st), 148(1st), 124(2nd), 125(2nd).
Bach-Riemenschneider: 40(5th), 200(1st), 68(1st), 275(2nd), 50(2nd).

IV⁷
#
4

Wonderlich: 45(8th), 54(6th), 60(3rd), 78(2nd), 85(3rd), 98(2nd).
Bach-Riemenschneider: 216(8th), 67(6th), 35(3rd), 105(2nd), 77(3rd), 338(2nd).

Wonderlich: 124(6th), 152(5th).
Bach-Riemenschneider: 275(6th), 121(5th).

DEDUCTIONS

II
#
4

1. The II is found in first inversion.
   #
   4

2. The II may follow I, IV, VI in normal progression. It may follow V in a retro-
   #
   4
gression.

3. The II progresses to the V.
   #
   4

4. The raised-four may be introduced as follows:
    (a) from below, a whole step.
    (b) from below, a chromatic inflection of the subdominant.
    (c) from above, a half-step.

5. The raised-four ascends to the dominant.

$$\text{II}^7_{\substack{\sharp \\ 4}}$$

1. The $\text{II}^7_{\substack{\sharp \\ 4}}$ is found in first inversion.

2. The first inversion of the $\text{II}^7_{\substack{\sharp \\ 4}}$ may follow VI, I, IV (root position or first inver-

    sion). The retrogression V to the first inversion of the $\text{II}^7_{\substack{\sharp \\ 4}}$ is possible.

3. The first inversion of the $\text{II}^7_{\substack{\sharp \\ 4}}$ progresses to the V (with or without a 4-3 suspen-

    sion). It occasionally resolves to the dominant bass with a $\substack{6\text{-}5 \\ 4\text{-}3}$.

4. The raised-four is approached from above as follows:
    (a) by leap of a third.
    (b) by step (usually a descending passing tone) from the submediant.
    (c) by leap of a diminished fifth from the tonic.

5. The raised-four ascends to the dominant.

$$\text{IV}_{\substack{\sharp \\ 4}}$$

1. The $\text{IV}_{\substack{\sharp \\ 4}}$ is found in first inversion.

2. The first inversion of the $\text{IV}_{\substack{\sharp \\ 4}}$ may follow:
    (a) the first inversion of the V.
    (b) the root position of the I.
    (c) the root position of the III (the IV will have a 7-6 suspension).

3. The first inversion of the IV progresses to the V.

$$\overset{\sharp}{4}$$

4. The raised-four is found in an inner part. It is approached from above by half-step.

5. The raised-four ascends to the dominant.

$$\text{IV}^7$$
$$\overset{\sharp}{4}$$

1. The IV^7 is most often found in fundamental position, occasionally in first in-
$$\overset{\sharp}{4}$$
version.

2. The IV^7 may follow:
$$\overset{\sharp}{4}$$

    (a) the fundamental position of VI.
    (b) the second inversion of I and occasionally the fundamental position of I.
    (c) the fundamental position of V^7
    (d) the first inversion of II or IV.

3. The IV^7 progresses to the V (with or without a suspension.) The partwriting
$$\overset{\sharp}{4}$$
of the IV^7–V is the same as that of the IV^7–V in Chapter 19.
$$\overset{\sharp}{4}$$

4. The raised-four is approached
    (a) from below, by chromatic inflection of the subdominant.
    (b) from above, by half-step.
    (c) from above, by leap of a third or diminished fifth.

5. The raised-four ascends to the dominant.

PARTWRITING EXERCISES USING VII^7, II, II^7, IV, IV^7
$$\overset{\flat}{6} \quad \overset{\sharp}{4} \quad \overset{\sharp}{4} \quad \overset{\sharp}{4} \quad \overset{\sharp}{4}$$

1) Before partwriting, always make a harmonic analysis of the exercise.

2) Approach the partwriting of the altered chord through the altered tone. The remaining voices are controlled by the diatonic procedures.

II II⁷ IV *
♭ ♭ ♭
6 6 6

* The IV⁷ is not used by Bach.
♭
6

Examine the following chorale phrases:

Ex. 505.   Jesu Leiden, Pein und Tod   Ex. 506.   Christus, der ist mein Leben

Ex. 507.   Warum sollt' ich mich denn grämen

At 1, the first inversion of the II opens the phrase and resolves to the dominant seventh.

The lowered-six in the tenor descends to the dominant. The normal doubling of the diminished triad is observed. This is the only example of the II in the chorales.

At 2, the first inversion of the II⁷ follows the tonic and progresses to the dominant triad. In the tenor the lowered-six is approached from below and descends to the dominant. The seventh of the chord is prepared and resolved by the suspension figure.

At 3, the first inversion of the IV follows the submediant and progresses to the dominant bass with a $\frac{65}{43}$. The lowered-six is derived by chromatic inflection of the submediant and resolves to the dominant.

Analyze the following examples which contain second classification chords with lowered-six according to the plan established in Chapter 23:

II

♭

6

Only the one II which is illustrated is to be found in the chorales.

♭

6

II⁷

♭

6

Wonderlich: 2(2nd), 45(8th).

Bach-Riemenschneider: 279(2nd), 216(8th).

IV

♭

6

Wonderlich: 79(2nd), 2(5th).

Bach-Riemenschneider: 59(2nd), 279(6th), 341(3rd).

DEDUCTIONS

II⁷

♭

6

1. The II⁷ follows chords of the third classification (VI⁷, I⁷) and I.

♭   ♯   ♭

6   1   7

2. The II⁷ usually progresses to the V or V⁷. It may be part of a chromatic chord

♭

6

progression involving modulation.

3. The lowered-six may be approached
   - (a) from below, by half-step.
   - (b) from above, by whole step from lowered-seven.
   - (c) from above, by chromatic inflection of the submediant.

4. The lowered-six descends to the dominant.

IV⁷ *

♭

3

Examine the following chorale phrase:

* This chord seems to disappear in musical composition by the close of the 18th century. The same sound reappears in the 19th century as an augmented-6th chord II⁷ in the first inversion. See Chapter 25.

♯

2

Ex. 508. Wenn mein Stündlein
vorhanden ist

At 1, the third inversion of the IV⁷ follows the first inversion of the tonic and pro-

$$♭\atop3$$

gresses to the first inversion of the leading-tone triad. The lowered-three is derived by chromatic inflection of the mediant and descends to the supertonic. This is a variation of the IV–VII (in first inversion) or IV⁷ (in third inversion)–VII (in first inversion).

Analyze the following examples which contain the IV⁷, according to the plan established in Chapter 23:

$$♭\atop3$$

Wonderlich: 36(5th), 45(4th), 73(3rd).
Bach-Riemenschneider: 34(5th), 216(4th), 89(3rd).

DEDUCTIONS

1. The IV⁷ is usually found in third inversion, occasionally in root position.

$$♭\atop3$$

2. The third inversion of the IV⁷ follows I (in first inversion) and III in a chro-

$$♭\atop3$$

matic chord progression. The IV⁷ may follow VI.

$$♭\atop3$$

3. The IV⁷ in fundamental position or third inversion progresses to the first inversion of VII.

4. The lowered-three is usually introduced by chromatic inflection of the mediant.

5. The lowered-three descends to the supertonic.

$$\text{IV}^7\atop{♭♯\atop34}$$

Examine the following chorale phrase:

Ex. 509.   Valet will ich dir geben

At 1, the IV⁷ follows the submediant and progresses to the dominant triad.   The

$$\begin{array}{c}\flat\sharp\\34\end{array}$$

raised-four is approached from above by the passing tone a, and ascends to the dominant.
The lowered-three is derived by the chromatic inflection of the mediant and descends to
the supertonic.   The remaining voices resolve in the same manner as the diatonic IV⁷ when
it resolves to the dominant triad.

Analyze the following examples which contain the IV⁷ according to the plan
established in Chapter 23: $\begin{array}{c}\flat\sharp\\34\end{array}$

Wonderlich: 14(4th), 36(5th), 69(9th), 79(2nd), 110(6th).
Bach-Riemenschneider: 340(4th), 34(5th), 107(9th), 59(2nd), 84(6th), 43(6th)

DEDUCTIONS

1. The IV⁷ is usually found in fundamental position.
$$\begin{array}{c}\flat\sharp\\34\end{array}$$

2. The IV⁷ follows I (in second inversion), IV, VI, and II (in first inversion).
$$\begin{array}{c}\flat\sharp\\34\end{array}$$

3. The IV⁷ progresses to the dominant triad (with or without the 4-3 suspension).
$$\begin{array}{c}\flat\sharp\\34\end{array}$$

4. The approach to the altered tones:
    (a) The raised-four is approached from below by chromatic inflection of the
        subdominant.
    (b) The raised-four is approached from above by half-step.
    (c) The lowered-three is approached from above or below by step or by
        chromatic inflection of the mediant.
    (d) The lowered-three is approached from below by leap of a third from the
        tonic.

5. The raised-four ascends to the dominant.
   The lowered-three descends to the supertonic.

PARTWRITING EXERCISES ADDING II, II⁷, IV, IV⁷, AND IV⁷

1) Before partwriting, always make a harmonic analysis of each exercise.

2) Approach the partwriting of the altered chord through the altered tone. The remaining voices are controlled by the diatonic procedures.

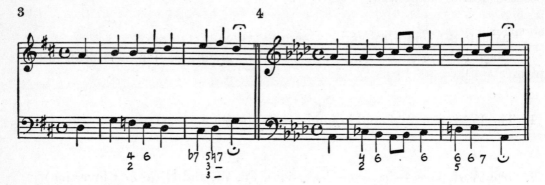

C. ALTERED CHORDS OF THE THIRD CLASSIFICATION

VI and VI⁷

Examine the following chorale phrases:

Ex. 510.   Herr Christ, der ein'ge Gott'ssohn

Ex. 511.   Meinen Jesum lass' ich nicht, Jesus

At 1, the VI opens the phrase and progresses to the supertonic. The raised-one ascends

$$\overset{\#}{1}$$

to the supertonic. The remaining voices progress to the supertonic based upon diatonic procedures.

At 2, the first inversion of the VI⁷ follows the mediant triad and progresses to the su-

$$\overset{\#}{1}$$

pertonic triad. The entire progression is fourth-third-second classification. The raised-one is approached from above by the passing tone e. The d-sharp, however, is delayed in its normal movement to e.

Analyze the following examples which contain VI and VI⁷, according to the plan established in Chapter 23:

$$\overset{\#}{1} \qquad \overset{\#}{1}$$

VI
#
1

Wonderlich: 63(2nd), 90(4th), 132(4th), 142(2nd), 125(4th).
Bach-Riemenschneider: 303(2nd), 83(4th), 38(4th), 139(2nd), 50(4th).

VI⁷
#
1

Wonderlich: 67(5th), 124(4th), 63(3rd), 102(5th), 6(3rd).
Bach-Riemenschneider: 284(5th), 275(4th), 303(3rd), 276(5th), 217(3rd).

DEDUCTIONS

VI
#
1

1. The VI is usually found in first inversion.

#
1

2. The VI may open a phrase.   Within a phrase it follows I or IV.

   #
   1

3. The VI progresses to II.   It may progress to II.

   #   #
   1   4

4. The raised-one is usually derived by chromatic inflection of the tonic.   The raised-one may be approached from above by a half-step.

5. The raised-one ascends to the supertonic.

VI^7
#
1

1. The VI^7 is found in fundamental position, first inversion, and third inversion.

   #
   1

2. The first inversion of the VI^7 may open a phrase.   It may follow I.   The VI^7 may follow VI, IV, III. #   #
                                    1   1

3. The VI^7 progresses to II.   It may also become a common chord in the modula-

   #
   1

tion to the supertonic key, VI^7 = V^7.

                       #   #
                       1   7

4. The raised-one may be derived as a chromatic inflection of the tonic.
The raised-one may be approached from above by half-step.
The raised-one may be approached by leap from above.

5. The raised-one ascends to the supertonic.

VI
♭♭
36

Examine the following chorale phrase:

    Ex. 512.   Vater unser im Himmelreich

At 1, the VI follows the dominant in the key of f-major. The progression creates a de-

$\flat\flat$
36

ceptive cadence. The lowered-six is approached by step from below, and the lowered-three is approached from above by a leap of a major third.

DEDUCTIONS

1. The VI is found in fundamental position in the deceptive cadence.

$\flat\flat$
36

2. The VI is rare in the Bach style.

$\flat\flat$
36

3. The lowered-three and the lowered-six are not introduced by chromatic inflection.

The lowered-three may be introduced from above by step or leap.

The lowered-six is introduced from below by step from the dominant.

I^7
$\flat$
7

Examine the following chorale phrases:

Ex. 513.   Gelobet seist du, Jesu
      Christ   Ex. 514.   Wenn ich in Angst und Not

Ex. 515. Christus, der ist mein Leben Ex. 516.   Vom Himmel hoch, da komm' ich her

At 1, the $I^{\flat 7}$ follows the first inversion of the tonic and progresses to the subdominant.

The lowered-seven is approached by half-step and descends to the submediant.

At 2, the first inversion of the $I^{\flat 7}$ follows the first inversion of the tonic and progresses to the subdominant. The lowered-seven is approached by half-step and descends to the submediant.

At 3, the third inversion of the $I^{\flat 7}$ follows the first inversion of the dominant and progresses to the first inversion of the subdominant. The lowered-seven is derived by chromatic inflection of the leading-tone and descends to the submediant.

At 4, the second inversion of the $I^{\flat 7}$ follows the dominant and progresses to the subdominant. The lowered-seven is derived by chromatic inflection and descends to the submediant.

Analyze the following examples which contain the $I^{\flat 7}$ according to the plan established in Chapter 23:

Wonderlich: 12(4th), 52(4th, 5th), 58(5th), 69(1st, 3rd, 10th).
Bach-Riemenschneider: 1(4th), 298(4th, 5th), 288(5th), 107(1st, 3rd, 10th).

Wonderlich: 73(3rd), 124(6th), 134(6th), 140(4th), 141(4th).
Bach-Riemenschneider: 89(3rd), 275(6th), 108(6th), 94(4th), 300(4th).

DEDUCTIONS

1. The $I^{\flat 7}$ is found in fundamental position and infrequently in any inversion.

2. The $I^{\flat 7}$ may follow I in fundamental position or in first inversion. It may also follow V.

3. The $I^{\flat 7}$ progresses to IV in fundamental position or in first inversion.

4. The lowered-seven is approached from above by a whole step.
The lowered-seven may be approached from above by chromatic inflection of the leading tone.
The lowered-seven may be approached from below by a leap of a minor third from the dominant or by half-step, usually a passing tone.

5. The lowered-seven descends a half-step to the submediant.

$$I^7$$
$$\sharp\flat$$
$$17$$

Examine the following chorale phrases:

Ex. 517.   Jesu, nun sei gepreiset

Ex. 518.   Herr Christ, der ein'ge Gott'ssohn

At 1, the I^7 is derived chromatically from the tonic and progresses to the supertonic.

$$\sharp\flat$$
$$17$$

The lowered-seven is approached from below by half-step (a passing tone) and descends to the submediant. The raised-one is derived by chromatic inflection of the tonic. It ascends to the supertonic.

At 2, the I^7 is derived chromatically from the tonic and resolves to the supertonic. The

$$\sharp\flat$$
$$17$$

lowered-seven is approached from above by whole step from the tonic. The raised-one is derived by a chromatic inflection of the tonic.

Analyze the following examples, which contain the I^7 according to the plan established in Chapter 23:

$$\sharp\flat$$
$$17$$

Wonderlich: 54(3rd, 6th), 102(4th), 147(4th).

Bach-Riemenschneider: 67(3rd, 6th), 276(4th), 322(4th), 165(4th), 274(2nd), 157(3rd).

DEDUCTIONS

1. The I^7 is found in fundamental position.
   #♭
   17

2. The I^7 follows the tonic in fundamental position and occasionally follows the
   #♭
   17
   first inversion of the I or fundamental position of the I^7.
                                                        ♭
                                                        7

3. The I^7 progresses to the fundamental position of the II.
   #♭
   17

4. The raised-one is usually derived by a chromatic inflection of the tonic. It
   may be approached from above by leap from the mediant. Under these conditions a cross relation occurs when the first inversion of the I progresses to I^7.
                                                                            #♭
                                                                            17
   The lowered-seven is approached from above by a whole step from the tonic.

5. The raised-one ascends to the supertonic.
   The lowered-seven descends to the submediant.

6. The I^7 may become a VII^7 in the supertonic key.
   #♭   #
   17   7

                        I
                        #
                        1

Examine the following chorale phrases:

Ex. 519. Gott lebet noch

Ex. 520. Ach Gott, wie manches Herzeleid

At 1, the I follows the V and progresses to the II. The raised-one is approached from

$$\sharp$$
$$1$$

below a whole step from the leading tone. The raised-one ascends to the supertonic.

At 2, the first inversion of the I follows the VI. The EG$\sharp$BD vertical sonority is a

$$\sharp$$
$$1$$

quadruple passing sonority. The raised-one is approached from below by step. The raised-one ascends to the supertonic.

Analyze the following examples which contain the I according to the plan established in Chapter 23:

$$\sharp$$
$$1$$

Wonderlich: 111(5th).
Bach-Riemenschneider: 32(5th), 52(4th).

DEDUCTIONS

1. The I is found in fundamental position or in first inversion.

$$\sharp$$
$$1$$

2. The I may follow:

$$\sharp$$ a) I in fundamental position or in first inversion.
$$1$$ b) IV, VI, or V.

3. The I progresses to the II.

$$\sharp$$
$$1$$

4. The I may frequently become the VII in the supertonic key.

$$\sharp$$ $$\sharp$$
$$1$$ $$7$$

5. The raised-one may be approached from above by half-step.
The raised-one may be approached from below by whole step.
The raised-one may be derived by a chromatic inflection of the tonic.

6. The raised-one ascends to the supertonic.

*PARTWRITING EXERCISES USING CHORDS WHICH HAVE THEIR ROOTS IN
THE FIRST, SECOND, AND THIRD CLASSIFICATIONS*

1) Before partwriting, always make a harmonic analysis of the exercise.

2) Approach the partwriting of the altered chord through the altered tone. The remaining voices are controlled by the diatonic procedures.

D. ALTERED CHORDS OF THE FOURTH CLASSIFICATION

$$\overset{\text{III}}{\underset{5}{\sharp}}$$

Examine the following chorale phrases:

Ex. 521.   In allen meinen Taten

Ex. 522.   Wie schön leuchtet der Morgenstern

At 1, the first inversion of the III opens the phrase and progresses to the VI.   The

$$\underset{5}{\sharp}$$

raised-five is derived by chromatic inflection of the dominant.

At 2, the III follows the VI and progresses to IV.   The raised-five is approached from

$$\underset{5}{\sharp}$$

below from the passing tone raised-four.

Analyze the following examples which contain the III according to the plan

established in Chapter 23: $\underset{5}{\sharp}$

Wonderlich: 116(10th), 38(2nd), 115(3rd), 126(4th).

Bach-Riemenschneider: 7(10th), 9(2nd), 257(3rd), 63(4th), 268(2nd, 10th), 317 (3rd), 366(4th), 217(3rd).

DEDUCTIONS

1. The III is found frequently in first inversion and less frequently in fundamental

$$\underset{5}{\sharp}$$

position.

2. The III is found most often opening the phrase. Within a phrase the III fol-
   #
   5

   lows I, VI, or the first inversion of IV.

3. The III progresses to IV in fundamental position or in first inversion. It fre-
   #
   5

   quently progresses to VI.

4. The raised-five is most often derived by chromatic inflection of the dominant. It may be approached from below by step from the raised-four or by leap from above from the tonic.

5. The raised-five ascends to the submediant.

III[7]
#
5

Examine the following chorale phrases:

Ex. 523.   In dich hab' ich gehoffet, Herr

Ex. 524.   Herr, wie du willst, so schick's mit mir

At 1, the first inversion of the III[7] follows the V and progresses to the first inversion
   #
   5

of the IV. The raised-five is derived by a chromatic inflection of the dominant. The seventh of the III[7] is introduced by the suspension preparation resolution figure.
   #
   5

At 2, the III⁷ follows the V and progresses to the VI. The raised-five is derived by a
$$\overset{\sharp}{5}$$
chromatic inflection of the dominant. Again the seventh of the III⁷ is introduced by the
suspension preparation resolution figure.
$$\overset{\sharp}{5}$$

Analyze the following examples which contain the III⁷ according to the plan
established in Chapter 23:
$$\overset{\sharp}{5}$$

Wonderlich: 95(2nd, last phrase).
Bach-Riemenschneider: 327(2nd, last phrase), 151(1st).

DEDUCTIONS

1. The III⁷ is found in fundamental position and in first inversion.
$$\overset{\sharp}{5}$$

2. The III⁷ follows V or VI. In the first chorale cited for analysis, the III⁷ is in-
$$\overset{\sharp}{5}$$ $$\overset{\sharp}{5}$$
troduced in a chromatic chord progression, producing a chromatic modulation
not involving a common chord. In the last phrase of the same chorale the
III⁷ follows the second inversion of the II.
$$\overset{\sharp}{5}$$

3. The III⁷ progresses to VI or the first inversion of IV.
$$\overset{\sharp}{5}$$

4. The raised-five is usually introduced by a chromatic inflection of the dominant.
   It may be approached from above by half-step.

5. The raised-five ascends to the submediant.

$$\overset{V^7}{\underset{\underset{5}{\sharp}}{}}$$

Examine the following chorale phrases:

Ex. 525. Valet will ich dir geben   Ex. 526. Erstanden ist der heil'ge Christ

At 1, the V⁷ follows the I and progresses to the VI. The raised-five is approached from

$$\sharp \atop 5$$

above by leap from the tonic. The seventh of the V⁷ is introduced by the passing tone preparation resolution figure.

$$\sharp \atop 5$$

At 2, the V⁷ follows the first inversion of the VI and progresses to the **VI**. The raised-

$$\sharp \atop 5$$

five is approached from above by half-step. The seventh of the V⁷ is approached by step

$$\sharp \atop 5$$

from above by the filled-in appoggiatura preparation resolution figure.

Analyze the following examples which contain the V⁷ according to the plan established in Chapter 23:

$$\sharp \atop 5$$

Wonderlich: 8(5th).
Bach-Riemenschneider: 313(5th), 54(4th).

DEDUCTIONS

1. The V⁷ is found in fundamental position.

$$\sharp \atop 5$$

2. The V⁷ may follow I, V, and VI in fundamental position or first inversion.

$$\sharp \atop 5$$

3. The V⁷ progresses to VI, a chord of the third classification.

$$\sharp \atop 5$$

4. The raised-five may be approached from above by half-step or by leap (usually from the tonic). The raised-five may be introduced by a chromatic inflection of the dominant.

5. The raised-five ascends to the submediant.

PARTWRITING EXERCISES USING ALL THE ALTERED CHORDS IN MAJOR

1) Before partwriting, always make a harmonic analysis of the exercise.
2) Approach the partwriting of the altered chord through the altered tone. The remaining voices are controlled by the diatonic procedures.

Chapter 25

Vertical Sonorities Containing the Interval of the Diminished Third or the Augmented Sixth

Thus far in the study of diatonic or altered chords, the structure of the chord has been composed of major and minor thirds. Under certain circumstances raising or lowering scale steps produces vertical sonorities containing either a diminished third or an augmented sixth. The vertical sonority resulting from raising or lowering scale degrees will be classified as an altered chord.

The following examples illustrate structures containing either a diminished third or an augmented sixth:

At *a*, in the key of c-minor the raised-four forms a II⁷ which contains a diminished third between the tenor and alto.

At *b*, in the key of c-minor the raised-four forms a II⁷ which contains an augmented sixth between the bass and alto.

At *c*, in the key of c-minor the raised-four forms a IV⁷ which contains a diminished third between the bass and tenor.

At *d*, in the key of c-minor the raised-four forms a IV⁷ which contains an augmented sixth between the bass and alto.

At *e*, in the key of c-minor the raised-four forms a II⁷ which contains an augmented sixth between the tenor and the alto. Compare this with the example at *a*.

The most frequent vertical sonority of this type encountered in music has the augmented sixth created by the bass and one of the upper voices. The next in frequency, but extremely rare, is the vertical sonority which contains the augmented

270

sixth in the upper voices. Vertical sonorities containing the diminished third are practically non-existent, especially in the 18th century. A brief historical approach to the use of these chords in the 18th century will clarify this point.

A. PRE–BACH USAGE *

Scholars studying the music of the late 16th century and the 17th century have located a few vertical structures containing the augmented sixth. Only two actual augmented sixths are found, and they are located as follows:

Ex. 528.

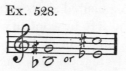

In both centuries the augmented sixth seems to be formed most often by use of the seven-six suspension. The following is from a madrigal by William Costeley:

Ex. 529.   Bauche qui n'as point de semblable *William Costeley (1531–1606)*

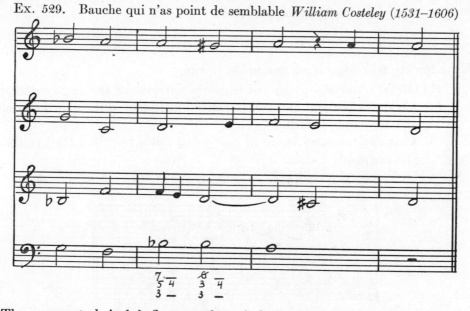

The augmented sixth b-flat to g-sharp is formed by the bass and soprano. The first beat of the measure contains the interval of the seventh between the bass and the soprano. The seventh dissonance is prepared and resolves as a suspension to the g-sharp, which is an augmented sixth above the bass. The resolution of the augmented sixth is an octave.

Although most of the appearances of the augmented sixth in the 16th and 17th centuries were without chromatic inflection, an occasional introduction of the interval of the augmented sixth appears in the late 17th century by chromatic inflection. The following example illustrates this procedure:

* This discussion is a brief summary derived from a thesis by Poland Miller, "The Augmented Sixth Chords: Their Historical and Theoretical Origin and Development," written under the author's guidance.

Ex. 530.   Toccata   *Domenico Zipoli (c. 1675–?)*

In the third measure the augmented sixth between the bass and soprano is approached by oblique motion and left by contrary motion. In the soprano the g-sharp is derived by chromatic inflection of the g-natural. The augmented sixth progresses by contrary motion to an octave. The vertical structure following the chord which contains the augmented sixth is a second inversion of a triad. The final chord is the a-major triad. Notice that the six-four chord avoids the parallel fifths which would result if the vertical sonority containing the augmented sixth had progressed directly to the a-major triad.

B. BACH'S USAGE

Examine the following Bach examples, noting

> (1) Melodic movement to and from the interval of the augmented sixth.
> (2) Classification and name of the chord introducing the chord containing the augmented sixth.
> (3) Classification and name of the chord following the chord containing the augmented sixth.

Ex. 531.   Ich hab' mein' Sach' Gott heimgestellt

Ex. 532.   Wer nur den lieben Gott lässt

Ex. 533.   Befiehl du deine Wege

At 1, the augmented sixth is approached by oblique motion caused by the seven-six suspension. The vertical sonority containing the augmented sixth is the first inversion of the C#E♭G. This sonority is preceded by the tonic in g-minor and is followed by the dominant. The sonority is therefore a first inversion of the subdominant with its root raised by the raised-four. The chord is the subdominant with raised-four and it belongs to the second classification. The augmented sixth progresses by contrary motion to an octave.

At 2, the augmented sixth is approached by contrary motion caused by the chromatic inflection of the bass and alto. The augmented sixth progresses by contrary motion to an octave. The vertical sonority containing the augmented sixth is the second inversion of BD#FA. This sonority is preceded by the first inversion of the subdominant triad with raised-six and is followed by the second inversion of the tonic in the key of a-minor. The BD#FA is a supertonic seventh with raised-four and belongs to the second classification.

At 3, the augmented sixth is approached by similar motion in the bass and tenor. The augmented sixth progresses by contrary motion to an octave. The vertical sonority containing the augmented sixth is the first inversion of G#B♭DF. This sonority is preceded by the tonic in d-minor, and is followed by the second inversion of the tonic, which is a passing chord to the root position of the IV⁷. The G#B♭DF is a subdominant seventh with

$$\frac{\#\#}{46}$$

raised-four and belongs to the second classification.

There are only four vertical sonorities containing an augmented sixth in the collection of 371 chorales harmonized by Bach. Three have been presented; the remaining one is #216, "Es ist genug, so nimm, Herr," eighth phrase, third chord from the beginning. The f-natural in the tenor should be enharmonically spelled as an e-sharp. Chord structures containing the augmented sixth are extremely rare in the compositions of Bach. Examples may be found in the following: *

Weihnachts Oratorium, Bach-Gesellschaft, Jahrg. V. 2, p. 119

    Cantate No. 114, "Ach lieben Christen, seid getrost," Bach-Gesellschaft, Jahrg. XXIV, p. 101

    Cantate No. 81, "Jesus schläft, was soll ich hoffen," Bach-Gesellschaft, Jahrg. XX. 1, p. 7

    Cantate No. 83, "Erfreute Zeit, im neuen Bunde," Bach-Gesellschaft, Jahrg. XX. 1, p. 63

* Due to the fact that examples of these chords are so rare and perhaps many sources listed above not available, the author lists in the deductions the common treatment of the chords. Also the partwriting exercises will include examples from a variety of composers, which will reveal through analysis the way in which the chords may be used.

Johannes Passion, Bach-Gesellschaft, Jahrg. XX, p. 51

    Cantate No. 101, "Nimm von uns, Herr, du treuer," Bach-Gesellschaft,
    Jahrg. XXIII, p. 6

B-minor Messe, Bach-Gesellschaft, Jahrg. VI, pp. 187, 227, 189

Kunst der Fuge, J. S. Bach

    Fuga XI, measure 69

    Fuga VII, third measure from the end

    Fuga IX, measures 76 and 102

    Fuga XV, measure 56

    Fuga III, measures 59 and 63

    Fuga XI, fourth measure from the end

DEDUCTIONS

1. There are three common chord structures containing the augmented sixth:

    (a) The augmented six-three (Italian Sixth)

Ex. 534.

    (b) The augmented six-four-three (French Sixth)

Ex. 535.

    (c) The augmented six-five (German Sixth)

Ex. 536.

2. The chords of the augmented sixth are found as first and second classification functions in major and minor keys. They are more frequent in minor, and they are usually found in the second classification. In the early part of the 18th century they are less frequent in major and again they are usually in the second classification.

The following table locates each of the functions which when in inversion becomes an augmented sixth chord structure:

MINOR KEY

First Classification (rare)		Second Classification	
	VII		IV
V^7	b♯		♯
b♯	27	II^7	4
27		♯	
	VII^7	4	IV^7
	b♯		♯
	27		4

MAJOR KEY

First Classification (rare)		Second Classification	
	VII		IV
V^7	b		♯b
b	2		46
2		II^7	
	VII^7	♯b	IV^7
	bb	46	♯b
	26		46

3. The characteristic interval is the augmented sixth. In practically every resolution of the augmented sixth chord, the augmented sixth spreads out to an octave. If the chord is a second classification chord, the augmented sixth resolves to an octave which is the dominant of the key. In like manner, if the augmented sixth chord belongs to the first classification, the augmented sixth resolves to an octave which is the tonic of the key.

When the resolution tone of the augmented sixth is on the dominant, the chord may be the dominant triad, second inversion of the tonic (either $\frac{65}{43}$ or a passing chord), or first inversion of the mediant triad.

When the resolution of the augmented sixth is on the tonic, the chord is practically always the tonic; in rare instances it is the second inversion of the subdominant, which is really tonic harmony as a $\frac{65}{43}$.

The following examples illustrate some of the common resolutions of augmented sixth chords:

(a) The augmented six-three and augmented six-four-three

Ex. 537.

(b) The augmented six-five

Ex. 538.

The resolution of the augmented six-five chord in the 18th century is carefully worked out to avoid parallel fifths. At *a* the fifths are easily avoided by its resolution to the tonic in second inversion. At *b* the six-five suspension avoids the fifths. At *c* the anticipation of the fifth of the dominant triad also avoids the fifths. Some strict theorists would call these parallel fifths; but in light of the fact that Bach uses the anticipation, the student may also utilize the device.

4. Chords of the augmented sixth, like any altered chord, may be introduced having the altered tones approached by diatonic procedures or by chromatic inflection.

5. In the chorales Bach usually has the diatonic tones of the augmented sixth chord in the soprano. This is due to the character of the choral melody. In recitatives, vocal, and instrumental composition, he uses the altered tones as well in the soprano.

6. In the early 18th century augmented sixth chords are rarely resolved in chromatic chord progression. It is interesting to observe that, all through the century, these chords appear near the cadence. This is especially true in connection with the half cadence on the dominant.

7. Since the chord structure containing the diminished third is so rare in this period, its study will be postponed to a later chapter. The following example illustrates the chord structure containing the diminished third in one of its early stages of development:

Ex. 539.   The Art of Fugue

J. Sebastian Bach

EXERCISES

Partwrite the following exercises using chords of the augmented sixth:

1) Make a harmonic analysis of each exercise before filling in the alto and tenor.

2) Work for smooth voice leading, and avoid parallel perfect fifths and octaves. Avoid doubling active tones.

The following partwriting exercises illustrate the use of the augmented sixth chords by composers of the 18th century.

Make a harmonic analysis of each exercise before filling in the alto and tenor.

1   Allegro

C. W. Gluck

2

Carl Heinrich Graun (1701–1759)

3

C. H. Graun

4

C. H. Graun

His spir-it is faint   His spir-it is faint,   is   faint   is faint

5

C. H. Graun

Joseph Haydn

6

| | 6 | 9 | 8 | 6 | 6 | | 6 | 6 | 6 | | 5 |
| | 5 | 4 | 3 | 5 | 5 | | 5 | 5 | 4 | | 3 |

7

Where from ash_es rise the sleep_ing quil_ty man to

W. A. Mozart 8

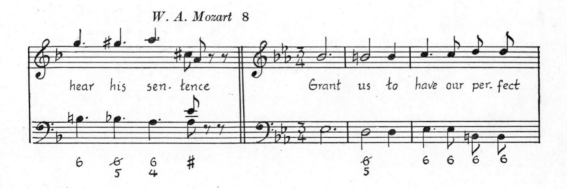

hear his sen_tence   Grant us to have our per_fect

W. A. Mozart

bliss ____ in Thy glo_ry e_ter_nal.

Chapter 26

Modulation to Foreign Keys

Although modulation has been practiced from the beginning of this manual, it has been confined to the system of closely related keys. There are not many of the 371 chorales harmonized by Bach which contain modulations to keys that have two or more accidentals more than the original key. Harmonic movement to such keys is called *foreign modulation*.

Examine the following Bach harmonization:

Ex. 540.   Jesu Leiden, Pein und Tod

The example begins with the cadence of the fourth phrase and extends through the sixth phrase. The seventh and eighth phrases are in the original key of e-flat major. The fifth phrase begins in e-flat major and by a chromatic modulation concludes in a half-cadence in the key of f-minor. In the sixth phrase, beginning at 1, the e-flat major triad becomes a IV in b-flat minor, and it progresses chromatically to the VI, which in turn moves by elision
#
6
to the cadence formula in b-flat minor. The final chord is a tonic with raised-three. The key of b-flat minor has five flats. The difference in accidentals between e-flat major and b-flat minor is two flats. The harmonic movement to the key of b-flat minor is a foreign modulation.

281

Examine the following Bach harmonization:

Ex. 541.　Ach Gott und Herr, wie gross und schwer

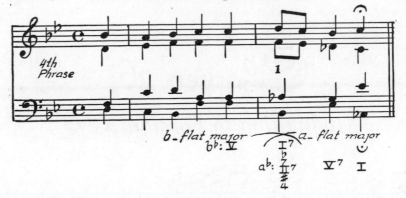

The phrase begins in the key of b-flat major and concludes in the key of a-flat major. At 1, the $B^{\flat}DFA^{\flat}$ seventh chord is derived chromatically as a I^7 in the key of b-flat major,

$$\overset{\flat}{7}$$

and it becomes the II^7 in the key of a-flat major. The key of a-flat major has two flats

$$\overset{\sharp}{4}$$

more than b-flat major. The harmonic movement from the key of b-flat major to the key of a-flat major is a foreign modulation.

Examine the following chorales for foreign modulation:

Wonderlich:　67, 81, 45, 90, 140.
Bach-Riemenschneider:　2, 5, 94, 83, 202, 216, 284, 309, 337, 340.

DEDUCTIONS

1. The majority of foreign modulations occur in chorales which are fundamentally based on a tonic major key relationship. For example, a modulation to the key of d-minor appears in a harmonization of a chorale that is basically in the key of g-major.

2. If the basic key is major, the majority of foreign modulations are up a fifth to a minor key. Less frequent modulations are to the parallel tonic minor or down a major second to a major key.

3. If the basic key is minor, a foreign modulation down a fifth to a major key and a modulation up a minor second to a major key are found in the chorales.

4. The modulations to a foreign key are derived directly from the basic tonic key, or they are derived from a closely related key of the basic tonic key.

5. The foreign modulation usually contains a chromatic chord progression.

6. The foreign modulations can be analyzed by the harmonic vocabulary established thus far in the manual.

In the works of Bach, the best sources for foreign modulation are in the type of writing which is more or less free, such as fantasies and recitatives.

The recitative's function is to link together larger units, such as the choruses and arias of oratorios and cantatas. It does not usually possess any definite basic tonic key. Examine the following recitative:

Ex. 542. Saint Matthew's Passion   *J. Sebastian Bach*

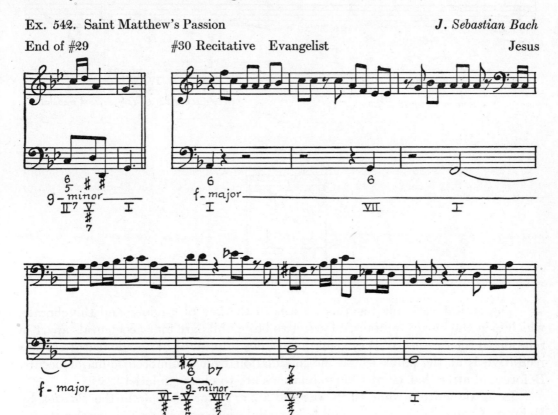

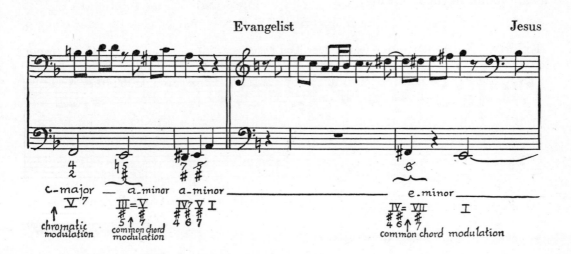

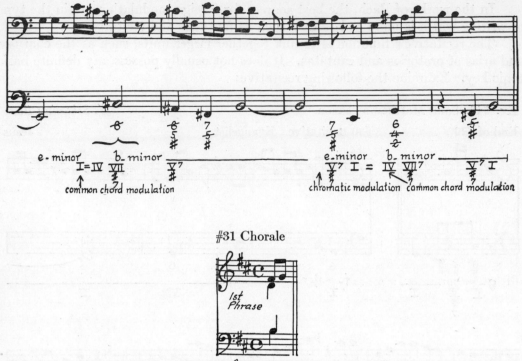

#31 Chorale

1st Phrase

b-minor

The recitative binds together an aria in the key of g-minor and the chorale, which is in the key of b-minor. These two large units are four accidentals apart in relation to their respective key signatures. The important harmonic feature of this recitative is at the point where the modulation from g-minor to c-major occurs. Before and after that point the modulations are to closely related keys.

In music written while Bach was still alive, as for example in the *Passion* by Heinrich Graun, quite extreme and bold modulations occur. In fact, such extreme modulations have not been found in the recitatives of Haydn, Mozart, and others as are found in the following:

Ex. 543.   No. 16 Recitative from "Der Tod Jesu"   *C. H. Graun*

Taking note of the keys in order, we see that they progress down a perfect fifth until a break occurs from the key of c-minor to f-sharp major. At this point the interval relationship will become a diminished fifth down from c-minor. This is important to consider, since the key of f-sharp major progresses down a perfect fifth to b-minor. In other words, the entire passage is down a fifth to the next key, with the exception of the modulation from c-minor to f-sharp major. This modulation is made possible by a common chord; an altered VII becomes enharmonically an incomplete diatonic V^7 in the new key. The harmonic movement at this point creates a foreign modulation in which the difference in accidentals of the keys is nine.

With the more general acceptance of equal temperament during the second quarter of the 18th century, composers gradually expanded the use of foreign modulation. Although every interval relationship between tonics might be tabulated, one outstanding relationship between tonics seems to appear during this century: change of mode. Many theorists recognize this type of modulation and call it *modulation by change of mode*. The following diagram illustrates the procedure:

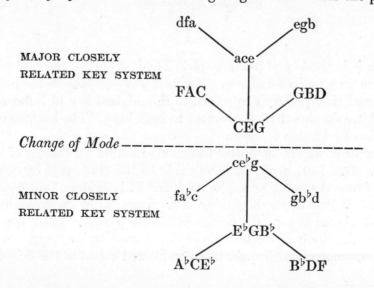

The diagram reveals the fact that there are two closely related key systems which appear at first foreign to one another. The tonic, subdominant, and dominant keys of both systems, however, are in parallel relationship. The important fact to bear in mind is that in the case of each key the first classification dominant chord is the same sound. Examine carefully the following diagram:

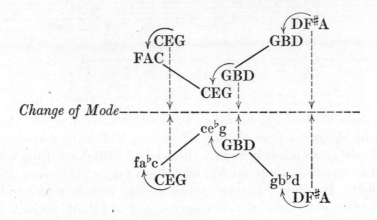

As an illustration of this method of changing key, examine the following example:

Ex. 544. No. 3, Aria, from "Der Tod Jesu"   C. H. Graun

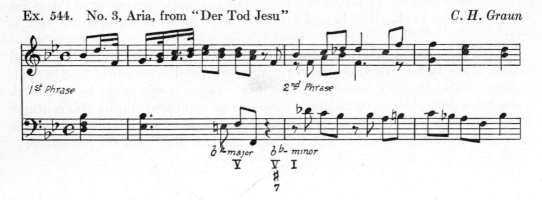

This aria is in the key of b-flat major. The last part of the first phrase which is given concludes on a half-cadence. The next phrase opens in the parallel key of b-flat minor and then proceeds to return to the original key of b-flat major. The f-major triad is a dominant triad common to both keys. The harmonic movement is a modulation by change of mode.

The manner in which composers utilize modulation by change of mode varies considerably. One fact, however, is valuable to the student if he chooses to use the device. From the many examples analyzed, it is evident that composers usually change mode first at the beginning of a phrase, as in the preceding example. Return to the original key usually occurs within the phrase. The return is gradual; that is, they utilize indirect modulation or direct modulation by means of common chord. The common chord is quite often an altered chord in the original key.

EXERCISES

1. Analyze and fill in the alto and tenor.

The exercises which follow are to contain modulations by change of mode. The first phrase is given and the modulation required is given. The student is to add the second phrase, ending it in the new key. If the instructor wishes to have the exercise return to the original key, it must contain four phrases in order to obtain a double period, in keeping with the style.

2. Modulate from g-major to e-flat major.

continue in the style

3. Modulate from g-minor to e-minor.
Allegro

continue in style

4. Modulate from c-major to e-flat major.

continue in the style

5. Modulate from a-major to e-minor.

continue
in the style

6. Modulate from f-major to b-flat minor.

continue
in style

Part 2

Harmonization

of the

Chorale Melody

Chapter 27

The Harmonization of the Chorale Melody: Introduction

The process of harmonizing a melody can be approached systematically without destroying one's artistic desires and aims. The following plan will be used:

1. Analyze the musical form of the melody to be harmonized.
2. Chord choice:
    (a) Work out the cadence formula.
    (b) Complete the harmonic scheme of the phrase leading to cadence formulas.
3. Compose the bass line to the melody in accord with the harmonies selected.
4. Fill in the alto and tenor.

A. THE MUSICAL FORM OF THE CHORALE MELODY

Authorities on Lutheran liturgical music inform us that the chorale melody was composed after the poem was written. Each line of the verse becomes a phrase in the musical setting. This accounts for the varying number of phrases which make up chorale tunes. The phrases do not combine into periods, double periods, and so on, as in dance forms. Study the following chorales, which illustrate the number of phrases that make up the chorale melody:

Wonderlich: 23, 20, 42, 14, 19, 62, 69.
Bach-Riemenschneider: 228, 6, 4, 340, 210, 70, 107.

Just as a chorale melody may vary as to the number of phrases it may contain, phrases within the chorale may vary in length. Study phrase lengths in the following chorales:

Wonderlich: 1, 27, 28, 69, 110, 132, 139, 153, 154.
Bach-Riemenschneider: 40, 232, 127, 107, 97, 38, 179, 323, 321.

The musical form of the chorale phrase depends upon the beat on which the phrase originates and upon the beat on which the phrase concludes. The relative importance of beats in a quadruple measure is as follows:

1. The first beat is heavy.
2. The second beat is light.
3. The third beat is less heavy than the first but not so light as the second beat.
4. The fourth beat is the lightest beat.

The quadruple bar may be illustrated graphically as follows:

$$1\,{}_2 3\,{}_4 \mid 1\,{}_2 3\,{}_4 \mid$$

The relative importance of beats in a triple measure is as follows:

1. The first beat is heavy.
2. The second beat is less heavy.
3. The third beat is light.

A triple measure may be illustrated graphically as follows:

$$1\,{}_2{}_3 \mid 1\,{}_2{}_3 \mid$$

The relative importance of the beats in a duple measure is as follows:

1. The first beat is heavy.
2. The second beat is light.

A duple measure may be illustrated graphically as follows:

$$1\,{}_2 \mid 1\,{}_2 \mid$$

Phrases are classified and named depending on the beat of the measure on which they originate and terminate. A masculine phrase begins on a heavy beat.

Ex. 545.   Das neugeborne Kindelein

A feminine phrase begins on a light beat.

Ex. 546.   Gelobet seist du, Jesu Christ

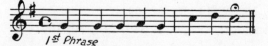

Phrases which end on a heavy beat have a masculine ending.

Ex. 547.   Mit Fried' und Freud' ich fahr' dahin

Phrases which end on a light beat have a feminine ending.

Ex. 548.   Freu' dich sehr, o meine Seele

Complete understanding of the form of a phrase depends upon its beginning and ending.   There are, therefore, four types of phrase forms:

1. A masculine phrase with a masculine ending.
2. A masculine phrase with a feminine ending.
3. A feminine phrase with a masculine ending.
4. A feminine phrase with a feminine ending.

Examine the following chorales and name each phrase:

Wonderlich: 49, 84, 7, 68, 55, 50, 151.
Bach-Reimenschneider: 238, 161, 25, 190, 8, 16, 62.

DEDUCTIONS

1. The feminine phrase with masculine ending is the most common type of phrase.
2. The masculine phrase with masculine ending is fairly common.
3. The masculine phrase with feminine ending is fairly rare.
4. The feminine phrase with feminine ending is rare.

Chorale melodies are found in duple, triple, and quadruple simple time.   The majority of Bach's settings of chorales are quadruple simple; most of the others are in triple simple, with rare instances of duple simple.

Knowledge of the form of a chorale melody has a direct bearing upon the selection of chords, especially at the beginning of a phrase, at the close of the phrase (cadence formula), and within the phrase.

B.   CHORD CHOICE

An organized plan which determines the selection of harmonies which will support the melody may be called *chord choice*.

The complete harmonization of a chorale melody rarely remains in the original key.   Bach's normal harmonizations make use of closely related keys.*

Memorize the following table of Bach usage:

Type Cadence	*Frequency*
1. Authentic cadence	
(a) Perfect authentic	(a) very frequent
(b) Imperfect authentic	(b) frequent
2. Plagal cadence	
(a) Perfect plagal	(a) very rare
(b) Imperfect plagal	(b) rare, but more frequent than the perfect plagal

* Introduction, page 19.

Type Cadence	Frequency
3. Half cadence on the dominant	Frequent
Half cadence on the subdominant	Rare
4. Deceptive cadence	More frequent than the plagal, but much less frequent than the half cadence.

PHRASES WITH MASCULINE ENDINGS

PERFECT AUTHENTIC CADENCE

Soprano line, supertonic-tonic or leading tone-tonic

Ex. 549.   Scale tone

DEDUCTIONS

1. Due to the nature of the chorale melody, the perfect authentic cadence with the soprano line supertonic-tonic is the most frequent.
2. The perfect authentic cadence must have the dominant and tonic triads in fundamental position and the tonic triad in the position of the octave.
3. The soprano line in the authentic cadence is either 7-8 or 2-1.
4. The perfect authentic cadence is the highest frequency cadence.

IMPERFECT AUTHENTIC CADENCES

1. Soprano line, supertonic to mediant

Ex. 550.   Scale tone

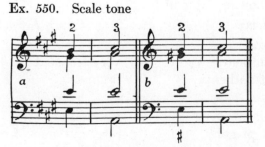

This imperfect authentic cadence is the most frequent in major and minor keys.

2. Soprano line, leading tone to tonic

Ex. 551.   Scale tone

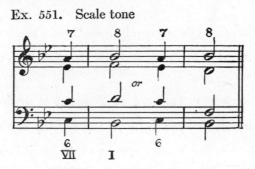

This cadence is infrequent in both major and minor keys.

3. Soprano line dominant to mediant

Ex. 552.   Scale tone

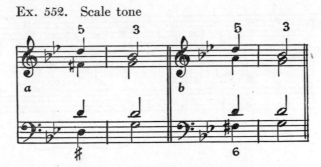

This cadence is rare in both major and minor keys.

4. Bass line, leading tone to tonic (Dominant chord in inversion) Soprano line, supertonic to tonic

Ex. 553.   Scale tone

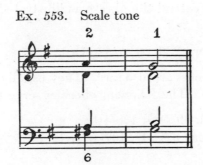

This cadence is rare.   It is not used in the last phrase of a chorale.

DEDUCTIONS

1. The tonic chord appears in the position of the octave or third in the imperfect authentic cadence.

2. The tonic chord rarely appears in the position of the 5th in the imperfect authentic cadence.

3. The imperfect authentic cadence rarely uses the first inversion of the dominant.

.4 The leading tone triad always appears in the first inversion in the imperfect authentic cadences.

5. Imperfect authentic cadences are not so frequent as perfect authentic cadences.

6. The imperfect authentic cadence is rarely used in the final cadence of a chorale.*

In authentic cadences, the V may appear on the first beat and extend through the second beat. Under these circumstances Bach utilizes non-harmonic tone devices to maintain the musical interest.

Ex. 554.   Was betrübst du dich, mein Herze

PLAGAL CADENCE

Perfect plagal cadences are extremely rare since the last two notes of the phrase of a chorale melody are rarely tonic-tonic. The only way in which the perfect plagal cadence can be used is to extend the phrase as illustrated in the following chorale:

Wonderlich: 105(2nd).
Bach-Riemenschneider: 239(1st), 252(6th).

Imperfect plagal cadences are also rare. They usually appear using the soprano line submediant-dominant. The following chorales serve to illustrate this cadence:

Wonderlich: 111(1st), 69(1st), 128(1st).
Bach-Riemenschneider: 32(1st), 107(1st), 12(1st).

HALF CADENCE

The half cadence on the dominant is not used in the last phrase of a chorale except in one instance.**

* In Part II, Chapter 32, under the harmonization of the Phrygian chorale melody, use of the imperfect authentic cadence in the final phrase will be discussed.

** This will be discussed in Part II, Chapter 32.

1. Soprano line, mediant-supertonic

Ex. 555.   Scale tones

(a) The above half cadences are the most frequent.

(b) Notice that the dominant triad is in the position of the fifth.

2. Soprano line, tonic-supertonic.

Ex. 556.   Scale tones

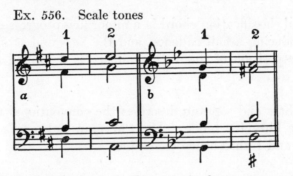

(a) The above half cadence is the next in frequency.

(b) Again the dominant triad is in the position of the fifth.

3. Soprano line, subdominant-supertonic

Ex. 557.   Scale tones

(a) The above half cadences are infrequent.

(b) Again the dominant triad is in the position of the fifth.

4. Soprano line, subdominant-dominant — Phrygian cadence

Ex. 558. Scale tones

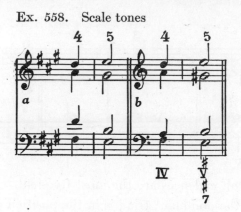

(a) The above half cadences are frequent.

(b) The half cadence in minor in example b is known as the Phrygian cadence.

When a second classification chord in a minor key progresses to the first classification chord, producing a half cadence, and the bass and soprano progress stepwise to the octave position of the V the cadence is described as *Phrygian.* The

$$\overset{\#}{7}$$

movement of the bass and soprano describes the conventional melodic movement to the final in the Phrygian mode. The Phrygian cadence is a half cadence in minor in the 18th and 19th century technique.

5. Soprano line, submediant-dominant

Ex. 559. Scale tones

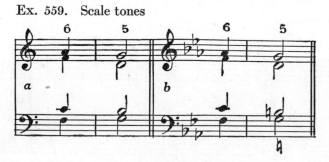

(a) This half cadence is less common.

(b) This half cadence is fairly common and is called a *Phrygian cadence.*

6. Soprano line, tonic-leading tone

Ex. 560.   Scale tones

The above half cadence is not common.

DEDUCTIONS

1. The final chord of a half cadence on the dominant is always a major triad. There are a few exceptions to this statement; they will be explained in Part II, Chapter 30.
2. The final chord V uses about equally the fundamental or the fifth in the soprano. The third appears less often in the soprano.

HALF CADENCE ON THE SUBDOMINANT

The half cadence on the subdominant is infrequent, compared with the half cadence on the dominant. The scale steps 5 to 6 or 3 to 1 in the soprano line of the cadence formula are usually harmonized as a half cadence on the subdominant.

Ex. 561.   Scale tones

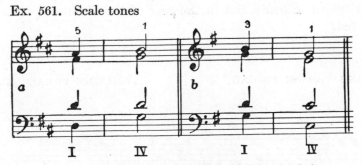

(a) is more frequent than (b). A variation of (b) which is more frequent contains an altered passing tone f-natural in the alto. This will be discussed in Part II, Chapter 31.

The half cadence on the subdominant is practically limited to a major key. This is due to the nature of the minor chorale melody, which rarely has the melodic line 5-6 or 3-1 in the cadence.

DECEPTIVE CADENCE

Bach's deceptive cadences are V–VI.

Soprano line, supertonic-tonic, dominant-tonic, and leading tone-tonic.

Ex. 562. Scale tones

Of these examples,

    (a) and (b) are the most common deceptive cadences,

    (c) is rare,

    (d) is extremely rare. This fact is important to observe because the use of this cadence increases after Bach.

Deceptive cadences are infrequent.

PHRASES WITH FEMININE ENDINGS

The harmonies which define the cadence of a phrase with a feminine ending appear in much the same relation with respect to the beats as in the phrases with masculine endings. As a basic example the following shows that the cadence harmonies fall on the same beats, but in the case of the feminine phrase ending this chord is repeated.

MASCULINE PHRASE ENDING *   FEMININE PHRASE ENDING

Ex. 563.

QUADRUPLE METER

The following authentic and half cadences closing a feminine phrase ending are taken from Bach chorale harmonizations:

*"L" means light, "H" means heavy.

Authentic Cadence   *Half Cadence*

Ex. 564.   Ex. 565.

The following examples are from Bach harmonizations:

Authentic Cadence

Ex. 566.

Half Cadence

Ex. 567.

The following examples are in the style but infrequent:

Ex. 568.

OPTIONAL CADENCE FORMULAS

Some phrase endings may have more than one type of cadence formula. This is especially true if the final tone of the phrase is the mediant.

Sing the melody below and determine the harmonic value of the final tone.

Ex. 569.

A majority of the class may arrive at the following conclusions:

Ex. 570.

TYPE CADENCE:	*Imperfect Authentic Cadence*
HARMONIC VALUE *	5M 3M **
SCALE TONE	2 3

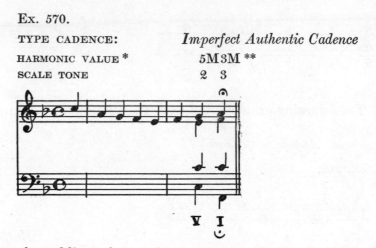

Sing the melody again and listen for another harmonic value for the final note. Some of the members of the class may find the following solution:

Ex. 571.

TYPE CADENCE:	*Phrygian Cadence*
HARMONIC VALUE	1m 1M
SCALE TONE	4 5

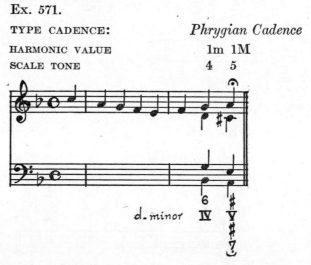

Changing the harmonic value of the last chord alters the entire musical effect of the phrase. The cadence decided upon for this phrase will control the entire harmonic thinking for the phrase.

---

* Harmonic value of a note is its position in the implied harmony. In this example the g is the fifth of the c-major triad.

** Capital M indicates *major;* small m *minor.*

EXERCISE: To select a cadence formula for the chorale phrase:

> (a) Sing or play each phrase and determine the harmonic value for the last tone of each phrase.
> (b) Select the type of cadence desired.
> (c) Write the melody on the staff and partwrite the cadence formula.

A complete chorale composed of three or more phrases rarely remains in the original key. The keys usually encountered are closely related. The first place to recognize the modulation is at the cadence. Play the following chorale melody, and determine, through singing, the harmonic value of the last tone of each phrase:

Ex. 572.

In example 572, at *a*, two possible harmonic values can be assigned to the tone d. It may be the fundamental of the d-major triad or third of the b-flat-major triad. In the first instance it is the V in the key of g-minor. In the second instance

$$\begin{matrix} \sharp \\ 7 \end{matrix}$$

it is the I in b-flat-major. Two cadences are possible with quite different harmonic implications. Play the first phrase twice using each cadence given below:

Ex. 573.

TYPE CADENCE:		Half Cadence (Phrygian)		Ex. 574.		Imperfect Authentic	
HARMONIC VALUE		1m	1M			5M	3M
SCALE TONE	g-minor	4	5	b♭-major		2	3

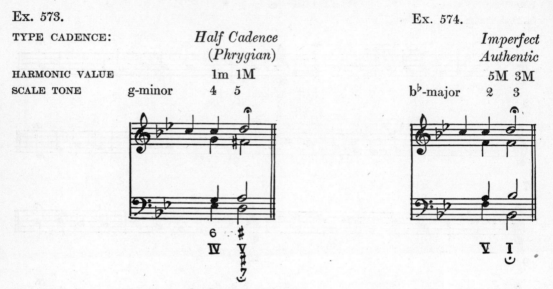

At *b*, in example 572, the harmonic value of g is fundamental of the g-minor triad.

Ex. 575.

TYPE CADENCE:		Perfect Authentic	
HARMONIC VALUE		5M	1m
SCALE TONE	g-minor	2	1

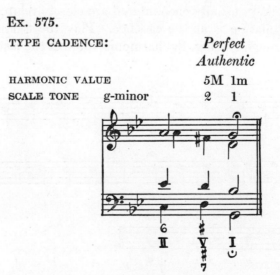

At *c*, in example 572, two possible harmonic values can be assigned to **c**. It may be the fifth of the f-major triad or the fundamental of the c-minor triad. In the style the following cadences are possible:

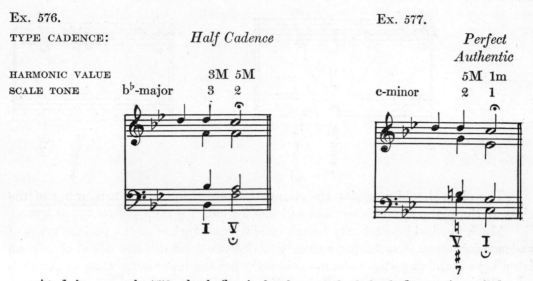

Ex. 576.

TYPE CADENCE:	*Half Cadence*		Ex. 577.	*Perfect Authentic*	
HARMONIC VALUE		3M 5M			5M 1m
SCALE TONE	b♭-major	3 2	c-minor		2 1

At *d*, in example 572, the b-flat is fundamental of the b-flat major triad.

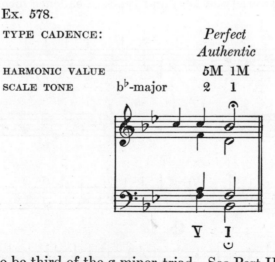

Ex. 578.

TYPE CADENCE:		*Perfect Authentic*	
HARMONIC VALUE			5M 1M
SCALE TONE	b♭-major		2 1

The b-flat can also be third of the g-minor triad. See Part II, Chapter 30, for discussion of cadences using the seventh chord.

At *e*, in example 572, the fundamental of the tonic triad must be assigned in accordance with the style. Fundamental major may be used at the final cadence of a chorale in a minor key. The g may, therefore, be fundamental of either the g-major or g-minor triads.

Ex. 579.   Ex. 580.

TYPE CADENCE:		*Perfect Authentic*	*Perfect Authentic*
HARMONIC VALUE		5M 1M	5M 1m
SCALE TONE	g-minor	2 1	g-minor 2 1

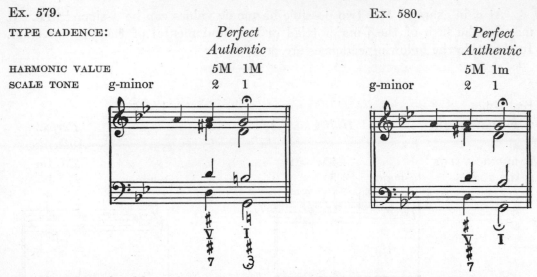

The class should now sing the chorale melody through and a member of the class at the piano should select the cadence formula for each phrase.

Much musical interest may be achieved by making use of the various types of cadence formulas. Combining a variety of cadence formulas and use of closely related keys is the first step to be made in selecting the harmonic setting of the melody. This procedure will be called *plotting the harmonic scheme.*

EXERCISE: Plot the harmonic scheme for the following chorale melodies. Write the melody on staff paper and partwrite the cadence formula for each phrase. Be sure to have some variety in keys and types of cadence formulas.

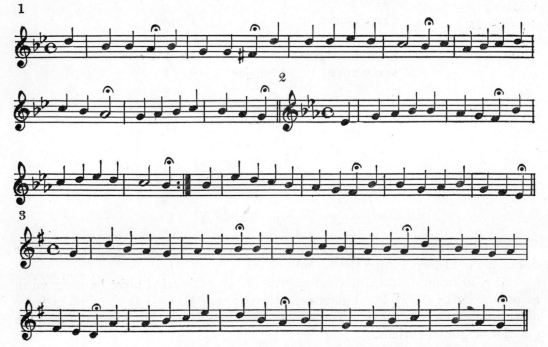

C. SELECTING THE CHORDS LEADING TO THE CADENCE FORMULA

As a background for the complete harmonization of a chorale, the student, by this stage in his understanding of the elements, should have acquired a knowledge of chord progression through dictation, keyboard, and analysis in connection with partwriting procedures.

Certain clear concepts, however, must be established before the harmonization of the chorale melody should be attempted. The first important factor is the frequency with which the classifications of root movement appear in the style. The following table illustrates the frequency of usage of the harmonic equipment, regardless of major or minor key:

4th classification	V	(altered)	.2	2%
	III		1.8	
3rd classification	I	(dissonance)	.6	
		(altered)		7%
	VI		6.4	
2nd classification	IV		11	19%
	II		8	
1st classification	VII		6	34%
	V		28	
tonic				38%

The data compiled in the preceding table show that Bach's harmonizations of the chorales are largely composed of tonic, first classification function, and second classification function. Less than ten percent of the entire harmonic equipment utilizes chords of the third and fourth classification functions. Considering the most popular roots upon which chords are erected, the most prominent are the tonic, next the dominant, next the subdominant. The supertonic and subdominant are about equally popular. The less frequent roots used are those on the leading tone and submediant. The mediant root is rare. The tonic harmony as a discord, either altered or diatonic, is rare. The rarest function is the fourth classification altered dominant with raised root.*

In addition to the varying frequency of classification of the functions, the frequency of the movement between classifications is of utmost importance. It was pointed out in the Introduction (page 10) that when a chord moves to another chord four types of progression are possible, namely normal progression, elision, retrogression, and repetition. The following table shows the relative frequency of usage of the four devices:

CHORD MOVEMENT **

Type of Progression	Frequency
Normal progression	76%
Repetition	14%
Elision	4%
Retrogression	6%

USE OF THE TONIC CHORD

At the outset of this discussion of the movement of chords, it must be understood that the tonic chord may progress to any function in its key. It also appears frequently between functions without disturbing the flow of the harmonic movement. This will be explained in the next subject, normal progression.

NORMAL PROGRESSION

When a classification of a function moves to the next classification nearer the tonic, it is a *normal progression*. A chord in the second classification progresses to a chord in the first classification as a normal progression. The following chorale phrase is harmonized by using normal progression:

Ex. 581. Herr Christ, der ein'ge Gott'ssohn

* See Part I, Chapter 24.
** The frequencies given here are based on a study of many chorales. The occasional chorales with unusual use of retrogression and elision are outbalanced by the many using normal progression. The student should master the conventional devices before indulging in less conventional ones.

In the above example, the third classification function VI progresses to the second classification function II which in turn progresses to the first classification function V. The first classification function V progresses to the I. The tonic then progresses to the first classification function V, which in turn progresses to the I in a perfect authentic cadence. The phrase is composed of a long series of normal progressions and a short normal progression near the end of the phrase.

Two chords in a normal progression may be separated by insertion of tonic harmony. Observe the tonic chord appearing here:

Ex. 582. Was Gott tut, das ist wohlgetan

At 1, the second classification IV progresses to the I. The insertion of the tonic at this point does not in any way disturb the fact that the normal progression is to the first classification function V. The tonic also appears frequently between the third classification function VI and the second classification II or IV. It may also appear between two chords of the same classification.

A normal progression is possible within a classification; namely, IV–II and occasionally VII–V. When diatonic chords are used, the movement of II–IV or V–VII is weak, and Bach avoids this harmonic movement.

REPETITION

The repetition of a function is controlled by the rhythm of the phrase. Within the phrase it is proper to repeat a function from a heavy beat to a light beat.

Ex. 583. Schmücke dich, o liebe Seele

Ex. 584.   Wie schön leuchtet der Morgenstern

At 1, 2, 3, and 4, the function is repeated from a heavy beat to a light beat.

At 1, 2, and 4, the harmony is tonic.

At 3, the harmony is dominant.

At 3 and 4, the bass note of each repetition is the same.

At the beginning of a feminine phrase the function is frequently repeated from light beat to heavy beat.

Ex. 585.   O Ewigkeit, du Donnerwort

Ex. 586.   Als der gütige Gott

At 1, the tonic triad is repeated from a light beat to a heavy beat at the beginning of a feminine phrase. The bass note remains the same.

At 2, the tonic triad is repeated as at 1; the bass note changes to the third of the tonic triad.

Phrases with feminine endings frequently repeat the last chord from the heavy beat to the light beat. Turn to the section on cadences for illustrations. The most common function to be repeated is tonic; next, dominant; and last, subdominant. Occasionally other functions are repeated.

ELISION

Harmonic elision occurs when a function avoids its normal progression and leaps to a function closer to the tonic.

Ex. 587.   Als der gütige Gott

At 1, the third classification function VI progresses to the first classification function V.

RETROGRESSION

The retrogression occurs when a function moves to a more remote function instead of observing the normal progression or elision.

Ex. 588.   Wach' auf, mein Herz, und singe

Ex. 589.   Wer weiss, wie nahe mir mein Ende

At 1, the third classification function VI retrogresses to the fourth classification function III. The III, in turn, moves by elision to the second classification function IV. The retrogression really retards the harmonic movement of the phrase until the second classification function IV appears and progresses normally toward the tonic.

At 2, the first classification function V retrogresses to the third classification function

$$\overset{\overset{\#}{7}}{\text{VI}},$$

which progresses normally through the classification functions to the half cadence.

CHROMATIC CHORD PROGRESSION

Occasionally a new key center may be established within a phrase by a chromatic chord progression. The second chord of the chromatic progression will establish a classification in the new key, but in no way can it be felt a function in the old key.

Ex. 590. Nun lob', mein' Seel', den Herren

At 1, the a-major triad, tonic of a-major, progresses chromatically to the e♯ diminished triad which is a VII in f-sharp minor. The chromatic progression in this case destroys a-major and establishes a chord of the first classification in the key of f-sharp minor.

$$\overset{\overset{\#}{7}}{}$$

D. THE BASS LINE

The bass and soprano help to bind together a musical composition just as the outside covers of a book help to keep the contents intact. The bass moves in four ways in relation to the soprano: stationary, oblique, similar, and contrary motion. Let us analyze the following chorale phrases and tabulate the motion of the bass to the soprano *:

Ex. 591. Herr, nicht schicke deine Rache

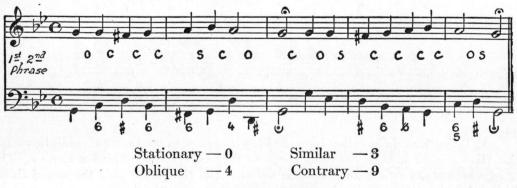

Stationary — 0	Similar — 3
Oblique — 4	Contrary — 9

* S = stationary; O = oblique; S = similar; C = contrary.

Taking the oblique movement instances in the order of their occurrence, the intervallic relationships between bass and soprano are as follows:

1. Octave — sixth
2. Fifth   — fifth (caused by leap of an octave.
   Frequent in the cadence formula.)
3. Octave — third
4. Sixth   — fifth

Taking the similar movement instances in the order of occurrence, the intervallic relationships between bass and soprano are as follows:

1. Third — third
2. Third — third
3. Fifth — octave (bass notes being roots of chords.)

Taking the contrary movement instances in the order of their occurrence, the intervallic relationships between bass and soprano are as follows:

1. Fifth — third
2. Third — sixth
3. Sixth — third
4. Third — fifth
5. Fifth — octave
6. Third — sixth
7. Sixth   — octave
8. Octave — third (tenth)
9. Third   — sixth

The following chorales illustrate the stationary bass and soprano:

Ex. 592. Nun preiset alle Gottes
Barmherzigkeit   Ex. 593.   Ich hab' mein' Sach' Gott heimgestellt

At 1, the stationary bass and soprano occur on the heavy beat and light beat.

At 2, the stationary bass and soprano occur at the opening of a feminine phrase. The stationary device is rare. It is usually encountered at the beginning of a phrase and it is occasionally found in a feminine cadence. It is extremely rare within the phrase from a heavy beat to a light beat.

The following table, based on an analysis of many chorales, illustrates the frequency of the four ways in which the bass and soprano lines travel simultaneously:

Contrary — 46%   Oblique   — 23%
Similar — 30%   Stationary — 1%

The discussion so far has been limited to intervals which are formed by utilizing a triad harmonic background. In the following chapters the intervals of the seventh, diminished fifth, and augmented fourth will be discussed in connection with the simultaneous movement of the bass and soprano.

THE BASS LINE MELODY

The bass, being an outer voice, should in addition to its own characteristics possess the qualities of a good melody. The first study to make concerning the bass line is its melodic intervallic movement. The following table lists the intervals encountered horizontally and their relative frequency:

Melodic Intervals	Direction	Frequency
Major and minor seconds	Ascending or descending	High frequency
Major and minor thirds	Ascending or descending	Frequent
Perfect fourths	Ascending	Moderately frequent
Perfect fourths	Descending	Less frequent
Perfect fifths	Ascending	Less frequent
Perfect fifths	Descending	Moderately frequent
Major or minor sixths	Ascending or descending	Rare
Minor sevenths	Ascending	Extremely rare
Minor sevenths	Descending	Practically non-existent
Major sevenths	Ascending or descending	None
Diminished fifths	Descending (subdominant to leading tone or tonic to raised 4)	Rare
Augmented fourths	Between phrases ascending	Extremely rare
Diminished fourths	Descending (mediant to leading tone)	Rare
Diminished sevenths	Descending (submediant to leading tone)	Rare
Octaves	Ascending	Rare
Octaves	Descending	Not too frequent

Almost any combination of intervals is possible between the bass and soprano line when they move in contrary motion. The only set of intervals which Bach avoids are the octave to octave or fifth to fifth.

Ex. 594.

At 1, these octaves are called *octaves by contrary motion*.
At 2, these fifths are called *fifths by contrary motion*.

Oblique motion provides many combinations of intervals. Due to the fact that one voice remains stationary while the other moves either toward or away from it, parallel fifths and octaves, which are out of the style, cannot occur between the bass and soprano.

Similar motion existing between the bass and soprano, however, presents some problems which must be thoroughly mastered. The following table shows the common intervals which follow each other in the similar motion of the bass and soprano.

Octave — fifth } Usually one voice moves by step.
Fifth   — octave} The bass notes are roots of chords.

Third   — third }
Sixth   — sixth } Most frequent

In similar motion a sixth to a fifth and a third to a fifth, forbidden by theorists, are occasionally found in the chorales; for instance:

Ex. 595. Heut' triumphieret Gottes Sohn   Ex. 596. Schwing' dich auf zu deinem Gott

Ex. 597. Auf meinen lieben Gott

At 1, the sixth in similar motion to a fifth appears in the progression of the first inversion of the I to V.

At 2, a third in similar motion to a fifth appears in the progression of the first inversion of the V to I.

At 3, a third in similar motion to an octave appears in the progression of the I to the first inversion of II with the third in the soprano.

The movement to the fifth at 1 and 2 is called *hidden fifths;* the movement to the octave at 3 is called *hidden octaves.* Bach does not often indulge in hidden fifths and octaves between the bass and soprano in similar motion. It is interesting to note that, whenever Bach uses hidden fifths and octaves, he consistently uses the tonic chord as one of the chords in the progression. The illustration at 1 is the most frequent of these rare examples of hidden fifths and octaves.*

* The student may use hidden fifths and octaves occasionally. If, however, he abuses the privilege, the instructor should immediately consider them errors in light of the fact that Bach uses the device sparingly.

Leaps in the same direction appear in the bass melody. They are not too frequent. The following table illustrates the varying frequency of this not-too-frequent melodic segment:

Type of Leaps	*Frequency*
A major third ascending or descending followed by a minor third	Frequent
A minor third ascending or descending followed by a major third	Frequent
A major or minor third descending followed by a perfect fourth	Low frequency
A major or minor third ascending followed by a perfect fourth	Rare
A perfect fourth ascending followed by a major or minor third	Rare
A perfect fourth descending followed by a major or minor third	Low frequency
A perfect fourth ascending followed by a perfect fifth	Low frequency
A perfect fourth descending followed by a perfect fifth	Low frequency
A perfect fifth ascending followed by a perfect fourth	Rare
A perfect fifth descending followed by a perfect fourth	Rare
A perfect fifth ascending or descending followed by a perfect fifth	None
A perfect fourth ascending followed by a perfect fourth	None
A perfect fourth descending followed by a perfect fourth *	Practically none
A perfect fifth ascending or descending followed by a minor third	Extremely rare

The instructor should afford the student opportunity to observe the information given in the last two tables through analysis of the bass line of quite a number of chorales.

The bass has many characteristics common to good melody writing. One of the most important factors in melody writing is concerned with contour. Although the bass melody is sometimes forced to give up good contour for harmonic reasons, the underlying qualifications of good melody writing prevail. Observe the contour in the following bass melodies:

Ex. 598.   Nun ruhen alle Wälder   Ex. 599.   Was Gott tut, das ist wohlgetan

As a general procedure Bach changes the direction of the bass melody, after a skip of a fifth, sixth, octave, and other wide intervals.

Ex. 600.   Herr Jesu Christ, du höchstes   Ex. 601.   Ich dank' dir schon durch deinen
              Gut   Sohn

Ex. 602.   Als der gütige Gott   Ex. 603.   Valet will ich dir geben

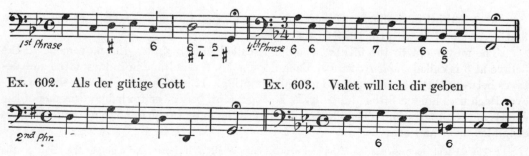

* The student should not use this melodic device.

Another characteristic of a good melody is avoiding too many repetitions of the same note. This is especially true of the highest or lowest note in the melodic line. In the following examples the highest and lowest notes for the entire phrase appear only once.

Ex. 604.   An Wasserflüssen Babylon   Ex. 605.   Ibid.

One of the features which characterize the bass melody is the descending leap of a fifth or ascending leap of a fourth at the authentic cadence. In fact, careful use of leaps in the bass, contrasting the more stepwise character of the chorale melody, adds interest to the setting of the chorale melody. The instructor should have the class sing the bass melodies of the chorale while the entire chorale is played at the piano or organ. This will help the student appreciate Bach's bass line as a melody.

Chapter 28

Harmonization of the Chorale Melody
Using Triads

In the last chapter, the important factors which contribute to making a harmonic setting of a chorale were presented. This chapter will develop the harmonization of the chorale melody utilizing the triads and their inversions.

Before the student begins to harmonize the chorale melody, he should give attention to the harmonic values of the notes which will precede the cadence formula.

To develop the student's background for the harmonic values of scale steps, two tables are presented which analyze the harmonic values of each scale step on a basis of relative frequency. To use these tables in a practical way, the student is urged to memorize the common frequencies; if he desires to use a less frequent harmonic value for a scale step, he can check on its use by referring to the tables. It is also suggested that, as the student studies the tables, he also sing the harmonic values of each scale step.

TRIAD HARMONIC VALUES OF THE SCALE STEP IN MAJOR

NAME OF SCALE STEPS	SCALE STEP	HARMONIC VALUE	FUNCTION	CLASSIFICATION	FREQUENCY
Tonic	1	1 M	I	Tonic	Common
		3 m	VI	3rd	Less common
		5 M	IV	2nd	Less common
Supertonic	2	5 M	V	1st	Common
		1 m	II	2nd	Less common
		3 dim.	VII	1st	Fairly common
Mediant	3	3 M	I	Tonic	Common
		5 m	VI	3rd	Quite rare
		1 m	III	4th	Very rare
Subdominant	4	1 M	IV	2nd	Fairly common

318

NAME OF SCALE STEPS	SCALE STEP	HARMONIC VALUE	FUNCTION	CLASSIFICATION	FREQUENCY
		3 m	II	2nd	Fairly common
		5 dim.	VII	1st	Less common
Dominant	5	5 M	I	Tonic	Common
		1 M	V	1st	Fairly common
		3 m	III	4th	Rare
Submediant	6	3 M	IV	2nd	Common
		1 m	VI	3rd	Rare
		5 m	II	2nd	Rare
Leading Tone	7	3 M	V	1st	Common
		1 dim.	VII	1st	Less common
		5 m	III	4th	Rare

TRIAD HARMONIC VALUES OF THE SCALE STEPS IN MINOR

NAME OF SCALE STEPS	SCALE STEP	HARMONIC VALUE	FUNCTION	CLASSIFICATION	FREQUENCY
Tonic	1	1 m	I	Tonic	Common
		3 M	VI	3rd	Less common
		5 m	IV	2nd	Less common
		1 M	I #3	Tonic	Fairly common in final cadence of a chorale
Supertonic	2	5 M	V #7	1st	Common
		1 dim.	II	2nd	Not common
		3 dim.	VII #7	1st	Less common
		5 m	V	1st	Rare
		1 m	II #6	2nd	Extremely rare
Mediant	3	3 m	I	Tonic	Common
		5 M	VI	3rd	Practically not used
		1 aug.	III #7	4th	Rare
		1 M	III	4th	Rare
		5 dim.	VI #6	3rd	Very rare

NAME OF SCALE STEPS	SCALE STEP	HARMONIC VALUE	FUNCTION	CLASSIFI- CATION	FREQUENCY
Subdominant	4	1 m	IV	2nd	Fairly common
		1 M	IV #6	2nd	In first inversion fairly rare
		3 dim.	II	2nd	Less common
		5 dim.	VII #7	1st	Not common
Dominant	5	1 M	V #7	1st	Quite common
		1 m	V	1st	Practically nonexistent
		5 m	I	Tonic	Rather rare
		3 M	III	4th	Practically nonexistent
		3 aug.	III #7	4th	Rare
Submediant	6	1 M	VI	3rd	Practically nonexistent
		3 m	IV	2nd	Fairly common
		5 dim.	II	2nd	Practically nonexistent
Raised- Submediant	#6	3 M	IV #6	2nd	Only a few instances in chorale melody
Subtonic	7	3 m	V	1st	Only a few instances, discussed in Chapter 32
Leading Tone	#7	3 M	V #7	1st	Fairly common
		1 dim.	VII #7	1st	Fairly common
		5 aug.	III #7	4th	Practically nonexistent

A. HARMONIZATION OF THE CHORALE PHRASE

The following chorale phrase is to be given a four-voice setting: *

Ex. 608.

* The student should always sing, using the conductor's beat, the melody which he intends to set.

The phrase is feminine with a masculine ending. The harmonic value of the final note of the phrase is fundamental of the g-major triad; the harmonic value for the second to last note of the phrase is fifth of a major triad of which d becomes the root. The resulting cadence will be a perfect authentic in the key of g-major.

Having established the cadence of the phrase, the next step is to find the most elemental implied harmonic background for the phrase. This is accomplished by carefully singing the melody, and grouping as many notes as possible under one basic harmonic background without considering any of the notes of the melody unessential (non-harmonic).*

VERSION I

Ex. 609. Version 1a   Ex. 610. Version 1b

Under 1a, the first three notes are linked together by implied tonic harmony. The a and c in the first measure are undoubtedly felt as the 5th and 7th respectively of the dominant seventh chord. Although this implied harmonic feeling is unquestionably fundamental, its use will have to be postponed until Chapter 30.

Under 1b, the a and c in the first measure are treated as the fundamental and third of a minor triad which is a chord of the second classification.

This basic harmonization will be called Version 1b.**

In continuing the harmonization, the next step is to decide the best places to retain the tonic harmony. Perhaps the tonic harmony should, for the present, be located as follows:

Ex. 611.

Locating the tonic as shown leaves the g at (1) without a harmonic value. Keeping the classification of function in mind, notice that the phrase has the limit of frequency in tonic harmony, low frequency of first classification, and the limit of second classification. This situation therefore suggests that the g at (1) might be a chord of the third classification. The harmonic value of 3 m to the g will create

---

* The instructor will play the harmonic background implied by the symbols, using inversions to put them in as good musical grammar as possible. It must be understood that in the following examples some of the implied harmonies are not always in good taste. The final decision concerning the harmonization will be a matter of taste.

** It must be remembered that, at this point, the class is interested in implied harmonic backgrounds, and that the matter of converting this rare harmonic material into usable form will be taken into consideration when the figured bass is composed to the melody, using the implied harmonic background for the melody.

a third classification function VI. The tonic triad appearing after VI does not in any way disturb the resolution of the third classification function to the second classification function:

VERSION 2

Ex. 612.

I   VI   I   II -   I   VI   I

So far the harmonization follows the principle of normal progression. One retrogression is possible for the phrase. The a on the third beat of the first measure may be assigned the value of 5 M, which has already been implied in Version 1a. Instead of linking a with c under the implied dominant seventh chord, the harmonic value for the c will remain 3 m as in Version 1b. This will cause a retrogression, the first classification function V moving to the second classification function II:

VERSION 3

Ex. 613.

I   VI   I   V   II   I   V   I

The phrase now has an elision, VI–(I)–V, and it has a retrogression V–II. Notice that the II eventually returns to the first classification function V in the cadence formula.

Instead of using 3 m for the g in the first measure, 5 M may be substituted. The resulting implied harmony will be a second classification function **IV**:

VERSION 4

Ex. 614.

I   IV   I   V   II   I   VI   I

Up to this point the implied harmonic possibilities have been conventional. A less conventional implied harmonic background is possible providing the tonic harmony is further reduced. The best location is at b in the first measure. If b is assigned a harmonic value of **1 m**, which is very rare, Version 2 can be revised as follows:

VERSION 5

Ex. 615.

I   VI   III   II -   I   V   I

The retrogression VI to III is followed by the elision III to II. A harmonization of a phrase like Version 5 should not appear more than twice in a complete chorale harmonization.

Before closing this discussion of the harmonization of the chorale, it is desirable to point out some practical suggestions concerning the harmonic values assigned to consecutive soprano notes. If the student analyzes the harmonic values which Bach uses, he will observe the absence of consecutive soprano notes given the harmonic value of 5 M–5 M, 5 M–5 m, or 5 m–5 m. The reason for avoiding the practice is in agreement with the style. Parallel perfect fifths, which are not in the style, will be avoided. The only exception to this practice is in connection with the fourth and fifth scale steps.

Ex. 616.   Wir Christenleut'   Ex. 617.   O Ewigkeit, du Donnerwort

At 1, the c-sharp is 5 m and the b is 5 d. Bach avoids the unequal fifths between the soprano and alto by use of the suspension in the first beat of the measure. Bach does not always use the suspension to avoid unequal fifths.

At 2, the b-flat is 5 d and the c is 5 M. Bach has unequal fifths with the perfect fifth as the last fifth.

Bach avoids unequal fifths, under all conditions, between soprano and bass.

Adding the figured bass melody in relation to the implied harmonic background established in the various versions will be the next step toward the complete four-voice setting of the chorale phrase. The last section of the previous chapter established the cardinal features of a good Bach bass.

The following basses may be used in connection with the harmonic background for Version 1b.

Ex. 618.

The element of taste will decide which one of the above basses might be desired. The figured basses just given are not the only possible basses that can be composed utilizing the established implied harmonic background.

Play at the piano and discuss the basses that may be written to Versions 2, 3, 4, and 5:

There are no errors in the above basses;* but as they are played some sound better than others. This is just the point to be stressed. This approach to harmonization rapidly develops one's ability to choose which one of his harmonizations is to his liking. This approach helps the teacher to guide the student toward a better understanding of the potential harmonic background of a melody.

EXERCISE: Find at least four harmonic backgrounds, and compose the figured bass melody, to the following chorale phrases. Some of the chorale phrases have more than one possible cadence. A phrase may use a first inversion of a triad as the first chord.

The last step will be to fill in the alto and tenor. Chapters 1 through 9 in Part I have established the partwriting procedures which will enable the student to partwrite the harmonic progressions he has selected. As an example, the following phrase illustrates the partwriting of one of the basses written to Version 3.

Ex. 623.

* It must be understood that more harmonic versions are possible.

EXERCISE: Make two four-voice settings of a chorale phrase using the method outlined in Chapter 27 and this chapter. Chorale phrases are to be assigned from Chapter 27, page 303.

B. THE FOUR–VOICE SETTING OF THE CHORALE MELODY

Change of key may be effected without use of diatonic or chromatic modulation; it may be achieved through musical form. At the initial announcement of a phrase, a related key may be established without any process of modulation. A few examples are cited as follows:

Wonderlich: 1(4), 111(6th), 49(3rd), 72(2nd), 95(3rd).
Bach-Riemenschneider: 40(1st), 32(6th), 238(3rd), 367(2nd), 327(3rd).

This is a useful method of achieving change of key as a contrast to the processes of modulation.

The chorale melody will be composed of four or more phrases. The four-voice setting of the chorale phrase can then be expanded to the complete chorale melody.

The student now has the tools with which to work. The musical interest which the setting will possess is made possible by carefully contrasting keys, cadence formulas, and types of harmonic movement. Overindulgence in elision or retrogression becomes an artistic error.

The best procedure to overcome such musical defects as lack of harmonic interest, excess of harmonic interest, or dull bass melody is to devote most of one's time and energy to studying the musical potentialities of the melody itself. This is best accomplished by musical planning. The approach to making the musical setting of a chorale melody is as follows:

1. Sing the chorale melody.
2. Study the form as a whole, and the form of the phrases.
3. Plot the key scheme by establishing the cadence formulas.
4. Find the potential harmonic possibilities of each phrase.
5. Write the bass melody and figured bass to determine the **inversion or** other necessary harmonic structures.
6. Add the alto and tenor.

EXERCISES: Harmonize the following chorale melodies, using four voices:

1

Chapter 29

Harmonization of the Chorale Melody
Using Non-Harmonic Tones*

From the standpoint of rhythmic interest, non-harmonic tones stimulate new ways in which harmonic movement may be used. Compare the following cadence formulas:

Ex. 624.

At *a*, the cadence is considered dull rhythmically, in light of the fact that harmonic movement before the cadence supports each beat.

At *b*, use of two chords corrects the style error of example *a*.

At *c*, the harmony is the same as at *a*. The dominant harmony is sustained from the heavy beat to the light, but the use of non-harmonic tones supports the musical interest of the cadence.

Non-harmonic tones are occasionally used to support the second classification function in the Phrygian cadence (half cadence in a minor key). Examine the following cadence:

Ex. 625.

---

* This chapter follows Part I, Chapter 14.

Two chords may appear in a progression within the duration of a beat. At times this device is used as a contrast to non-harmonic tones, which usually appear on the last half of the beat.

Ex. 626.   Alles ist an Gottes Segen

At 1, the harmonic progression is I–VI.
At 2, the harmonic progression is I–VII.
At 3, the harmonic progression is I–IV.

This device makes it possible to repeat frequently a series of normal progressions within one phrase. Analyze the classification of root movement in the preceding chorale example.

Non-harmonic tones tend to increase the melodic interest of the bass melody. Many of the leaps of a third and fourth are filled in by passing tones. Occasionally a bass note may be held from a light beat to a heavy beat, by making use of the suspension.

The method of approach to harmonization of the chorale remains unchanged. The student must first approach the harmonization as if he intended to use triads. After the framework is decided upon, the four-voice solution may be worked into a contrapuntal harmonic style.*

Harmonize the following chorales in four parts in contrapuntal harmonic style using a triad basis:

* Contrapuntal harmonic style means an increased melodic interest in each voice line.

NOTE: The instructor is urged to have his students transpose the preceding melodies in order to gain experience in harmonizing in more than a few common keys.

Chapter 30

Harmonization of the Chorale Melody
Using Seventh Chords*

The chapters in **Part I** established the relative frequency of triads and seventh chords in Bach's style; the relative frequency of the functions of seventh chords; the relative frequency of the root position and inversions of seventh chords. This chapter will be devoted to presentation of some of the practical ways to utilize seventh chords in harmonization of the chorale.

The perfect authentic cadence and the imperfect authentic cadence may use the first classification function V^7 in major and minor keys.

Ex. 627.

The imperfect authentic cadence may occasionally use the first classification function VII^7 in a minor key. The following examples are used by Bach:

Ex. 628.

* This chapter follows Part I, Chapter 20.

331

Use of a first classification function dissonant chord is occasionally found in the half cadence. Examine the following examples:

Ex. 629. O Herzensangst, o Ban-
    gigkeit

Ex. 630.   Jesu Leiden, Pein und Tod

For further examples in the chorales examine the following:

Wonderlich: 102(4th).
Bach-Riemenschneider: 216(1st), 276(4th).

Use of seventh chords in the first classification functions in the half cadence are extremely rare. In light of this fact, the student is urged to avoid the device.

Contrary to what may be expected with an increase of the harmonic equipment by use of seventh chords, Bach uses them sparingly and restricts many of the seventh chords to specific harmonic movements. Much of this information has been discussed in Part I. To aid, however, in finding suitable places to use seventh chords, the following table enumerates the functions and the scale steps which are used most often in the soprano.

MAJOR KEY

ROOT CLASSIFI-CATION	FUNC-TION	POSITION IN BASS	SCALE STEP IN SOPRANO			REMARKS
			Common	*Less common*	*Rare*	
1st	V^7	root	2, 4, 7	5		
		1st inv.	4	2, 5		
		2nd inv.	4		7, 5	
		3rd inv.	7, 5		2	
	VII^7	root	4			Chord is rare. See Chapter 20, p. 212.
2nd	II^7	root	4	1, 2	6	
		1st inv.	1, 2		6	
		3rd inv.	4		2, 6	
	IV^7	root	3		1	
		1st inv.	4			
		3rd. inv.	6		1	

ROOT CLASSIFICATION	FUNCTION	POSITION IN BASS	SCALE STEP IN SOPRANO *Common*	*Less common*	*Rare*	REMARKS
3rd	VI⁷	root	5			
		1st inv.	5			
		2nd inv.	5			Passing chords
		3rd inv.	3			
	I⁷	root	7, 1, 3			
	III⁷	root	5, 3			

MINOR KEY

ROOT CLASSIFICATION	FUNCTION	POSITION IN BASS	SCALE STEP IN SOPRANO *Common*	*Less common*	*Rare*	REMARKS
1st	V⁷ ♯7	root	2, 4, ♯7	5		
		1st inv.	4	2, 5		
		2nd inv.	4		♯7, 5	
		3rd inv.	♯7, 5		2	
	VII⁷ ♯7	root	4, 2, 6			
		1st inv.	4, ♯7			
		2nd inv.	♯7, 6, 2			
		3rd inv.	♯7, 2, 4			
2nd	II⁷	root				Rare in minor.
		1st inv.	2, 1			⎰6th scale step is so rare
		3rd inv.	2, 4			⎱its use is negligible.
	IV⁷	root	3			
		1st inv.	4			
		3rd inv.	6			
	IV⁷ ♯6	root				⎰See Introduction
		1st inv.	4			⎱and Chapter 19
		3rd inv.	♯6			

ROOT CLASSIFI- CATION	FUNC- TION	POSITION IN BASS	SCALE STEP IN SOPRANO *Common Less common Rare*			REMARKS
3rd	VI^7	root	5			Other examples practically non-existent
	VI^7 #6	root	5			
4th	III^7 #7					Negligible
	III^7					

Inversions of the seventh chords provide stepwise motion in the bass melody in the same manner as inversion of the triads. Occasionally within a phrase a bass note may be repeated from a light beat to a heavy beat, providing the chord on the heavy beat becomes the third inversion of a seventh chord.

Ex. 631. Herr, nun lass in Frieden

Ex. 632. Allein zu dir, Herr Jesu Christ

At 1, the c in the bass line becomes the seventh of the IV^7, change of harmony.

The bass line at this point seems to possess the feeling of an ornamental resolution of a suspension.

At 2, the c-sharp is repeated from a light beat to a heavy beat. The harmonic progression is V to I[7].

One should remember that

(1) Overuse of seventh chords retards the use of non-harmonic tones.
(2) Overuse of two seventh chords in succession will weaken the style.

Harmonize the following chorale melodies using non-harmonic tones and inversion of triads and seventh chords, following the method of approach established in Part 2, Chapter 28.

In addition to these melodies, the instructor may use other chorale melodies found in Wonderlich or Bach-Riemenschneider.

Chapter 31

Harmonization of the Chorale Melody Using Altered Non-Harmonic Tones and Altered Chords *

Altered non-harmonic tones and altered chords are occasionally found in the cadence formula. They are not used in the authentic cadence.** In the half cadence, however, both altered non-harmonic tones and altered chords are used. Examine the altered non-harmonic tones in the following half cadences:

Ex. 633. Nun preiset alle Gottes Ex. 634. Lobet den Herren, denn er ist sehr
Barmherzigkeit   freundlich

Ex. 635. Es woll' uns Gott genädig
sein   Ex. 636. Freu' dich sehr, o meine Seele

* This chapter follows Part I, Chapter 24.

** In the latter part of the 18th century altered chords of the first classification begin to appear. At first they are used sparingly but they never attain a high frequency until the last part of the 19th century.

At 1, and 2, the altered passing tones, lowered-7, appear in the half cadence on the subdominant.

At 3, the lower neighboring tone, raised-4, appears in the half cadence on the dominant.

At 4, the altered passing tone, raised-4, appears in the half cadence on the dominant.

In the preceding examples, which reveal Bach's usual procedure, the altered non-harmonic tones are in the tonic harmony.

The following examples illustrate the altered subdominant chord which occasionally appears in the half cadence on the dominant:

Ex. 637. Des heil'gen Geistes reiche
Gnad'   Ex. 638.   Nun ruhen alle Wälder

At 1, the IV⁷ progresses to the V.   The altered IV follows the I in first inversion.

At 2, the second inversion of the IV⁷ follows the I and progresses to the V.   Occa-

sionally the II, II⁷ and IV⁷ in a major key are used before the V in the half cadence.

Altered chords may appear at the beginning of a phrase and within a phrase. The altered tone practically never appears in the soprano in the chorales. Keeping this in mind, one can readily understand that restrictions are placed on use of altered chords under the soprano. Providing the altered note is not in the soprano, the remaining preferences for the position in the soprano of the diatonic triads and seventh chords continue. For example, the II⁷ harmonizes the first and second degrees of the major scale and rarely the sixth degree. Turn to the diatonic seventh chord in major table in Chapter 30, and verify this analysis. Since more restrictions in harmonizing the soprano are placed on seventh chords rather than on the triads, the following tables outline only the altered triads:

ALTERED TRIADS IN MAJOR

CLASSIFICATION			SCALE TONE IN SOPRANO	
			Common	*Occasional*
	II # 4		2	6
2nd	II ♭ 6	(1st inv.)	2	4
	IV # 4	(1st inv.)	6, 1	
	IV ♭ 6	(1st inv.)	1	4
	VI # 1		3	6
3rd	I # 1	(1st inv.)	3	5
	VI ♭♭ 36		1	
4th	III # 5		3, 7	

ALTERED TRIADS IN MINOR

CLASSIFICATION			SCALE TONE IN SOPRANO	
			Common	*Occasional*
	II ## 46		2	
2nd	IV ## 46		1	See special use, Part I, Chapter 23.
	II ♭ 2	(1st inv.)	4	

Altered non-harmonic tones are found in the bass. In the following bass the lowered-7 appears in the subdominant chord in the key of e-flat major.

Ex. 639. Wo soll ich fliehen hin

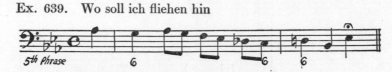

For further examples refer to Part I, Chapter 21.

When altered chords are used, one frequently finds the altered tone in the bass. The approach to and resolution from the altered tone in the bass is by step, by chromatic inflection, and by leap.

Raised-4 may be approached by leap of a third, diminished fifth, and diminished seventh.

Ex. 640. Wo Gott der Herr nicht bei uns hält

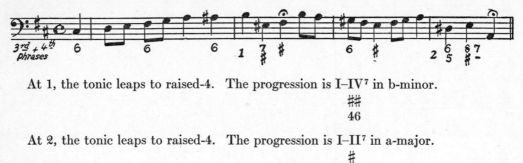

At 1, the tonic leaps to raised-4. The progression is I–IV[7] in b-minor.

$$\begin{array}{c} \text{\#\#} \\ 46 \end{array}$$

At 2, the tonic leaps to raised-4. The progression is I–II[7] in a-major.

$$\begin{array}{c} \text{\#} \\ 4 \end{array}$$

Ex. 641.   Du Lebensfürst, Herr Jesu
            Christ   Ex. 642.   O Haupt voll Blut und Wunden

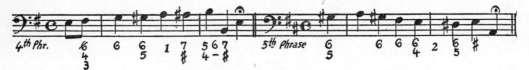

At 1, the chromatic chord progression into the IV[7] in the key of e-minor has the chro-

$$\begin{array}{c} \text{\#\#} \\ 46 \end{array}$$

matic inflection in the bass as well as in an upper voice.

At 2, the raised-4 is approached by half-step from above. The phrase is in the key of a-major. The chord is a II[7].

$$\begin{array}{c} \text{\#} \\ 4 \end{array}$$

For further examples refer to Part I, Chapters 23 and 24.

Harmonize the following chorale melodies, using altered non-harmonic tones and altered chords:

The instructor is urged to select other chorale melodies in addition to those presented here, and to assign the melodies to be harmonized in less common keys.

Chapter 32

Harmonization of Modal Chorale Melodies

Before starting this chapter, the student should review the modes. (See Appendix.)

The following chorale melodies were Aeolian when they were introduced during the Reformation in Martin Luther's time:

"Nun komm, der Heiden Heiland"
"Dies sind die heil'gen zehn Gebot'"
"Jesus Christus, unser Heiland"
"Christ, unser Herr, zum Jordan kam"

The following chorale melodies were Dorian:

"Mit Fried' und Freud' ich fahr' dahin"
"Wir glauben all' an einen Gott, Schöpfer"
"Christ lag in Todesbanden"
"Vater unser im Himmelreich"
"Erhalt' uns, Herr, bei deinem Wort"

The following chorale melodies were Phrygian:

"Aus tiefer Not schrei' ich zu dir"
"Es woll' uns Gott genädig sein"
"Mitten wir im Leben sind"
"Christum wir sollen loben schon"

The following chorale melodies were Mixolydian:

"Komm, Gott Schöpfer, heiliger Geist"
"Gott sei gelobet und gebenedeiet"
"Verleih' uns Frieden gnädiglich"
"Gelobet seist du, Jesu Christ"
"Der du bist drei in Einigkeit"

Very few of the original modal melodies retained their general melodic outline by the time Bach began to use them in his cantatas, oratorios, and other works. It is safe to say, in general, that the only melodies which consistently adhered to the modal feeling were the Aeolian and Phrygian ones.   The trends toward fundamental bass in the style of composition during the 17th century affected the melodic contour to such a degree that many Aeolian, Mixolydian, and Dorian melodies crystallized into either major or minor tonal systems.   For example, let us observe the transformation of the melody "Christ lag in Todesbanden" from its original form in the 16th century to its form in Bach's time:

Ex. 643.   Christ lag in Todesbanden   *Martin Luther (1483–1546)*
                                                          Erfurt Enchiridion (1524)

The harmonic treatment given the modal chorale melody by Bach is not original with him.   He carried on the tradition established in the 17th century by Schein, Scheidt, Schütz, Böhm, Buxtehude, and others.   Each phrase of the chorale melody is in a definite key.   The modulations which occur in the chorale are determined by the key established by the last chord of the chorale.   An analysis made of nearly a hundred harmonizations of Bach's settings of modal chorale melodies shows that the last chord is either a dominant or a tonic chord.   The melodies which are Aeolian, Mixolydian, Dorian, and modified Dorian * have their final note harmonized as fundamental of a triad. The Phrygian melodies are an exception to this basic procedure.   To clarify this point, each mode will be taken up separately and Bach's treatment analyzed.

   * *Modified Dorian* means that the melody adheres to the basic feeling of the mode but contains one or two scale steps which are raised or lowered for harmonic reasons.

The key signature * of Bach's treatment of the modal chorale melodies is in the tradition of the transposed modes. For example, if the final note of a Phrygian melody is f-sharp, the key signature will be two sharps. If the final note of a Mixolydian tune is c, the signature will be one flat.

EXERCISE: What is the signature for the following transposed modes?

> Dorian with the final note on f.
> Aeolian with the final note on f-sharp.
> Mixolydian with the final note on a-flat.
> Mixolydian with the final note on b.
> Phrygian with the final note on g-sharp.
> Dorian with the final note on e.

AEOLIAN CHORALE MELODIES

Analyze the key system in each of the following chorales:

Wonderlich: 9, 11, 18, 31, 49, 65, 96, 100, 104, 114, 127, 156.
Bach-Riemenschneider: 13, 304, 245, 167, 287, 30, 45, 358, 28, 219, 285.

DEDUCTIONS

1. The final note is fundamental of a major triad. The major triad at the end of the chorale is a I in tonic minor key.

    ♯
    3

2. The most common modulations are to the mediant major key and the subtonic major key.
3. Modulation to the subdominant minor is rare.
4. The pure dominant minor triad is used in the harmonization, and it usually appears near the beginning of the phrase.

MIXOLYDIAN CHORALE MELODIES

Analyze the key system in each of the following chorales:

Wonderlich: 26, 57, 99, 62.
Bach-Riemenschneider: 154, 160, 187, 70.

DEDUCTIONS

1. The tone a fourth above the final note is frequently raised in the Mixolydian mode to obtain an authentic cadence in the dominant. The whole tone below the tonic is occasionally raised.
2. The final note is the fundamental of a major triad.
3. The final major triad is a tonic triad controlling the system of keys used in the harmonization of the Mixolydian chorale melody.

---

* See Appendix, p. 433.

4. The common modulations are subdominant, supertonic, and to either a dominant major or minor key. The dominant minor is a foreign key to the normal closely related system.*

DORIAN CHORALE MELODIES

Dorian melodies are modified in every instance for harmonic or *musica ficta* reasons.

Analyze the key system in the following chorales:

Wonderlich: 107, 108, 10, 14, 19, 27, 32, 83, 113, 135.
Bach-Riemenschneider: 49, 325, 180, 340, 210, 232, 87, 19, 185, 267.

DEDUCTIONS

1. The subtonic, mediant, and subdominant are raised for harmonic reasons and the raised submediant is lowered, for either *musica ficta* or harmonic reasons.
2. The final note is the fundamental of a major triad, which is considered a tonic triad in a minor key with the raised third.
3. The key system is based on the closely related keys to the minor tonic built on the final tone.
4. The common modulations are to the subtonic, mediant, dominant, and subdominant. Occasionally a major subdominant key is used.
5. In the modulation to the dominant, Bach occasionally uses the tonic with the raised third.

PHRYGIAN CHORALE MELODIES

Phrygian chorale melodies are rarely modified for harmonic or *musica ficta* reasons.

Analyze the key system in each of the following chorales:

Wonderlich: 13, 21, 36, 50, 61, 72, 73, 74, 75, 121, 3, 4.
Bach-Riemenschneider: 10, 81, 34, 16, 181, 367, 89, 74, 80, 82, 3, 262.

DEDUCTIONS

1. The final note of the Phrygian chorale melody may be given three harmonic values. In each instance the triad is major.
2. If the final note is fundamental or fifth of a major triad, the last chord is a $V_7^{\#}$ in a minor key. If the final note is third of a major triad, the chord is a tonic of a major key. The final cadence encountered most often, however, contains the final note harmonized as fundamental of a major triad.
3. The key system used is dependent upon the characters of the final chords. The following key system chart is based on e as the final note:

* See Part I, Chapter 26.

FINAL CHORD	CHARACTER OF FINAL CHORD	BASIC KEY FOR HARMONIZATION	KEY SYSTEM
e-major	V ♯ 7	a-minor	Closely related keys to a-minor.
c-major	I	c-major	Closely related keys to c-major.
a-major	V ♯ 7	d-minor	Closely related keys to d-minor.

4. Occasional foreign keys may occur.

EXERCISE: Determine the mode, and make a four-voice setting, employing the entire harmonic and non-harmonic equipment, of the following chorale tunes:

Part 3

Contrapuntal

Harmonic Style

Chapter 33
Two-Voice Harmonic Counterpoint*

Counterpoint is the art of combining two or more voices, emphasizing in each the principles of melodic composition. The composer selects a melody, either composed by him or borrowed from other sources, to which he may add other voices. The melody selected as the basis for the contrapuntal composition is called the *cantus firmus*. The voices which are composed to the *cantus firmus* are called the *counterpoints*.

When two or more voices are added to the *cantus firmus* under the guidance of the classification of root movement, the type of composition is called *harmonic counterpoint*. Owing to the fact that the triad is the smallest tone combination used by composers in the style being studied, many of the vertical intervals formed by the two voices imply chords. These intervals are called *essential intervals*. The remaining vertical intervals in a two-voice harmonic passage which do not imply chords are called *unessential intervals*.

Sing the following two-voice composition, then study the analysis:

Ex. 644.   Allein Gott in der Höh' sei Ehr'   *George Bohm (1661–1733)*

* This chapter follows Part I, Chapter 13.

351

1. Chorale prelude composers frequently vary the chorale melody. The devices range from varying the meter and time values of the original melody to creating elaborate ornamental variations of the original. Compare the chorale melody used as the *cantus* for the preceding composition with the original found in the following collections:

Wonderlich: 8.
Bach-Riemenschneider: 313.

2. The numbers under the notes of the counterpoint indicate the essential intervals which imply the basic harmony. In this composition, thirds and sixths motivate the harmonic progressions.

3. Non-harmonic tones appear in both the *cantus firmus* and the counterpoint. The following abbreviations will be used to indicate the type of non-harmonic tone:

P. T.	Passing tone	App.	Appoggiatura
S.	Suspension	E. S.	Escape tone
N. T.	Neighboring tone	A.	Anticipation
	C. T.	Changing tone	

In the third measure an ornamental suspension appears on the first beat and a normal suspension on the last beat. In each case the suspension of a second resolves to an essential harmonic interval of a third. This suspension is called the *two-three suspension*; it is found only in the lower part in two-voice harmonic counterpoint.

4. Below the composition on a third staff are the notes which imply the function of the chord from which the classification of root movement may be established. Two-voice harmonic counterpoint introduces nothing new in harmonic progression. It is based on the principles established for four-part writing and harmonization. Due to the fact that there are only two parts, it is quite logical that the implied harmonies will be triad structures unless the melodic contour of the parts suggests seventh chord structures. Certain intervals created by the two parts at times imply seventh chords. They will be explained later in the chapter.

ANALYSIS

Analyze the following two-voice compositions according to this plan:

1. Determine the essential harmonic intervals. Directly beneath the lower voice indicate the essential interval by an Arabic number.
2. Determine the non-harmonic tones in each voice. Write the type of non-harmonic tone in abbreviation above each non-harmonic tone.
3. Determine the manner in which the essential interval is approached, namely, similar, oblique, contrary, or stationary. Collect this information in a table.
4. Add a staff below the composition and write the roots of the implied harmonies.

5. Indicate the function of the harmony by use of Roman numerals. If modulations occur, indicate the type, using the same procedure as was used in Part I and Part 2.
6. Indicate the root classification below the Roman numerals.

(Each composition analyzed should appear in the form of the example cited at the beginning of this chapter.)

Ex. 645.   Allein zu dir, Herr Jesu Christ   *J. Christoph Bach (1732–1795)*

1st Phrase

Ex. 646.   Allein Gott in der Höh' sei Ehr'   *J. Christoph Bach*

1st Phrase

Ex. 647.   Es ist das Heil uns kommen her   *J. Christoph Bach*

Ex. 648.   Ach Gott, vom Himmel sieh' darein   *J. Christoph Bach*

Ex. 649. Ach Gott,vom Himmel sieh' darein   *Johann Pachelbel (1653–1706)*

Ex. 650. Gott hat das Evangelium   *Johann Pachelbel*

Ex. 651. Nun lob', mein' Seel', den Herren   *Dietrich Buxtehude (1637–1707)*

1st Phrase

Ex. 652. Fugue in **C**   *Dietrich Buxtehude*

Subject

Ex. 653. Du Friedensfürst, Herr Jesu Christ   *Johann Bernhard Bach (1676–1749)*

1st Phrase

Ex. 654. Gott hat das Evangelium   *Johann Gottfried Walther*

DEDUCTIONS

The following table lists the essential intervals used in harmonic counterpoint:

| | IMPLIED HARMONIC | |
INTERVAL	FUNCTION	SCALE STEPS [*]
3rd (major or minor)	Any function	Any combination of scale steps.
6th (major or minor)	Any function	Any combination of scale steps.

[*] In this column the names of the scale steps represent the vertical interval.

INTERVAL	IMPLIED HARMONIC FUNCTION	SCALE STEPS
Perfect 5th	Usually I or V	Tonic-dominant or dominant-supertonic
	Occasionally II or III	Supertonic-submediant or mediant-leading tone
	Rarely IV or VI	Subdominant-tonic or submediant-mediant
Perfect octave	Usually I or V and rarely other functions	Tonic-tonic or dominant-dominant
Perfect unison	Usually I and rarely V	Tonic-tonic Dominant-dominant
Diminished 5th	VII or V^7	Leading tone-subdominant
Augmented 4th	V^7	Subdominant-leading tone
Minor seventh	Usually V^7; rarely any other function	Dominant-subdominant
Major 2nd	V^7; rarely any other function	Subdominant-dominant
Diminished 7th	VII^7 in minor $\overset{\sharp}{7}$	Leading tone-submediant
Augmented 2nd	VII^7 in minor $\overset{\sharp}{7}$	Submediant-leading tone

The following table lists the use of unessential intervals found in two-voice harmonic counterpoint:

1. Passing tone

  Passing tones will produce the following intervals between the two voices: Major and minor 2nds, perfect 4th, major 6th and occasional minor 6th, major and minor 7ths; perfect 5th, occasional augmented 4th or diminished 5th.

2. Suspension

  The most common suspension in the upper voice is the 7-6. The 4-3 is less frequent and the 9-8 is practically non-existent. The 2-3 suspension in the lower part is common.

3. Neighboring tone

  The two types of neighboring tones will produce the following intervals between the two voices:

  Common intervals: major 2nd and minor 7th; less common intervals: 5th and 6th.

4. Changing tone

The changing tone figure usually begins on a harmonic interval of a 3rd or 6th and occasionally on an octave or perfect 5th. The non-harmonic tones in the changing tone figure will form intervals with the other voice according to the harmonic relationship of the first tone in the figure. The changing tone figure usually uses the scale of the key in which it is found. For instance, the ascending form of minor will determine the notes used if the figure is on the leading tone.

5. Escape tone, appoggiatura, and anticipation:

These types of non-harmonic tones rarely appear in two-voice harmonic counterpoint. When they do appear, they are found in tonic or dominant harmony.

THE HORIZONTAL MOVEMENT OF TWO–VOICE COUNTERPOINT

When the two voices progress in similar motion, intervals of the 3rd and 6th are most frequent. The two parts progressing in similar motion to a 5th (perfect or imperfect) are not used, except in the progression called the *horn-fifth*:

Ex. 655.

The fifth is interlocked here between two positions of the implied f-major triad. The interlocking implied harmony is either tonic or dominant. In measure 2 of Example 646 the 5th on the fourth beat of the measure is interlocked between the same position of the f-major triad (I). This is an extremely rare example of a legitimate 5th approached by similar motion.

The perfect octave is not approached by similar motion within the phrase. In the cadence, however, a fifth may progress to an octave in similar motion. The harmonic background is dominant to tonic.

From a study of examples it is quite apparent that two 4ths, two 5ths (both perfect or one perfect and the other diminished), two 7ths, and two octaves do not appear in similar motion in the style. Occasionally 4ths in similar motion appear as unessential, as in Example 695.

Contrary motion between the two voices introduces in succession practically any combination of different intervals. The following examples illustrate the approach to some of the unusual intervals:

Ex. 656.

Oblique motion is useful in introducing a 5th, major 2nd, or minor 7th:

Ex. 657.

Suspension requires oblique motion:

Ex. 658.   Wir Christenleut'   *Wilhelm Friedemann Bach (1710–1784)*

MELODIC CHARACTERISTICS OF COUNTERPOINT

The old battle among musicians concerning the distinguishing characteristics between vocal and instrumental counterpoint is of no concern in this study. If the ranges of voices or instruments are established for the composition, the characteristics of the melodic movement of the parts, whether instrumental or vocal, must contain the elements which constitute the style. Eliminating the problem of range, the real distinction between vocal and instrumental counterpoint lies in the fact that the voice has technical limitations. Instruments can reproduce any vocal style, but the reverse is not always possible.

In harmonic contrapuntal style the feeling for good melodic composition does not become a slave to harmonic progression. A counterpoint to a given *cantus firmus* may possess all the elements of a good melody and at the same time supply the harmonic movement which the style demands.

Every melody must have good contour, which is achieved by carefully observing the movement of the melody from its starting point. Three directions of the melodic movement are possible from a given point. It may ascend, descend, or remain stationary. The melody should never be permitted to continue step-wise in the same direction for more than five notes of different pitch.

The melody should reverse direction as illustrated in the following examples:

Ex. 659.

If a wide leap occurs in the melody, the direction should be changed:

Ex. 660.

If it is at all possible, every counterpoint should have in its contour a high note and a low note which are not repeated. The high note is sometimes called the *climax note*; the low note is called the *anti-climax note*. It is not always possible to write a counterpoint which will contain both notes. An investigation of many counterpoints reveals that, if they contain only one, the climax tone is favored.

Certain melodic intervals are avoided by composers of harmonic counterpoint. This is true for the most part in instrumental style as well as in vocal style. The intervals avoided are the augmented 2nd, the augmented 4th, and the major 7th. The minor 7th and diminished 7th are extremely rare, and they are used in chords of the first classification.

The rhythmic construction of a counterpoint is of major importance. Poor administration of the rhythmic structure of a counterpoint may retard the musical flow of the two parts.

A counterpoint should be a contrast to a given *cantus firmus*, but at the same time it should not overshadow the importance of the *cantus firmus*. Observe the counterpoint which Bach composed to the fugue subject in the following example:

Ex. 661.   Well-Tempered Clavichord No. 37   *J. Sebastian Bach*

In this example the counterpoint is not only a contrast to the fugue subject but also supports the rhythmic flow of both parts. In addition the counterpoint has a rhythmic continuity of its own. In practically every example analyzed at the beginning of this chapter, the rhythmic patterns are established within four or five beats at the beginning of the counterpoint. Avoid inventing too many rhythmic patterns because they produce a meaningless musical result. As the study of counterpoint progresses, the student will become increasingly conscious of the organic development of a musical idea.

THE OPENING OF A TWO–VOICE CONTRAPUNTAL COMPOSITION

The two voices rarely begin at the same time. The usual procedure is to begin with the *cantus firmus* and start the counterpoint anywhere from a half beat to two or three beats later. Study the examples at the beginning of the chapter to verify this statement. Since the *cantus firmus* may begin on the tonic, mediant, or dominant and at the same time may be either the upper voice or the lower voice, composers have established certain conventional procedures concerning the interval at which the counterpoint may begin.

If the *cantus firmus* is in the upper voice and the first note is the tonic, the following beginnings are possible:

Ex. 662.

If the *cantus firmus* is in the lower voice and the first note is the tonic, the following beginnings are possible:

Ex. 663.

If the *cantus firmus* is in the upper voice and the first note is the mediant, the following beginnings are possible:

Ex. 664.

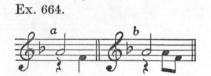

If the *cantus firmus* is the lower voice and the first note is the mediant, the following beginnings are possible:

Ex. 665.

If the *cantus firmus* is the upper voice and the first note is the dominant, the following beginnings are possible:

Ex. 666.

If the *cantus firmus* is the lower voice and the first note is the dominant, the following beginnings are possible:

Ex. 667.

If the *cantus firmus* in the lower voice begins with the dominant note followed by the tonic, the counterpoint may begin in the implied harmonic background of the tonic:

Ex. 668.

Complete the following exercises in two-voice harmonic counterpoint:

1   2

3   4

5

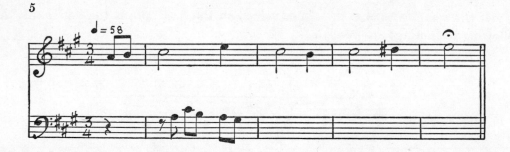

6

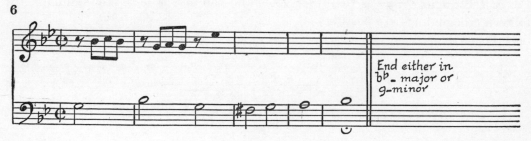

End either in
b♭ major or
g-minor

Compose a counterpoint to the following melodies: *

* The melodies may be transposed. A counterpoint should be written above as well as below. The instructor should provide other melodies if the class needs additional practice.

DOUBLE COUNTERPOINT AT THE OCTAVE

A composer frequently found it desirable to write counterpoint which could be used either above or below the *cantus firmus*. Examine the following excerpt from a chorale prelude:

Ex. 669.   Ein Lämmlein geht und trägt die Schuld

Johann Gottfried Walther

The counterpoint in the preceding example becomes the top voice when the *cantus firmus* is rewritten an octave lower. Comparing at the same places the intervals of the original with those of the modification of the original, the 3rd becomes the 6th, the 6th becomes the 3rd, and so on. The implied harmonic background remains the same in both versions.

The process of composing a counterpoint to a given melody in such a way as to make it possible to have either part above or below the other, while at the same time the implied harmony satisfies the classification of root movement, is called *double counterpoint*.

Double counterpoint at the octave is achieved if either part is written an octave above or below the other. When this occurs the following table illustrates what happens to each interval if it is inverted at the octave:

Original   1 2 3 4 5 6 7 8

Inverted   8 7 6 5 4 3 2 1

Essential and unessential intervals will be used in double counterpoint, as practiced in the first part of the chapter. One exception is the use of the unessential interval of a perfect 5th. The inversion of a perfect 5th is a perfect 4th (an unessential interval). In the original counterpoint which is to be inverted at the octave, the interval of a perfect 5th must not be used as an essential interval. The diminished 5th and augmented 4th may be used in composing double counterpoint because their inversions respectively are the augmented 4th and diminished 5th.

Double counterpoint at the octave may also be achieved by transposing both voices and inverting them at the same time, providing the intervallic transposition of the one part is the complement of the other. The Walther example (No. 669) is transposed here so that the key is e-minor:

Ex. 670.

The same example is transposed to c-major:

Ex. 671.

In the preceding examples the intervals are modified to conform to the harmonic and melodic characteristics of the major or minor keys.

The only further guidance the student needs in connection with composing double counterpoint in the octave is as follows:

(1) The interval of a perfect 5th must not be used as an essential interval in the original counterpoint which is to be inverted.

(2) The counterpoint which is to be inverted should not have too wide a range.

EXERCISES

Compose double counterpoint to the melodies on page 360:

Chapter 34

Strict Imitation: The Real Answer

Imitation is the process of repeating a figure, motif, or subject in another voice at the unison or at other intervals.

The following example shows a subject imitated at the octave:

Ex. 672.   Ricercare

Girolamo Frescobaldi (1583–1643)

An *answer* is the imitation of a subject in another voice. If the imitation is an exact reproduction of the figure, motif, or subject, it is called *strict imitation*. A *real answer* is a strict imitation of a subject.

Frequently the time value of the first note of an answer is shortened, especially when the first note of the subject is held for more than a beat. The time value of the first note of an answer may be varied for rhythmic or harmonic reasons.

Ex. 673.   Ricercare

Girolamo Frescobaldi

The preceding example, which was composed during the first half of the 17th century, reveals that the essential intervals were thoroughly established.

The next example, from the English composer Henry Purcell, again clearly shows the trend of the 17th century toward a feeling for the classification of root movement implied by use of the essential intervals of the 3rd and 6th.

Ex. 674.   Old Hundred   *Henry Purcell (1658–1695)*

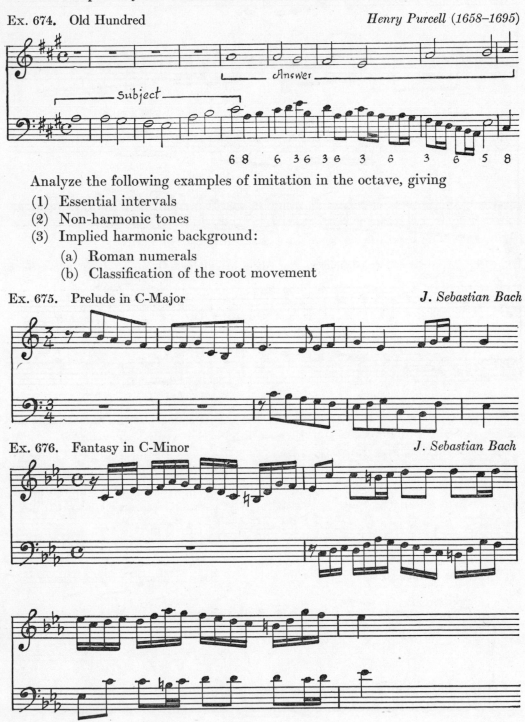

Analyze the following examples of imitation in the octave, giving
(1) Essential intervals
(2) Non-harmonic tones
(3) Implied harmonic background:
   (a) Roman numerals
   (b) Classification of the root movement

Ex. 675.   Prelude in C-Major   *J. Sebastian Bach*

Ex. 676.   Fantasy in C-Minor   *J. Sebastian Bach*

Ex. 677.   Prelude — Noten-Büchlein von Anna Magdalena Bach   *J. Sebastian Bach*

Ex. 678.   Minuet — Noten-Büchlein von Anna Magdalena Bach   *J. Sebastian Bach*

(imitation broken here)

Ex. 679.   Gigue   *Georg Friedrich Handel*

(imitation broken at this point)

Ex. 680.   Andante   *Georg Friedrich Handel*

Andante

Ex. 681. Gigue   *Georg Friedrich Handel*

EXERCISES: Write the imitation in the octave and the accompanying counterpoint to the following subjects in the style of the examples previously analyzed:

1   *J. Sebastian Bach*

2   *J. Sebastian Bach*

3   *Wilhelm Friedemann Bach*

4   *J. Sebastian Bach*

5   *George Phillip Teleman (1681–1767)*

The most frequent imitation encountered in music is at the fifth. By the time of Bach, the imitation at the fifth involved the process of modulation. If the imitation is at the fifth above (a fourth below) the answer is in the **dominant key**. The following example shows the answer in the dominant key:

* Begin imitation at this point.

Ex. 682.   In dich hab' ich gehoffet, Herr   Johann Michael Bach (1648–1694)

At 1, the c is an altered passing tone.   (See Part I, Chapter 21.)

At 2, the e is an appoggiatura.

At 3, the implied triad GBD which is tonic in g-major becomes the subdominant in the key of d-major.

The next examples are taken from the music of Bach and his contemporaries. In the first example, the subject should move at a fairly good tempo; this is taken into consideration in the following analysis:

Ex. 683.   Allein Gott in der Höh' sei Ehr'   J. Sebastian Bach

At 1, the e and g are passing tones.

At 2, the g is a passing tone.

At 3, the g and e are the 7th and 5th of the V^7.

In the next example the chorale melody is in the Aeolian mode.   In order to clarify the harmonic background, the author has added a third voice.   The answer begins in the key of d-minor, modulates to f-major, and returns to d-minor:

Ex. 684.   Nun komm, der Heiden Heiland   J. Sebastian Bach

Comparing the subject of the next example with the first phrase of the chorale melody, one finds that the melody has been ornamentally converted into a lively subject.   The real answer is in the subdominant minor key:

Ex. 685.   Christ lag in Todesbanden   *J. Sebastian Bach*

At 1, the e is an accented lower neighboring tone.

At 2, the c-sharp is an accented lower neighboring tone.

At 3, the f is an accented passing tone to e.   The entire measure is the V in d-minor. The real answer is found most often in the dominant key.

Analyze the following real answers and accompanying counterpoint,* giving

- (1)   Essential intervals.
- (2)   Non-harmonic tones.
- (3)   Implied harmonic background:
    - (a)   Roman numerals.
    - (b)   Classification of the root movement.
- (4)   Compare the subject with the first phrase of the chorale melody found in either Wonderlich or Bach-Riemenschneider.

Ex. 686.   Christ, der du bist der helle Tag   *George Böhm*

* The instructor should also dictate two-part counterpoint illustrating the subject and answer with its accompanying counterpoint.

Ex. 687.   Wir danken dir, Herr Jesu Christ   *Wilhelm Friedemann Bach*

Ex. 688.   In dich hab' ich gehoffet, Herr   *J. Christoph Bach*

Ex. 689.   Gelobet seist du, Jesu Christ   *Johann Pachelbel*

Ex. 690.   Erhalt' uns, Herr, bei deinem Wort   *J. Christoph Bach*

Ex. 691.   Gelobet seist du, Jesu Christ   *Johann Pachelbel*

The next examples contain, at the conclusion of the answer, a modulatory section returning to the original key. This short section is called an *episode*. * Analyze the answer, with its accompanying counterpoint, and the episode.

Ex. 692.   Gott Vater, der du deine Sohn   *Johann Pachelbel*

Ex. 693.   Erhalt' uns, Herr, bei deinem Wort   *Dietrich Buxtehude*

Ex. 694.   In dich hab' ich gehoffet, Herr   *J. Christoph Bach*

* In three-voice and four-voice fugues, the episodical material composed before the entrance of the third voice is sometimes called a *codetta*.   See Chapter 39, section B.

Ex. 695.   Fugue in D Minor   *J. Sebastian Bach*

Ex. 696.   Es woll' uns Gott genädig sein   *Johann Pachelbel*

EXERCISES: Write the answer and the accompanying counterpoint to the following subjects:

1   Answer at the 5th above   2   Answer at the 4th below

3   Answer at the 5th above   4   Answer at the 5th above

5   Answer at the 5th below   6

In the following exercises compose the counterpoint to the answer as double counterpoint at the octave:

7   Answer at the 5th above   8   Answer at the 4th below

9   Answer at the 4th below   10   Answer at the 4th below   *Georg Friedrich Handel*

* Explain the interval of the fourth at each place indicated by the asterisk. This example was selected because of these intervals.

In the following exercises follow the answer with its accompanying counterpoint by an episode ending in the original key.

11 Answer at the 5th above   **12** Answer at the 4th below   *J. Christoph Bach*

13 Answer at the 4th above

In the following exercises have the answer in the subdominant key; compose for at least one of the exercises an episode ending in the original key:

1   **2**

Chapter 35

Free Imitation: The Tonal Answer

Free imitation occurs when the succession of intervals in the answer does not exactly correspond with the intervals in the subject. The *tonal answer* is a type of free imitation at the fifth above or below. The reasons for using a tonal answer are based upon the character of the subject. Subjects which require a tonal answer are grouped into four types.

TYPE 1

If a subject ends in the dominant key, a tonal answer is required. Compare the subject and answer in the following example:

Ex. 697.   Herr Jesu Christ, dich zu uns wend'   *J. Christoph Bach*

At 1, the interval is changed to a major third. If this tonal adjustment had not been made, the answer would have modulated to the key of a-major, as follows:

Ex. 698.

To decide where the tonal adjustment should take place, a harmonic analysis of the subject will be compared with a harmonic analysis of the answer. In this analysis the counterpoint composed to the answer does not influence the basic implied harmonic background of the answer. Furthermore, the implied harmonic background must be as simple and basic as possible. With this in mind study the analysis of the subject and answer in the following example:

Ex. 699.

The tonal adjustment at 1 takes place when the tonic triad in the key of g-major becomes the subdominant triad in the key of d-major. The entire tonal answer is in the key of g-major. The last four notes of the answer in the key of g-major are the same scale steps as the last four notes of the subject in the key of d-major, namely, 5-6-7-8. From this example it is to be noted that if a subject modulates to the dominant key the tonal answer is in the tonic key.

Not all the subjects of type 1 are as obvious in their modulation to the dominant key. The following example illustrates an implied modulation to the dominant key:

Ex. 700.   O Lamm Gottes, unschuldig   *Johann Pachelbel*

Again the tonal answer adjustment takes place in the immediate vicinity where the fundamental implied harmonic background of the subject reveals the tonic triad of f-major becoming the subdominant triad in the key of c-major. The entire answer is in the key of c-major. The last four notes in the subject and answer are the same scale steps, namely 1-1-2-1 in both keys.

In the examples cited thus far the composer has retained practically all the melodic characteristics of the subject in the answer.

For further examples examine the following subjects and answers:

Ex. 701.   O Mensch, bewein' dein' Sünde gross   *Johann Pachelbel*

Ex. 702.   Ein' feste Burg ist unser Gott   *J. Christoph Bach*

Ex. 703.   Fugue from "Prelude, Fugue, and Chaconne"   *Dietrich Buxtehude*

Ex. 704.   Fughetta on "Lob sei dem Allmachtigen Gott"   *J. Sebastian Bach*

Ex. 705.   Fughetta on "Gottes Sohn ist Kommen"   *J. Sebastian Bach*

DEDUCTIONS

1. A subject which ends in the dominant key must have a tonal answer.
2. The tonal adjustment in the answer takes place in the immediate vicinity of the common chord modulation to the dominant in the subject.
3. The implied harmonic background of the tonally adjusted note is either **I** or **V**.
4. Since the common chord modulation in the subject occurs near the beginning, the tonal adjustment will occur near the beginning of the answer.
5. The answer must retain the basic melodic characteristics of the subject.

TYPE 2

A subject which opens with a leap tonic-dominant or dominant-tonic, and which does not modulate to the dominant, is usually given a tonal answer. The answer will begin in the tonic key and modulate to the dominant key.

Ex. 706.   Magnificat   *Johann Pachelbel*

Two intervals are changed in the answer. At 1, the fourth answers the fifth in the subject. At 2, the second answers the third in the subject. The remaining succession of intervals in the answer corresponds to the remaining succession of intervals in the subject.

The tonal answer is composed before the counterpoint is added. With this in mind, the composing of the tonal adjustments is based upon a knowledge of the harmonic implications of the subject. In the following example the subject and answer of the example cited above are combined as one melodic line. The class is to sing the illustration:

Ex. 707.

At 1, the a to d are felt as the fifth and root of the d-minor triad. As the melody progresses from this point, the implied harmonic feeling is in the dominant key. The harmonic analysis shows that the d-minor triad which is tonic in d-minor becomes a subdominant triad in the dominant key of a-minor.

The basic fact thus far established in this discussion is as follows:

If a subject begins with a leap of tonic to dominant or dominant to tonic, the answer begins with a leap of dominant to tonic or tonic to dominant. These two tones imply in the answer at first tonic harmony in the original key of the subject, but this harmony changes its function to subdominant in the dominant key.

The next step is to decide the tonal adjustment which will make it possible to give the remainder of the answer the exact succession of intervals found in the subject. Examine the following analysis of the subject and answer:

Ex. 708.

Note that in the subject the next melody note after the first a is f, which is the third of the tonic triad. Directly below in the answer the d is followed by c, which is also the third of the tonic harmony in the key of a-minor. The composer established as early as possible in the answer the implied harmony of the subject. This obviously transposes the greater part of the subject into the dominant key.

The following example further illustrates the principle of composing the tonal answer upon the implied harmonic analysis of the subject:

Ex. 709.   Fugue VIII — Well-Tempered Clavier   *J. Sebastian Bach*

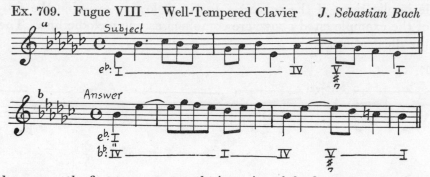

In the answer, the first two notes are the inversion of the first two notes of the subject, and the implied harmony is tonic in e-flat minor. This tonic harmony immediately becomes the subdominant harmony in the dominant key of b-flat minor. The tonal adjustment takes place in this harmonic background in order to establish as early as possible the implied harmonic background of the subject. Again this implies the fact that the answer is conceived in the dominant key, which is established by a common chord modulation at its beginning.

For further examples examine the following subjects and answers:

Ex. 710.   Art of Fugue No. 1   *J. Sebastian Bach*

Ex. 711.   Art of Fugue No. 4   *J. Sebastian Bach*

Ex. 712.   Wir glauben all' an einen Gott, Schöpfer   *J. Sebastian Bach*

Ex. 713. Wie schön leuchtet der Morgenstern *Dietrich Buxtehude*

Ex. 714. Magnificat *Johann Pachelbel*

DEDUCTIONS

1. A subject which opens with the leaps tonic to dominant or dominant to tonic is usually (not always: see Chapter 34) given a tonal answer.

2. The first tonal adjustments are as follows:
    (a) The tonic of the subject is answered by the dominant.
    (b) The dominant of the subject is answered by the tonic.

3. The answer is in the dominant key. At the beginning a common chord modulation occurs, involving a tonic changing its function to subdominant in the dominant key.

4. The second tonal adjustment which frequently takes place is in the immediate vicinity of the common chord modulation. The second adjusted note will be in either implied tonic, subdominant, or dominant harmony in the dominant key, depending upon the implied harmonic analysis of the subject.

5. The tonal answer retains the basic melodic characteristics of the subject.

TYPE 3

When the subject begins on the dominant tone, the answer is frequently tonal and begins on the tonic tone.

As in type 2, the answer is for the most part in the dominant key.

Ex. 715. Fugue XXI — Well-Tempered Clavier *J. Sebastian Bach*

The subject begins on f, which is the fifth of the b-flat major triad. The dominant f is answered by the tonic b-flat. As in type 2, the first note of the answer is harmonized as tonic in b-flat major and becomes the subdominant in the key of f-major, the dominant key.

The only difference between type 2 and type 3 is in the first note. In both types the answer begins with the tonic harmony of the original key becoming the subdominant harmony in the dominant key. The tonal adjustment occurs in both types in the immediate vicinity where the common chord modulation takes place. This adjustment occurs near the beginning of the answer.

For further examples examine the following subjects and answers:

Ex. 716.   Stabat Mater No. 8   *Giovanni B. Pergolesi (1710–1736)*

Ex. 717.   Vater unser im Himmelreich   *Johann Schneider (1786–1853)*

Ex. 718.   Capriccio   *Friedrich W. Marpurg (1718–1795)*

Ex. 719.   Fuga VI   *Georg Friedrich Handel*

Ex. 720.   Durch Adams Fall ist ganz verderbt   *Wilhelm Friedemann Bach*

Ex. 721.* Fugue VII — Well-Tempered Clavier *J. Sebastian Bach*

Ex. 722.* Komm, heiliger Geist, Herre Gott *J. Sebastian Bach*

DEDUCTIONS

1. When a subject begins on the dominant and the next note is a submediant, sub-dominant, or mediant, the answer is tonal.

2. The answer is in the dominant key. The first note of the answer will be the tonic in the tonic key. The implied tonic harmony becomes the subdominant triad in the dominant key.

3. The tonal adjustment takes place in the immediate vicinity of the common chord modulation to the dominant. The tonally adjusted note will be in either subdominant or tonic harmonies of the dominant key.

4. The tonal answer retains the basic melodic characteristics of the subject.

* Examples 721 and 722 illustrate a combination of Type 1 and Type 3.

TYPE 4

A subject which begins with the tonic tone followed by the leading tone is frequently given a tonal answer.

Ex. 723.   Fugue XXIII — Well-Tempered Clavier   *J. Sebastian Bach*

At 1 and 2, the melodic line of the answer contains the tonal adjustment.   The answer begins in the key of b-major and ends in the key of f-sharp major.   The following example illustrates the analysis and the reasons for the melodic modifications in the answer:

Ex. 724.

As in the case of the preceding types, the tonal adjustment takes place in the vicinity of the implied subdominant harmony.   Like types 2 and 3, the subject which begins with tonic followed by the leading tone is given a tonal answer which begins in the tonic key and modulates by implied common chord to the dominant key.

EXERCISES: Compose the tonal answer and complete the counterpoint to the following subjects:

Chapter 36

Mirror, Augmentation, and Diminution Imitation

The kind of imitation studied thus far has retained the basic melodic characteristics of the subject. The types of imitation which are to be presented in this chapter are based upon varying one of the two elements of melodic composition, namely, the time values of the notes or the melodic succession of the pitches. These types of imitation in the 18th century style are less frequent, but composers have found it practical to use them as additional contrapuntal devices.

A. MIRROR IMITATION

Sing and carefully examine the following 17th century examples:

Ex. 725.   Capriccio VI   *Johann J. Froberger (1616–1667)*

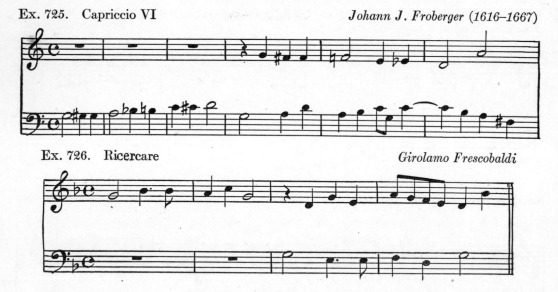

Ex. 726.   Ricercare   *Girolamo Frescobaldi*

Theorists describe this kind of imitation as *imitation by inversion* or *imitation by contrary motion*. Both terms are slightly ambiguous in light of the meaning given the terms earlier in this text, or, for that matter, in other treatises.

If the subject of either example is placed before a mirror, the notes nearest the observer on the printed page will be the farthest removed in the mirror and the notes farthest away on the printed page will be the nearest in the mirror. Now observe the answer to the subject on the printed page and compare it to the subject as it is seen in the mirror. The contour of the subject as seen in the mirror will be the same as the contour of the answer on the printed page. This type of imitation is properly called *mirror imitation*.

In mirror imitation, composers begin the answer in the following manner:

(1) If the first note of the subject is the tonic, the mirror imitation begins on either the tonic or the dominant.

(2) If the first note of the subject is the dominant, the mirror imitation begins on either the tonic or dominant.

In mirror imitation, notes may be raised or lowered for implied harmonic reasons. Composers also break the mirror imitation near its conclusion, depending on how they choose to continue the composition.

Analyze the implied harmonic background of the following examples:

Ex. 727.   From Toccata Sexta   *Georg Muffat (1645–1704)*

Ex. 728.   Fugue V from "Art of Fugue"   *J. Sebastian Bach*

Ex. 729.   Wenn wir in höchsten Nöten sein   *J. Sebastian Bach*

Ex. 730. Chorus No. 64 — Judas Maccabaeus *Georg Friedrich Handel*

Ex. 731. 30 Variations *J. Sebastian Bach*

Ex. 732. 30 Variations *J. Sebastian Bach*

Ex. 733. Fugue VIII from "Art of Fugue" *J. Sebastian Bach*

Ex. 734.   Canon at the fifth above, as Mirror   *Wolfgang A. Mozart (1756–1791)*

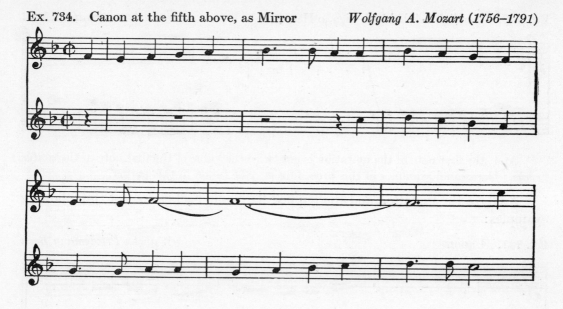

B. AUGMENTATION IMITATION

The type of imitation just studied was based upon the pitches of the notes. *Augmentation imitation* is based upon the time values assigned to the pitches.   In this type of imitation the time values assigned the pitches in the answer are twice the values of the notes in the subject: A quarter-note in the subject will become a half-note in the answer and so on.   This type of imitation is quite rare in 18th century composition.   The idea back of augmentation, however, is frequently used in the construction of thematic material which is derived from chorale melodies. This subject will be discussed in the next chapter.

Sing and carefully examine the following 17th century examples:

Ex. 735.   Wir glauben all' an einen Gott, Schöpfer   *Samuel Scheidt*

Ex. 736. Herzlich lieb hab' ich dich, o Herr   *Samuel Scheidt*

At 1, the first note of the imitation is not twice the value of the first note of the *cantus firmus*. Occasional examples of this procedure may be found in this period.

Analyze the imitation and the implied harmonic background of the following examples:

Ex. 737. Canon   *Wilhelm Friedemann Bach*

Ex. 738. Canon I from "Art of Fugue"   *J. Sebastian Bach*

C. DIMINUTION IMITATION

In *diminution imitation* the time values assigned the pitches in the subject are half the values of the notes in the subject. This type of imitation is extremely rare in the 18th century.

Analyze the imitation and implied harmonic background of the following example:

Ex. 739. Fugue VI from "Art of Fugue" *J. Sebastian Bach*

EXERCISES: Write the imitation as directed and complete the counterpoint to the imitation:

1. Mirror at the octave

2. Mirror at the fifth below and modulate to the dominant key

3. Tonal answer in augmentation

4. Diminution at the octave above, beginning at the asterisk

Chapter 37

Two-Voice Compositions

A. THE CHORALE WITH ACCOMPANYING COUNTERPOINT

Two-voice compositions of a chorale with accompanying counterpoint are found in sets of variations or partitas on a chorale melody. The chorale melody as *cantus* is found in either the upper voice or lower voice. It is also possible in one composition to alternate the phrases between the voices: first phrase in the upper voice, second phrase in the lower voice, and so on. The most satisfactory form of this type of composition opens with a motive from one to two measures in length at which point the chorale *cantus* appears in the second voice. After the first phrase of the chorale *cantus* is completed, a short interlude in the other voice, usually the same length as the introduction, binds the first phrase to the opening of the second phrase. This process continues until the entire chorale melody has been stated. The final cadence of the chorale *cantus* is frequently extended into a coda commensurate in length with the interludes. The following plan illustrates the manner in which this form should be outlined before the actual composition begins:

	1ST		2ND		3RD		4TH	
INTRODUCTION	PHRASE	INTERLUDE	PHRASE	INTERLUDE	PHRASE	INTERLUDE	PHRASE	CODA

Analysis of compositions reveals that composers used two methods for working out the material in the accompanying counterpoint. The thematic material is either an original motive or a motive which is a variant of the first phrase of the *cantus*.

The following student examples illustrate the beginning of a two-voice treatment of a chorale *cantus*.

The first phrase of the chorale *cantus*:

Ex. 740.   Christus, der ist mein Leben

(a) The accompanying voice is based on an original motive:

Ex. 741. *Virginia Bradshaw*

Ex. 742. *Ellen Riggio*

Ex. 743. *Robert Ottman*

(b) The accompanying voice is based on a variant of the chorale *cantus*:

Ex. 744. *Mignon Prendergast*

Ex. 745. *Jack Lowe*

Ex. 746.   *Ray Berry*

Ex. 747.   *Elizabeth Rhodes*

The *interlude* serves as a connecting link between phrases.   It should retain the melodic and rhythmic characteristics of the accompanying counterpoint.   The following student example illustrates the interlude:

Ex. 748.   Christus, der ist mein Leben   *Robert Ottman*

In some instances the composer may make a rhythmic variant of the coming phrase during the interlude and at the same time retain the style of the counterpoint:

Ex. 749.   Nun lob', mein' Seel', den Herren   *Dietrich Buxtehude*

Occasionally, at the cadence of the last phrase and through the coda, the composer adds a third and even a fourth voice to give a more complete ending to the composition.   Examine the following student example:

Ex. 750.   Christus, der ist mein Leben *Robert Ottman*

Further examples of this type of composition may be found in the following publication: Max Seiffert, *Dietrich Buxtehudes Werke für Orgel* von Philipp Spitta. Zweiter Band; Leipzig, Breitkopf und Härtel, 1904.

EXERCISES: Write a composition using the chorale as a *cantus* with accompanying counterpoint.   The student may choose any chorale melody he wishes.

B.   THE TWO–VOICE INVENTION

Historical research reveals that Bach was the first composer to write two-voice compositions with the title "Two-Part Invention." *   His comments concerning the inventions point out the necessity for a good musical idea and its development.   A careful examination of the inventions shows that they are constructed for the most part from one musical idea and its contrapuntal associate.   The invention, therefore, teaches the young composer how to develop a composition based on limited material.

If a musical idea is short and in many instances lacking a cadence, it is called a *motive*.   A *subject* is a musical idea, usually longer than a motive, having a well developed cadence.   Nine of Bach's two-part inventions are built on a motive and six are based on a subject.   The following table shows which of the fifteen inventions use a motive or subject:

Motive	*Subject*
1, 3, 4, 7, 8, 9, 10, 13, 14	2, 5, 6, 11, 12, 15

After studying the motives and subjects in the inventions by Bach, examine the following motives and subjects which have been used by students:

Ex. 751.   Original *Alfio Micci*

Ex. 752.   Borrowed — Based on "Christ lag in Todesbanden" *J. Sebastian Bach*

* The student should purchase for analysis the *Two- and Three-Part Inventions* by J. S. Bach.   (Mason, *Two-Three Part Inventions by J. S. Bach;* G. Schirmer, N. Y.)

Ex. 753. Original — Invention for Violin and 'Cello   *Florence Reynolds*

Ex. 754. Original   *Earl George*

Ex. 755. Original — Invention for Violin and 'Cello   *Barbara Shattuck*

Ex. 756. Borrowed   *Michael Keller*

Ex. 757. Original — Invention for Two Flutes   *Louise Johnson*

Ex. 758. Original   *Helen DeJager*

Ex. 759. Original   *Betty Shaefer*

Ex. 760. Original — Invention for Trumpet and Trombone   *Sidney Mear*

The invention opens with a statement of the motive or subject in the upper voice. Six of the inventions have the motive or subject begin the composition without the second voice accompanying them. After the upper voice has completed the motive or subject, the answer appears in the lower voice at the octave or fifth. The following table illustrates Bach's method of imitation:

	Motive			Subject	
At octave	At fifth		At octave		At fifth
1, 3, 4, 7, 8, 13	10		2, 6, 11		5, 12, 15

Nos. 9 and 14 do not begin with imitation.

The first section of the two-voice invention is composed of the statement of the motive or subject followed by its imitation in the lower voice. This section is called the *exposition*. The contrapuntal associate to the answer may be in double counterpoint if the composer intends to use it in connection with other entries of the motive or subject. Invention No. 6 uses double counterpoint at the octave; compare measures 1-4 and 5-8. Invention No. 2 also uses double counterpoint at the octave; compare measures 3-4 and 13-14. The use of double counterpoint is not necessary if the composer intends to write a new counterpoint with each entrance of the motive or subject.

The following student examples illustrate the exposition of a two-voice invention:

Ex. 761. Allegretto   *Alfio Micci*

Ex. 762. Allegro Moderato   *Earl George*

Ex. 763. Borrowed   *Michael Keller*

Ex. 764. Allegro   *Barbara Shattuck*

The portion of the invention between the exposition and the next statement of the motive or subject is called the *episode*. The episode is constructed by utilizing the melodic and rhythmic elements of the motive or subject and their respective contrapuntal associates. The implied harmonic movement of the episode is toward the key in which the next statement of the motive or subject happens to appear. If the opening statement is in a major key, the next statement is usually in the dominant major key. If the opening statement is in a minor key, the next statement is usually in the mediant major key or the dominant minor key. The problem of the first episode is to link the exposition to the next statement of the motive or subject.

The episode is probably the most difficult part of the invention to compose. The pitfalls the composer must avoid are these:

(a) An aimless wandering of the melodic lines.

(b) Inventing new melodic and rhythmic material.

(c) Over anticipation of the implied harmonies which constitute or belong to the next statement of the motive or subject.

To avoid (a) and (b) Bach frequently utilizes the device of *sequence*. (See inventions Nos. 4, 8, 9, and 10.) The episode is not entirely constructed out of the sequence; the sequence, when it is used, is usually found in the first part of the episode. Episodes not containing sequence are more difficult to compose. The student should analyze episodes in the inventions and look for devices of pedal-point, repetition, mirror use of thematic material, and so on. Whenever these devices are utilized, they seem to appear at the first part of the episode and break off into the preparation of the cadence. For this point see any episode in the inventions.

As in the harmonization of the chorale melodies, the composer must decide the cadence of the episode before he proceeds to write the episode. After he has decided the key in which the next statement will occur, the episode ought to develop harmonically by either common chord modulation or, occasionally, by chromatic modulation toward the second classification harmony of the new key. This will avoid harmonic movement away from the key in which the next statement is planned. For example, if the exposition is in g-major and the next entry is in d-major, avoid the keys of c-major and a-minor because they introduce implied harmonies which are foreign to d-major. The a-minor triad would be difficult to convert into an a-major triad, which must be used as the dominant triad of the key of d-major. There are no cut-and-dried rules concerning procedures on this matter, and the only recourse is analysis of the masters.

The following examples are episodes selected from student two-voice inventions:

Ex. 765.   *Robert Baustian*

g-major

Ex. 766.   *Alfio Micci*

d-major

Subject

Ex. 767.   *James Buffington*

a-minor

Subject

Two important factors in reference to the second statement are to be taken into consideration; first, the voice in which the reoccurrence of motive or subject will appear; second, the manner in which the contrapuntal associate will appear.

The motive or subject usually appears in the reverse voice order of their appearance in the exposition. This is not a rule, but it seems to be the common practice.

The motive or subject may appear alone or with a contrapuntal associate. If a contrapuntal associate is used, it may be a new counterpoint, or it may be a former contrapuntal associate if it was composed as double counterpoint to the answer in the exposition.

Locate the second statement and analyze the key in which it appears, the order of appearance of the motive or subject, and the use of the contrapuntal associate in the following inventions: Nos. 1, 2, 4, 8, 10, 13.

The second statement of the motive or subject is followed by an episode which links the second statement to the third statement.* The key of the third statement is a related key to the key of the exposition. The following table lists the usual keys of the third statement:

Exposition	*Third Statement*
Tonic major key	Submediant minor or subdominant major
Tonic minor key	Subtonic major or dominant minor

If a new counterpoint is written to the motive or subject in the second statement, the melodic and rhythmic elements of this counterpoint may be used in the episode.

The third statement usually has one appearance of the motive or subject. It may appear in either voice. The contrapuntal associate may be an old one, or another counterpoint may be composed.

The third statement of the motive or subject is followed by a third episode which links the third statement to the fourth or final statement. The final statement is in the key of the exposition. Two entries of the motive or subject appear in this final statement. The contrapuntal associate may be old or new.

At the close of the final statement a short coda is usually added. The coda is composed by utilizing the melodic and rhythmic elements found in the invention. If the invention is in a major key and the motive or subject did not appear in the subdominant key, the coda should contain a brief modulation to the subdominant key before the final cadence.

EXERCISE: Compose a two-voice invention, following these instructions:

    (a) Use a motive or subject, either borrowed or original.

    (b) Compose for any of the following instruments or combination of instruments:

---

* An invention may or may not have a third statement before the final statement.

1. Piano
2. Violin and viola or 'cello.
3. Two flutes, oboe and bassoon, clarinet and bassoon.
4. Trumpet and trombone.

(c) Do not consider the invention completed until tempo, dynamic, phrasing, and other marks have been added.

C. OTHER TWO–VOICE COMPOSITIONS

Two-voice fugue, canon, and movement of suites are suitable forms in which to compose. Examples of two-voice fugues are rare. Bach and Handel composed a few. In the *Well-Tempered Clavier* by Bach, Fugue No. 10 is a two-voice fugue. Most of the texts pay little attention to the two-voice fugue. Chapters 34 and 35 presented one of the most important features of the fugue, the real and tonal answer. The two-voice invention presented another important feature, the episode. If the student wishes to compose a two-voice fugue, his training, thus far, coupled with outside reading and study of the two-voice fugues by Bach and Handel, will equip him to venture into the form.

Two-voice canons are extremely rare. In a sense this type of composition has been more or less relegated to student training. A canon maintains throughout the composition the imitation in the second voice. This strict imitation is broken only at the cadence. Canons may have the imitation at any interval. The types of imitation which have been studied thus far in Chapters 34 and 36 are practical applications of the canon. Students interested in composing canons may refer to the following texts: *Applied Counterpoint* by Percy Goetschius (G. Schirmer); *Double Counterpoint and Canon* by Ebenezer Prout (Augener).

Two-voice compositions are found in the French and English Suites by Bach. The two-voice compositions in the suites are either in two-part or three-part form. The style of these compositions is in the melodic and rhythmic character of the title given them. They contain many characteristics of the invention style, with the exception of the treatment of thematic material. The following plans illustrate the common two-part and three-part forms:

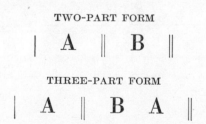

TWO-PART FORM

| A ‖ B ‖

THREE-PART FORM

| A ‖ B A ‖

In the two-part form, the first and second parts are usually separated by a double-bar. The second part is frequently longer than the first part and breaks up into two sections. The second section, however, is not a return to the first motive or subject in the true sense. The thematic material used in the second part is the motive or subject clearly stated or slightly modified with old or new contrapuntal associates from the first part. A mirror of the motive or subject is not uncommon. The key scheme is as follows: the first part usually ends in the dominant key and the second part either begins in the old tonic key or continues in the dominant key. The second part ends in the tonic key.

In the three-part form the general scheme of the two-part form is retained. After the double-bar the composition breaks up into two sections of which the second is in the tonic key, and it begins with a reoccurrence of the motive or subject in either the upper or lower voice.

With this brief outline the student who wishes to compose in these forms is urged to analyze two-voice compositions and submit them to his instructor for criticism and help.

EXERCISE: Compose for piano or combinations of orchestral instruments any of the following two-voice compositions: Prelude; Gigue; Allemand; Air; Minuet; or Courante. The compositions must be completely edited.

Chapter 38
Three-Voice Harmonic Counterpoint

Three-voice contrapuntal compositions are frequent in the late 17th and 18th centuries. The harmonic background of the three-voice counterpoint has a high frequency of triads and an extremely low frequency of seventh chords. The style of voice-leading established in the two-voice counterpoint and four-voice chorale remains basically the same. Perfect octaves and perfect fifths in similar motion are not used by the composers. Imperfect fifth to perfect fifth or the reverse in the outer voices are avoided. In the cadence formula, however, similar motion in the outer voices to a perfect octave or perfect fifth are used.

Analyze the following three-voice contrapuntal examples according to the following plan: *

1. Spacing between the consecutive voices.
2. Method of doubling in the root position of a triad.
3. Method of doubling in the inversions of a triad.
4. Method of selecting the chord members for the root position of a seventh chord.
5. Method of selecting the chord members for inversions of a seventh chord.
6. Classification and frequency of types of non-harmonic tones used.
7. Classification of root movement and function of chord.

Ex. 768. Nun lob', mein' Seel', den Herren   *Dietrich Buxtehude*

* The instructor should give three-voice dictation, preferably from works of the late 17th and 18th centuries in the character of the above examples.

Ex. 769. Gelobet seist du, Jesu Christ   *Johann Gottfried Walther*

Ex. 770. Christus, der ist mein Leben   *Johann Pachelbel*

Ex. 771. *Ibid.*   *Johann Pachelbel*

Ex. 772. Herzlich tut mich verlangen   *Johann Pachelbel*

Ex. 773.   Was Gott tut, das ist wohlgetan   *Johann Pachelbel*

Ex. 774.   Von Gott will ich nicht lassen   *Johann Michael Bach*

Ex. 775.   Von Gott will ich nicht lassen   *Johann Michael Bach*

DEDUCTIONS

1. Spacing between the consecutive voices:

   The upper and middle voices are rarely found more than an octave apart. The lower voice in its relation to the middle voice has a surprising intervallic range; it may range from a unison to two octaves.

2. Root position of a triad:

   Major and minor triads appear most often with the fundamental, third, and fifth. When the triad is incomplete, it is found with two fundamentals and a third, rarely with a fundamental and two thirds.

3. Inversions of a triad:

   (a) The first inversion of a major or minor triad usually has the fundamental, third, and fifth present. If the chord is incomplete it may have two fundamentals and a third, or two thirds and a fifth. The incomplete first inversion of a triad is rare; when it appears it implies the tonic or occasionally the dominant harmony.

   (b) The diminished triad is most often found with a fundamental, third, and fifth.

   (c) The augmented triad is rare, and all tones must be present.

   (d) The second inversion of a major or minor triad is rare.

4. Root position of the seventh chord:

   The seventh chord appears with a fundamental, third, and seventh. The seventh of the seventh chord is prepared and resolved according to the function of the seventh chord.

5. Inversions of the seventh chord:

   The first and third inversions of the seventh chord are used. In both inversions the seventh chord has a fundamental, third, and seventh. The first inversion is more frequent than the third inversion. The seventh of the seventh chord is prepared and resolved according to the function of the seventh chord.

6. Non-harmonic tones:

   (a) The order of frequency of the non-harmonic tones in three-voice harmonic counterpoint is as follows: Passing tones, neighboring tones, suspensions, changing tone figures, appoggiaturas, escape tones, and anticipations. The last three are less frequent than the first four.

   (b) In this style the 4-3 and 7-6 suspensions are the most common. The 9-8 and the 5 suspensions are less frequent.

2

7. Classification of root movement:

It is important to observe that in this style the classification of root movement is practically always tonic, first classification, second classification, with infrequent use of third and fourth classifications. The functions most frequently encountered are tonic, dominant, and subdominant. Supertonic and leading tone are less frequent. The submediant and mediant functions are infrequent.

EXERCISE: Complete the following three-voice contrapuntal phrases:

1

2

3

4   5

6

7

EXERCISES: The student is to select the first phrase of a chorale melody, to which a second and third voice are to be added in the style of three-voice contrapuntal harmony. The chorale *cantus* may be used in the upper, middle, or lower voice.

A more elaborate three-voice contrapuntal style may be achieved by ornamenting the *cantus* and accompanying it with an imitation of a motive or motives. In the following examples compare the *cantus* with the given chorale melody, and observe the motive imitation carried out in the three voices:

Ex. 776. Allein Gott in der Höh' sei Ehr'

Johann Gottfried Walther

Ex. 777. Was Gott tut, das ist wohlgetan

Johann Pachelbel

EXERCISE: Complete the following examples in three-voice contrapuntal style, carrying out the motive imitation and occasionally ornamenting the chorale *cantus*:

1. Christus, der uns selig macht

2. Christus, der ist mein Leben

3. Du Friedensfürst, Herr Jesu Christ

3a

4. Freu' dich sehr, o meine Seele

4a

5

The chorale melody may be converted into a subject which is answered at the fifth, creating an exposition in the style of the invention or fugue. This exposition serves as an introduction to the appearance of the chorale melody in the third voice. The introductory voices continue as an accompaniment to the chorale melody, using melodic or rhythmic figures already established in the introduction.

Examine the following examples according to the following plan:

1. Compare the subject with the chorale *cantus*.
    (a) What time values are assigned to the notes of the subject?
    (b) To what extent do the notes of the subject vary in their relationship to the chorale *cantus*?
2. How is the subject answered in the introduction?
3. Compare the nature of the melodic lines of the two voices which accompany the chorale *cantus* with the introduction.

Ex. 778. Wenn wir in höchsten Nöten sein cantus

Johann Pachelbel

cantus

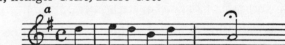

Ex. 779.   Komm, heiliger Geist, Herre Gott

Johann Gottfried Walther

Ex. 780. Wo Gott zum Haus nicht gibt sein' Kunst?

Johann Gottfried Walther

Chorale cantus

DEDUCTIONS

1. (a) The time values of the notes of the subject, when it is not an ornamented variant of the chorale *cantus*, are usually half the value of the notes of the chorale *cantus*.

   (b) If the subject is not an ornamented variant of the chorale *cantus*, the notes of the subject will be in the same order as those found in the chorale *cantus*.

   (c) The subject, however, may be converted into an ornamental variant of the chorale *cantus* and the notes are usually in short time values.

2. The answer will be tonal or real depending on the melodic characteristics of the subject.

3. When the two voices of the introduction accompany the chorale *cantus*, they retain the rhythmic and melodic characteristics established in the introduction.

EXERCISE: Convert a chorale phrase into a subject which is to be answered at the fifth, and have these two voices continue as an accompaniment to the chorale phrase used as a *cantus*.

If the *cantus* is in the top voice, the composition may begin in either the middle or lower voice. If the *cantus* is in the lower voice, the composition may begin in either the middle or top voice.

If the introduction ends in the dominant key, a brief modulation by use of an interlude must be written to bring about a return to the tonic key of the *cantus*.

The following chorale phrases were used by composers of the late 17th and 18th centuries:

1   2

(a real answer may be used.)

STRETTO IMITATION

When the answer begins before the subject has been completed, the type of imitation created is called *stretto*. This kind of imitation is usually classified as free imitation because the complete answer is not required. In stretto enough of the subject and answer must appear to give it the musical effect of being made out of the subject. The stretto is found in inventions and fugues, and it appears at any time after the exposition and first episode. Most of the strettos, however, are found in the latter part of the composition.

Not every subject is harmonically equipped to lend itself to stretto imitation. Composers therefore find out the potentialities of their motives or subjects. If they want to use stretto, they are forced to consider the implied harmonic possibilities of the motive or subject.

In the following examples the entire fugue subject is given, and a three-voice stretto imitation is quoted:

Ex. 781. Fugue XI from "Well-Tempered Clavier"

J. Sebastian Bach

The following example illustrates stretto and free imitation of a motive:

Ex. 782. Three-part Invention No. 14

J. Sebastian Bach

The following example illustrates a stretto containing mirror and augmentation as well:

Ex. 783. Well-Tempered Clavier, Vol. II, No. 2

J. Sebastian Bach

For further examples of stretto consult the following:

J. S. Bach, *Well-Tempered Clavier*

      Vol. I: No. 1 (measures 7–8; 17–18)

             No. 6 (measures 21–25)

             No. 20 (measures 27–31; 64–68)

      Vol. II: No. 3 (measures 1–3)

             No. 6 (measures 14–15)

             No. 24 (measures 70–73)

EXERCISES: Write stretto imitation for each problem presented. Each problem is to be terminated by an authentic cadence.

1. Compose a tonal two-voice stretto at the fifth above to the following subject:

2. **Compose** a three-voice stretto using the subject in the upper voice. The first answer is tonal and should appear at the fourth below in the middle voice. The second answer is real and should appear at the octave to the subject:

3. **Compose** a three-voice stretto using the subject in the upper voice. The first answer is mirror imitation at the fifth below. The second answer is real, at the octave to the subject:

4. **Compose** a three-voice stretto using the subject in the lower voice. This is a canonic stretto because each voice will appear at the interval of a fourth above the previous statement:

5. **Compose** a three-voice stretto using the subject in the upper voice. The first answer is at the fourth below and the second answer at the octave below the subject:

6. **In** the following exercise the subject is given, and the student is to compose a three-voice stretto. There are no leads concerning the proper place to bring in the two answers:

THE PEDAL POINT

Pedal point is found more often in three- and four-voice harmonic counterpoint compositions than in the four-voice chorale harmonization. Its order of appearance frequency is as follows:

Lower voice   frequent
Upper voice   much less frequent
Middle voice   least frequent

Pedal points in the late 17th and 18th centuries are generally found as either tonic or dominant tones of a key. The mediant is extremely rare. At the moment the pedal point makes its appearance, the pedal point tone is a chord member. As the music progresses, the harmonies formed by the remaining voices may or may not contain the pedal point tone.

The aural effect of pedal point is polychordal, that is, two chords sounding at the same time. The reason for this is the fact that the tones selected for the pedal point are either tonic, dominant, or mediant. Analysis of many pedal points shows that at the moment the pedal point appears the pedal point tone is either the fundamental of the tonic or the dominant triad or the third of the tonic triad.

Examine the following examples of pedal point:

Ex. 784.   Well-Tempered Clavier, Vol. II, Prelude 1   *J. Sebastian Bach*

Ex. 785.   Well-Tempered Clavier, Vol. II, Fugue 18   *J. Sebastian Bach*

For further examples of pedal point in Bach's works consult:

Well-Tempered Clavier
  Vol. I: Prelude 1 (measures 24–27)
            Fugue 2 (measures 29–31)
            Prelude 5 (measures 32–35)
            Prelude 10 (measures 21–22)
            Prelude 18 (measures 27–29)
            Fugue 20 (Coda)

Vol. II: Prelude 9 (measures 1–2; 51–54)
Prelude 19 (Coda)
Three-Part Inventions: No. 11 (measures 24–29; 57–64)
No. 12 (measures 28–30)
Two-Part Inventions: No. 4
No. 7

The student will apply the use of pedal point in the exercises of Chapter 39, page 425.

Chapter 39
Three-Voice Compositions

A. THE CHORALE PRELUDE

The *chorale prelude*, which is a composition for the organ, is based on a chorale melody. In the chorale prelude the entire chorale melody appears. The manner in which composers of the late 17th and 18th centuries treated the chorale melody in the chorale prelude can stretch one's imagination to the limit.

Up to this point the student has been given the basic elements which constitute the style. It is now up to him to follow the leads through research of his own.

The chorale prelude as a form is found in the following fundamental types:

TYPE 1

SPECIFICATIONS

1. The chorale melody appears without ornamentation, usually in the upper voice.
2. The composition begins immediately with the first phrase of the chorale melody accompanied by the two contrapuntal associates which establish during the first phrase motives developed as the composition progresses to its completion.
3. Each phrase is separated from the next by a transition which is a half measure to two measures in length. The contrapuntal associates continue during the transition.

Ex. 786.   Herzlich tut mich verlangen   *Johann Pachelbel*

416

Ex. 787.   Komm, heiliger Geist, Herre Gott   *Frederick W. Zachow (1663–1712)*

TYPE 2

SPECIFICATIONS

In this type the chorale melody is ornamented. In other respects type 2 is the same as type 1.

Ex. 788.   Jesu, meine Freude

Johann Gottfried Walther

Ex. 789.   Auf meinen lieben Gott

Johann N. Hanff
(1630–1706)

TYPE 3

SPECIFICATIONS

1. The chorale melody appears without ornamentation. The chorale melody used as the *cantus* is usually found in the upper voice, sometimes in the lower voice, and rarely in the middle voice.

2. The chorale prelude begins with imitation at the fifth above or the fourth below. The subject is usually based on the melodic line of the chorale *cantus*. The notes of the subject are usually in shorter time values than those assigned to the chorale *cantus*. This serves as an introduction to the entrance of the first phrase of the *cantus*.

3. Each phrase of the *cantus* is separated from the next by a transition. The transition is frequently shorter than the introduction. The motive material may be old or new. If it is new, it should be in the style which has been used up to this point. Sometimes chorale prelude composers use thematic material derived from the melodic line of the coming phrase of the *cantus*.

4. To give the chorale prelude well rounded design the last note of the last phrase of the *cantus* may be extended from one to three and even four measures to form a pedal point for a coda.

Ex. 790.   Wenn wir in höchsten Nöten sein   *Johann Pachelbel*

chorale cantus

Ex. 791.   Christ, unser Herr, zum Jordan kam   *Johann Pachelbel*

Chorale Cantus

TYPE 4

SPECIFICATIONS

1. The chorale *cantus* is ornamented.
2. Type 4 is the same as type 3 in the rest of its design.

TYPE 5

SPECIFICATIONS

1. The chorale *cantus* is not ornamented.
2. The *cantus* is the leading voice of a canon. The strict imitation is usually found in the lower voice. The canon can be theoretically at any interval, but canon at the octave and fifth or fourth are the most frequent. The remaining voice accompanies the canon.

   This type of chorale prelude is less frequent. It is quite obvious that most chorale melodies will not lend themselves to this kind of treatment. Type 5 challenges the ingenuity of the composer.

Ex. 792.   Christus, der ist mein Leben   *Friedrich Marpurg*

In the following example the composer uses imitation at the unison for the first phrase and imitation at the fourth below for the second phrase:

Ex. 793.   Ach was soll ich Sünder machen   *Friedrich Marpurg*

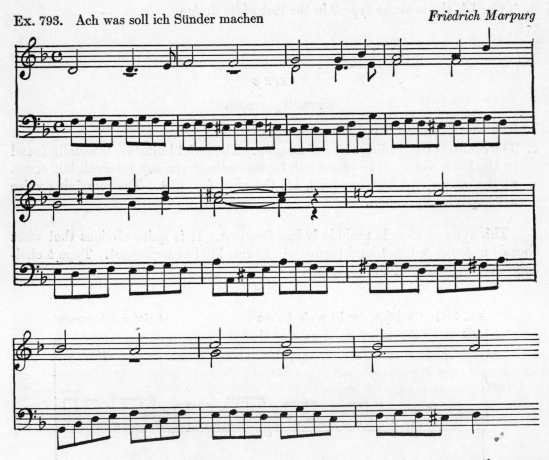

For further examples, although they are not in three-voice counterpoint, consult the following chorale preludes by Bach as published in Johann Sebastian Bach's *Compositionen*, Vol. V, C. F. Peters, Leipzig:

Canon at the octave — "Erschienen ist der herrliche Tag"
Canon at the octave — "Gott, durch deine Güte"
Canon at the fifth — "Hilf Gott, das mir's gelinge"
Canon at the octave — "In dulci jubilo"
Canon at the fifth — "Liebster Jesu, wir sind hier"
Canon at the fifth — "O Lamm Gottes, unschuldig"

The *Einige canonische Veränderungen*, which appear over the chorale tune "Vom Himmel hoch da komm' ich her" (published in the same volume) are for the most part in three-voice counterpoint and they contain practically every canonic device.

TYPE 6

SPECIFICATIONS

1. The chorale *cantus* is not ornamented; it appears in the lower voice,* and occasionally in the middle voice.

2. The other two voices form a two-voice composition. The third voice, which contains the chorale *cantus*, appears at regular intervals during two-voice composition.

Study the following chorale preludes by J. S. Bach in Peters, Vol. VII:
"Es ist gewisslich an der Zeit"
"Wachet auf, ruft uns die Stimme"
"Auf meinen lieben Gott"

TYPE 7

A free composition based on a chorale *cantus* is to be considered type 7. Study the following chorale prelude by J. S. Bach in Peters, Vol. VII:
"Fantasia super: Komm, heiliger Geist, Herre Gott"

B. THE THREE–VOICE FUGUE

The elements necessary to compose a fugue have been presented. Fundamentally, the fugue is divided into three parts. Although there are many modifications, the large number of fugues investigated tend to support this concept.

The three parts of a fugue are:

PART I	PART II	PART III
Exposition	Middle Section	Closing Section
Tonic Key	Related Keys	Tonic Key (basically)

* Be careful to take note of the *cantus* when it is written for the pedal in three-voice organ compositions. In some cases the registration for the pedal may be an eight-foot stop, which would place its tones in the ensemble as a middle voice.

It may be stated that the harmonic structure of a fugue is as important as manipulation of the entrances of the subject. It is the harmonic nuclear concept that clarifies the form. The exposition is tonic; lack of tonic key sets off the middle section from the closing section, which is again strongly tonic key. With this in mind the characteristics of the exposition will be discussed.

EXPOSITION

In the three-voice fugue the subject is announced without accompanying counterpoint. The subject is immediately answered in a second voice at the fifth above or fourth below. The answer may or may not be followed by a codetta leading to the statement of the subject in the third voice. The voice order in which the subject, answer, and subject appear is not a set procedure. In an analysis of twenty-six three-voice fugues from the forty-eight fugues found in the *Well-Tempered Clavier* by J. S. Bach, the following facts are found:

Number	Order followed
13	Upper, middle, and lower voices
9	Middle, upper, and lower voices
2	Lower, middle, upper voices
2	Lower, upper, middle voices

The answer to the subject will be real or tonal, depending upon the characteristics of the subject. After the answer is completed, a codetta or even an episode* may be used before the statement of the subject in the third voice. The form of the exposition is as follows:

PART I

Exposition

Upper voice:	Subject-Counterpoint	Codetta	. . . . . .	End
Middle voice:	Answer		. . . .	of
Lower voice:			Subject . . .	Exposition

The answer will be imitation at the fourth below (real or tonal). The subject in the lower voice will be imitation at the octave below the original subject (real).

A counterpoint which is composed to the answer and which appears quite consistently throughout the fugue as a contrapuntal associate of the subject is called a *countersubject*. The countersubject must be composed as double counterpoint, so that it may appear either above or below the subject. Countersubjects do not necessarily accompany the entire subject. In the case of a subject which requires a tonal answer, the countersubject usually begins immediately after the last tonal adjustment takes place. Quite often the first few notes at the beginning and at the ending of a countersubject may be different from those of the original. The reasons for these variants are found in the harmonic and melodic conditions of the compo-

---

* If the codetta is unusually long some theorists consider it an episode.

sition at the time the composer wishes to introduce the countersubject. The student must not fail to recognize a countersubject if these variants occur.

THE MIDDLE SECTION

The middle section begins at the close of the last subject entry in the exposition. In a three-voice fugue the exposition ends in the tonic key. The middle section is composed of episodes and grouped statements of the subject which are usually in keys closely related to the basic key of the fugue.

The middle section begins with an episode which links the exposition to the next statement of the subject. The thematic material in the episodes is usually derived from the exposition. This is for the most part true in the *Well-Tempered Clavier*, but in the organ fugues this procedure is not always practiced. New motives may be used to compose the episode. An excellent example of this procedure may be found in the organ *Toccata and Fugue* in d-minor by J. S. Bach.

At the close of the episode the subject appears in any of the three voices. Questions concerning a composer's procedure at this point may be asked. Is there only one statement of the subject which is immediately followed by an episode? Is the subject followed by an answer which is immediately followed by an episode? Is there any set plan when the subject group appears? In the light of the many fugues analyzed, any one of the following procedures may be used:

1. The subject alone may appear.
2. The subject and answer may appear.
3. The subject may appear in stretto.
4. The subject may be answered by mirror, augmentation, and other devices.

When the statement of the subject appears, its contrapuntal associate may be the countersubject or a new counterpoint.

The middle section has at least two places at which the subject group occurs. The following plan serves to illustrate a middle section:

PART I						PART III
Exposition		*Middle Section*				*Closing Section*
	Episode	Subject Group any one of the four listed possibilities	Episode	Subject Group any one of the four listed possibilities	Episode	
Tonic key		Related key		Related key		Tonic key

THE CLOSING SECTION

The beginning of the closing section is usually identified by recurrence of the subject in the tonic key. As in the case of the middle section, the composer may utilize any method of imitation of the subject which he feels is in keeping with the composition as a whole.

Quite often the subject is not quoted exactly. In the following example notice that the eighth notes at the beginning of the subject are ornamented in the subject as it appears in the closing section:

Ex. 794.   Fugue No. 11 — Well-Tempered Clavier

As it is stated in the closing section

It is also important to observe the stress on the subdominant key at the beginning of the subject as it appears in the closing section. In Fugue No. 21, Vol. I of the *Well-Tempered Clavier*, the episode leading to the closing section modulates to the subdominant key; the subject is changed at the very beginning to outline the e-flat major triad which is tonic in e-flat major, but it is used in a modulation as a common chord since the subject turns out to be in the key of b-flat major. The example is as follows:

Ex. 795.   Fugue No. 21 — Well-Tempered Clavier

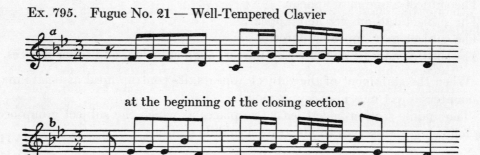

at the beginning of the closing section

In the closing sections of fugues which are in a major key, Bach seems to like to play up subdominant harmony at some point, either at the beginning or near the end.

The closing section is in reality two parts, the recurrence of the subject and the coda. The coda is constructed out of thematic material presented during the composition of the fugue. It is short and frequently has a pedal point, especially if the fugue has more than three voices.

PART III

Closing Section

Subject Group | Coda
Basically tonic key

Analyze * the following three-voice fugues:

Well-Tempered Clavier, J. S. Bach, G. Schirmer

Volume I	Volume II
Nos. 2, 3, 6, 8, 9, 11, 15, 21	Nos. 3, 4, 6, 11, 12, 13, 14, 15, 18, 19, 20, 21, 24

The following three-voice fugue by Bach, using a subject based on a chorale melody, is important to analyze:

"Allein Gott in der Höh' sei Ehr'"   Peters Ed., Vol. VI

C. THE FUGHETTA

The *fughetta* is a little fugue; like the fugue, it has an exposition; but it differs from the fugue in its composition after the exposition.   There is no specified structural plan for the fughetta; those investigated show a variety of procedures.   After the exposition one may find any one of the following situations:

1. A middle section with only one appearance of the subject group, followed by a brief closing section

2. The middle section replaced by an episode leading to a subject group in the tonic key, which closes the composition

3. The middle section omitted entirely

Among the chorale preludes by J. S. Bach, the following are three-voice fughettas:

"Allein Gott in der Höh sei Ehr'"	Peters Edition, Vol. VI
"Gottes Sohn ist kommen"	Peters Edition, Vol. V
"Herr Christ, der ein'ge Gott'ssohn"	Peters Edition, Vol. V
"Lob sei dem allmächtigen Gott"	Peters Edition, Vol. V
"Nun komm, der Heiden Heiland"	Peters Edition, Vol. V
"Vom Himmel hoch"	Peters Edition, Vol. VII
"Wir glauben all' an einem Gott, Schöpfer"	Peters Edition, Vol. VII

OTHER THREE-VOICE COMPOSITIONS

Among the other three-voice compositions, students will find it worthwhile to analyze the movements in the suites of J. S. Bach; his Trio Sonatas from the *Complete Organ Works*, Vol. V, published by G. Schirmer; and the Preludes using three voices in his *Well-Tempered Clavier*, Vols. I and II.

EXERCISE: The student should compose at least two three-voice compositions. The compositions may be for piano, organ, or combinations of three orchestral instruments.   The instructor and the student should work together in selecting the kind of composition, the instrumentation, and the thematic material.   The composition is not to be considered finished until a copy written in ink, with all tempo, phrasing, and dynamic marks, is completed.

* One fugue may be assigned to three students to give the analysis as a report to the class.

Chapter 40

Four-Voice Harmonic Counterpoint

The harmonization of the chorale in four voices using triads, non-harmonic tones, and seventh chords is fundamentally the basis from which the elaborate four-voice vocal and instrumental style is evolved.

As in the case in three-voice counterpoint, the bass voice (vocal or instrumental) has the widest range. The remaining voices, especially the tenor and alto, have the narrowest range. On the whole the soprano, alto, and tenor remain close together, but the bass may be removed from the tenor as far as two octaves. It is also important to note that, if the four-voice counterpoint is composed for keyboard instruments, the handling of the ranges of the voices is considered in relation to the technical problems of performance. For example, four-voice counterpoint for the clavier is slightly more restricted than four-voice counterpoint for the organ, where the pedal usually takes the bass and where the middle voices are distributed between the right and left hands. If four-voice counterpoint is composed for orchestra, the ranges of the instruments used must be taken into consideration.

If one makes a study of four-voice counterpoint, he will be strongly convinced that crossing of voices is low in frequency. This is true in vocal as well as instrumental four-voice counterpoint.

The vast amount of four-voice counterpoint investigated shows that composers constantly drop out a voice in a passage. Some theorists maintain that the composers realized the fact that the ear can assimilate just so much independent movement of voices. Probably a better reason for reducing the number of voices is in the very nature of counterpoint itself. The devices of imitation become more intelligible when there are fewer voices. A voice which has been dropped, as the composition progresses, can be brought back with new interest to the listener, even though it does not contain imitative characteristics. In any of the four-voice fugues from the *Well-Tempered Clavier*, one will find that Bach seldom keeps four voices in motion for more than six or seven measures at a time.

Although there is a little more freedom demonstrated in connection with the conventional doublings for the fundamental position and inversions of triads and

426

seventh chords, the student should not entertain the idea that the basic concepts of doubling are to be forgotten.

The order of frequency of non-harmonic tones is as follows:

Passing tone	frequent
Neighboring tone	
Suspension	somewhat less frequent
Changing tone figure	not frequent
Appoggiaturas	
Escape tone	for the most part rare
Anticipation	

The style of the composition also determines the relative use of the non-harmonic tones. For example, a fugue would hardly need an anticipation, but a chorale prelude of type 2 might find anticipations extremely useful.

With these points in mind analyze the following four-voice contrapuntal passages:

Ex. 796.   Vater unser im Himmelreich   *Dietrich Buxtehude*

Ex. 797.   Ach Herr, mich armen Sünder   *Dietrich Buxtehude*

Ex. 798.   Vater unser im Himmelreich   *Johann Pachelbel*

Ex. 799.   Christ lag in Todesbanden   *J. Sebastian Bach*

Ex. 800. Gelobet seist du, Jesu Christ

J. Sebastian Bach

FOUR-VOICE COMPOSITIONS

The purpose of this section of the chapter is to outline the most common compositions in four-voice harmonic contrapuntal style. Little or no explanatory material will be found. References are given to editions of music which contain material for analysis.

The student has now reached a point in his development where he must do his own analysis. He should have acquired a mastery of the elements which constitute the period. His mastery of the elements coupled with his own research will enable him to write in whatever style of composition he chooses.

THE CHORALE PRELUDE

The seven types of chorale preludes discussed in Chapter 39 may be composed in four-voice as well as in three-voice harmonic contrapuntal style.

Four-voice chorale preludes which may be used for study may be found in the following editions.

Choralvorspiele, Peters Edition, many different composers
Alte Meister, Peters Edition, many different composers
Dietrich Buxtehudes Werke für Orgel, Zweiter Band, Breitkopf & Härtel
Johann Sebastian Bach's Kompositionen für Orgel, Bände V, VI, VII, Peters
    Edition
Method of Organ Playing, Harold Gleason, F. S. Crofts and Co.

THE FOUR-VOICE FUGUE

The construction of a four-voice fugue follows basically the design of the three-voice fugue. In the exposition, however, the entrances of the subject, answer, and interlude are controlled by certain established procedures.

In the four-voice fugue the name of each voice from the highest voice to the lowest voice is as follows: soprano, alto, tenor, and bass. In vocal fugues the ranges of voices correspond to the voice, but in instrumental fugues the range has little or no relation to the vocalist's range.

The order of appearance of subject and answer in the nineteen four-voice fugues from the *Well-Tempered Clavier* by J. S. Bach is as follows:

		Number of the Fugue	
Number of Occurrences	Order	Vol. I	Vol. II
4	B T A S	5	9, 23, 7
4	T A S B	18, 23	5, 16
3	A S T B	1	2, 17
3	A S B T	16, 20	22
2	T A B S	12, 14	
2	A T B S	24	8
1	T B S A	17	

Fugues 1, 12, 14 in Vol. I and Fugue 17 in Vol. II are the only ones which do not observe the normal procedure of subject-answer subject-answer.

In the four-voice fugue an interlude of one or two measures usually appears between the first answer and second appearance of the subject.   There is no codetta in the exposition in the following fugues:

Vol. I   Vol. II

1, 18, 23   5, 9, 16, 17, 23

Of the remaining fugues which contain the normal interlude in the exposition, a short interlude appears between the second entrance of the subject and its answer.   This procedure is found in the following fugues:

Vol. I   Vol. II

12, 14, 24   7, 22

In Fugue 2, Vol. II, the interlude does not appear until the completion of the second appearance of the subject.

The exposition of a four-voice fugue usually ends in the key of either the dominant or the tonic.   This is determined by the key of the answer.   The exposition will end in the key of the dominant if the subject requires an answer in the dominant key.   The reverse is found if the subject requires an answer in the tonic key.   If the order of subject-answer in a four-voice fugue is changed, for example, to subject-answer answer-subject, the exposition will end in the tonic key.   For an illustration of this exceptional order of subject and answer, see Fugue 1, Vol. I of the *Well-Tempered Clavier*.

Following the exposition, Bach's procedure in the four-voice fugue is more or less the same as in the three-voice fugue.   As was stated earlier in this chapter, Bach rarely keeps four voices in motion for more than six measures; consequently much of the four-voice fugue after the exposition is in three-voice counterpoint. The last part of the fugue, especially the coda, uses the four voices.

EXERCISE: Select one of the following:

(1) Compose a chorale prelude for organ or woodwind quartet or string quartet.

(2) Compose the exposition of a four-voice fugue for piano, organ, woodwind quartet, or string quartet.

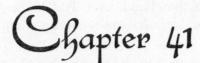

Chapter 41

Some Typical 18th Century Compositions

In this chapter are presented some of the larger forms of composition. The student will select one of these forms, perform his own research, and finally write a composition in the form. As in the case of the assignments in previous chapters, the compositions may be written for combinations of orchestral instruments or keyboard instruments. Whatever the student's project may be, the instructor must guide him in his research as well as in his composition.

THE PRELUDE AND FUGUE

The prelude and fugue may be composed for piano, organ, woodwind quartet, or string quartet. The thematic material for both the prelude and the fugue may be original or borrowed. If it is borrowed, the title should be "Prelude and Fugue on a Theme by ——." If the thematic material is based on a chorale melody, a most successful form is to place a complete harmonization of the chorale melody between the prelude and the fugue. The title of the composition will be "Prelude, Chorale, and Fugue on ——."

Investigation of the *Well-Tempered Clavier* reveals that the prelude or the fugue may be in either two, three, or four voices. The prelude, for example, may be in invention style in either two or three voices and may be followed by a fugue in four voices. In short, any number of voices may be used in either the prelude or fugue — except that the student is urged to avoid five-voice counterpoint, which has not been studied.

THE CHORALE AND VARIATIONS

Chorales and variations were composed by pre-Bach composers as well as by Bach and his contemporaries. The number of voices used in variations ranges from two to four. Variations having three voices are the most common. The variations vary in tempo and meter. Usually one variation is in the opposite parallel mode of the theme and appears near the middle of the set of variations. A variation may be one of the seven types of chorale prelude, or a fughetta, or an invention. The student will find examples of the chorale and variations in the bibliography listed in Chapter 40, page 429.

THE SUITE

The student will find this an interesting composition. Suites may be composed for keyboard instruments or orchestral combinations. A suite for an orchestral instrument and piano is also a suitable combination.* Dietrich Buxtehude composed a suite for organ based on the chorale melody "Auf meinen lieben Gott." The movements are: chorale, double, sarabande, courante, gigue.

THE PASSACAGLIA AND CHACONNE

Both the passacaglia and chaconne are based primarily upon the variation form. Pachelbel, Buxtehude, and Bach wrote compositions in these forms. The student should write a short paper on the history of either one, then proceed with analysis before writing this style of composition. The passacaglia should be composed for organ. The chaconne should be composed for piano, organ, or unaccompanied violin.

THE CANTATA

The author has had a number of students who have composed cantatas based on a chorale melody and the words of the chorale. Excellent translations of the chorales may be found in the Evangelical Lutheran hymnals. Many of Bach's cantatas using English words are to be found in the libraries of the following publishers: Novello; E. C. Schirmer; G. Schirmer; and Oxford Press. A possible form for a cantata may be as follows:

1. Chorale in four voices
2. Recitative
3. Aria
4. Chorale treated in the style of the chorale prelude type 3, four voices with accompaniment
5. Recitative
6. Duet
7. Final chorus: a fugue or a chorale prelude type 3

The student should be given at least three to four weeks to complete the assignment in this chapter. The instructor must carefully guide the student in selecting any one of these projects, must insist upon research, and must be sure that the student has suitable thematic material with which to work.

* If a harpsichord is available, substitute it for the piano.

Appendix

THE MODES

Some chorale melodies are modal. In Chapter 32 of Part II, Bach's treatment of modal chorale tunes is discussed. As a background for this discussion it is necessary for the student to know the modes and the transposition of the modes. The following table lists the modes and two transpositions of each mode:

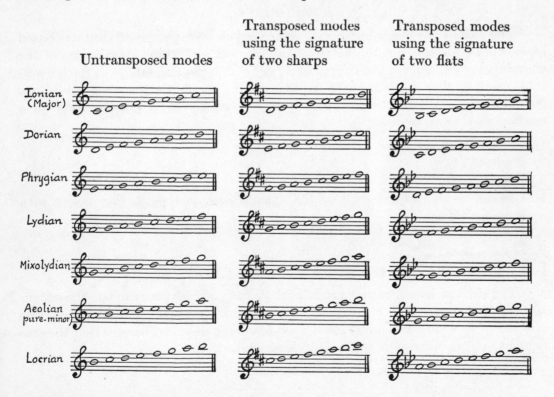

The above table illustrates the method Bach uses when transposing the modes. Bach's signature for the chorale melody which is in the Dorian mode is the signature of the Ionian scale a major second below the final note of the Dorian mode. For example, if the final note of the Dorian chorale melody is f-sharp, Bach will use the key signature of e-major.